The Economics of t

edited by Roger Clarke and Tony McGuinness

BLACKWELL
Oxford UK & Cambridge USA

Copyright © Blackwell Publishers 1987

First published 1987
Reprinted 1991

Blackwell Publishers
108 Cowley Road, Oxford, OX4 1JF, UK

Three Cambridge Center
Cambridge, Massachusetts 02142, USA

British Library Cataloguing in Publication Data
A CIP catalogue record for this book is available from the British Library.

Library of Congress Cataloging in Publication Data
The Economics of the firm.
  Bibliography: p.
  Includes index.
  1. Industrial organization (Economic theory)
  2. Managerial economics.   I. Clarke, Roger.
II. McGuinness, Tony.
HD2326.E243   1987   338.6   86–27057
ISBN 0–631–14075–1
ISBN 0–631–14076–X (pbk.)

Typeset in 10 on 12 pt Times
by Photo·graphics, Honiton, Devon
Printed in Great Britain by Billing & Sons Ltd, Worcester

Contents

Preface

The main aim of this book is to introduce current thinking on the economic analysis of the firm, paying particular attention to some of the rapid developments that have taken place in recent years. The past ten or fifteen years have seen a great deal of activity in the field, including developments of ideas on principals and agents, markets and hierarchies and strategic firm behaviour. Such ideas, however, have not received widespread attention in currently available textbooks. This reflects, in part, the recent development of the ideas, but also the variety and breadth of the literature which makes comprehensive treatment by a single (or several) author(s) a formidable task. Consequently, new and recent thinking in the area has not permeated into undergraduate teaching as much as might be desired.

This book attempts to overcome these problems, and notably the problem of the breadth of the literature, by using a multi-author format to introduce the economics of the firm. Each of the substantive chapters in this book has been written by a specialist author who was asked to provide an up-to-date and readable treatment of work in his field. Whilst individual authors were allowed the freedom to select topics and organize material in their own way, they were asked to emphasize recent work where appropriate. It is hoped in this way that this book will be of use in introducing students to the field.

Broadly speaking, the book divides into two parts, dealing, respectively, with recent theoretical developments and more specific applications. The first half of the book (Chapters 2–4) looks at three areas in which important theoretical developments have taken place: principals and agents, economic analysis of organizational form, and strategic firm behaviour. The second half (Chapters 5–7) then looks at current ideas on vertical integration, and conglomerate and multinational firms. Chapters 1 and 8 also offer an introduction and conclusions.

Whilst the variety and breadth of the literature (or, more accurately, literatures) on the economics of the firm inevitably give rise to considerable diversity in the material, it is hoped that this book will provide some useful insights into developments which have recently taken place.

The editors would like to thank each of the chapter authors for their cooperation in preparing this book and their willingness to take on board our comments as the book progressed. We would also like to thank the anonymous reader for his comments on each chapter and Sue Corbett of Basil Blackwell for her patience and cooperation throughout.

Roger Clarke
Tony McGuinness
October 1986.

1 Introduction

ROGER CLARKE AND TONY McGUINNESS

1.1 Introduction

Recent years have seen important new developments in the theory of the firm. Whilst it has been recognized, at least since the 1930s, that firms are important institutions worthy of study in their own right, they received only intermittent attention in the economics literature up to the 1960s. This trend was partly reversed, in the 1960s, however, with the growth in interest in managerial and behavioural theories of the firm. Moreover, the development of ideas on firms as alternatives to markets, following the pioneering work of Coase (1937), led to a substantial burst of activity in the 1970s and more recently. These (and other) developments have led, and are leading, to important revisions of our ideas on how and why firms operate and some of these ideas are the subject matter of this book.

Since ideas on the economics of the firm have developed in a number of different directions, it is difficult to make general statements about their common attributes. In contrast to standard managerial approaches to the firm, however, more recent work has been concerned to look in greater depth at the process, and environment, of firm operation. In this literature, it is recognized in particular that firms are complex organizations operating in situations of uncertainty (or limited information). These (and other) factors raise much more complex questions as to the nature and operation of firms than are discussed, for example, in managerial maximization models. They raise questions of why firms exist, and what determines the nature and extent of their activities; how firms organize their internal decision-making processes and what implications this has for their overall development; and how they deal with problems of control loss in the absence of perfect information. Such questions previously had been considered only vaguely in the economics literature, although it is now recognized that they are of considerable importance to our understanding of the nature of the firm.

Whilst firms come in various forms and sizes particular attention has been devoted over the years to large corporations which have come to dominate many sectors of country or, indeed, world production. In the UK, for example, the largest 100 firms, by 1970, controlled 40 per cent of manufacturing net output (Prais, 1976, p. 4). In the US, the corresponding figure (for the largest 100 firms in manufacturing net output in 1977) was 33 per cent (Weiss, 1983, p.432). In both countries, therefore, large firms play a major role in manufacturing, and similar findings also apply to other sectors in these countries (e.g. financial services).

Large firms, moreover, can be large in absolute terms. General Motors, for example, with 691,000 employees in 1983 employed approximately the same number of persons as were employed in all manufacturing in the Netherlands in that year (cited by Radner, 1986, p. 1). Clearly an understanding of how and why such firms operate, together with what effects they have in national and international markets, is of considerable interest and these issues receive particular attention in this book.

The remainder of this chapter sets the scene for subsequent chapters by reviewing some of the ideas in the development of the theory of the firm since the 1930s. Section 1.2 briefly reviews developments up to the 1970s including managerial models and the important work of Coase (1937). Section 1.3 then considers some post-1970 developments in more detail, focusing in particular on analysis of principals and agents, internalization of market transactions, and strategic firm behaviour. This material serves as an introduction to the more detailed treatment given in Chapters 2–4. Finally, Section 1.4 provides a summary and plan of the rest of the book.

1.2   Developments up to 1970

1.2.1   Managerial and Behavioural Theories

We begin by briefly reviewing the development of managerial and behavioural theories of the firm. Whilst these theories were developed primarily in the 1960s they owe their intellectual origins to several earlier developments.

The publication in 1933 of work by Robinson (1969) and Chamberlin (1966) indicates the interest that economists were beginning to take in markets whose structures seemed to be depicted inadequately in models of either pure competition or pure monopoly. It seemed important to analyse markets whose firms possessed a certain amount of market power, reflected in the negative slope of their demand curves. Having recognized that monopoly power existed in a wider sphere of economic activity, questions were raised about the goals of the firm. The assumption of a profit-maximizing goal seemed reasonable within the purely competitive model, where it was required as a condition of survival in the industry's long-run equilibrium. But was the assumption always appropriate for firms in non-competitive markets?

The need to address this question, which brought the firm to the centre of a theoretical framework previously dominated by the industry, was prompted by the publication of several influential empirical studies of the form and behaviour of contemporary business corporations. Berle and Means (1932)[1] emphasized that ownership of the typical, large US corporation was thinly spread over a large number of shareholders, leaving control in the hands of managers who themselves owned a very small fraction of a firm's equity. In these circumstances managers could steer the firm away from profit maximization in pursuit of their own interests. Second, Hall and Hitch (1939) reported on a series of interviews with businessmen, from which it appeared that business decisions were not made in the 'marginalist' way that characterized traditional economic theory. The uncertainty that surrounded decision-making led to the adoption of rules of thumb rather than marginalist techniques in setting prices.

Beyond pushing the firm itself to the forefront of analysis, these developments threw out two distinct challenges to economic theory. They suggested, first, a call for more attention to the motivation of firms; second, a call for greater realism in the assumed process by which business decisions are made.

The first of these ideas led, eventually,[2] to the development of managerial theories of the firm. Given that share ownership is often diffuse in large corporations, with managers having (typically) a minor equity stake, it seemed reasonable to assume that managers would pursue their own interests at least to some degree. Somewhat surprisingly, development of this idea into explicit managerial models took place only in the early 1960s (or, more specifically, in the case of Baumol's sales maximization model, in 1959). In this period, however, a variety of models were produced ranging from static models proposed by Baumol (1959) and Williamson (1964) to quasi-dynamic (growth) models proposed by Baumol (1962), Marris (1964) and Williamson (1966). These models all suggested that managers would seek to maximize their own utility and considered implications of this assumption for firm behaviour in contrast to the profit-maximizing case.[3]

An important feature of managerial models is their recognition that separation of ownership from control gives rise to problems of controlling managers. In more recent literature this idea is incorporated in so-called 'principal–agent' analysis. In a large corporation, shareholders can be regarded as principals in a contract engaging managers as agents to control the company. Shareholders, of necessity, do not have full information on the actions taken by managers nor the conditions surrounding those actions. Hence, in a world of uncertainty, they cannot (costlessly) infer how managers are behaving. This means that managers can pursue their own interests to an extent determined partly by the monitoring abilities of shareholders. (Other constraints, of course, may also be operative.) Details of this analysis are considered further in Section 1.3.1 and Chapter 2.

Traditional managerial models proceed by abstracting from many features of real-world decision-making, assuming typically that managers maximize a simple objective function subject to an arbitrarily given profit constraint. The behavioural approach to the economics of the firm, in contrast, seeks to introduce greater realism into the description of actual decision-making processes. In this approach, exemplified, in particular, in the work of Cyert and March (1963), the emphasis is less on economic predictions and more on explaining how firms actually take decisions given the complexity and uncertainty of their environment. This approach inevitably presents a much more detailed picture of the firm than presented in the managerial approach, drawing also on a much broader field of inquiry than found in traditional neoclassical economics.

Much of the inspiration for this wider viewpoint was provided by the work of Herbert Simon. In the 1950s (e.g. Simon, 1955) Simon was already questioning whether economists' notions of rationality were suitable for the analysis of behaviour in situations of uncertainty, suggesting that preoccupation with the results of rational choice led to neglect of the process by which choice is made. But attention to this process is needed as economists move beyond their traditional concern with questions of price theory to the analysis of more complex problems: for example, to institutional analysis in which choice must be made amongst discrete structural alternatives. Simon argued that people possess limited cognitive ability and so can exercise only 'bounded rationality' when making decisions in complex, uncertain situations.

Individuals and groups tend to 'satisfice': that is, attempt to meet attainable goals, rather than to maximize utility, profits or whatever.

These ideas were taken up in particular by Cyert and March. They argued that firms in general, and managers in particular, could not be regarded as a single cohesive group but rather as a coalition of individuals with conflicting interests. Different individuals or groups within the firm have their own aspirations and objectives and a problem of resolving conflicting objectives arises. Whilst this conflict is an inescapable element within the firm, organizational mechanisms exist for its amelioration. Amongst these they suggest that 'satisficing', the use of sequential decision-taking, and organizational slack may all help to reduce conflict as well as to economize on 'bounded rationality'. The result is an essentially 'organizational' view of the firm in which the detailed behaviour of participants within the firm is crucial in determining the decisions that are made.

The importance of these ideas is that they focus attention on the process of decision-taking; on what Simon (1978) refers to as 'procedural' as opposed to 'substantive' rationality. Their main weakness, however, is that they offer little in the way of prediction concerning how aspiration levels are set, how sequential decisions are ordered, and, more generally, how firms will respond to different market circumstances. For this reason, behavioural analysis has not been adopted widely in the economics literature. Nevertheless, it can offer valuable insights into how firms behave, and (as is shown below in Chapter 3), Simon's work on 'bounded rationality', in particular, has been an important input into Williamson's analysis of the firm.

1.2.2   The Nature of the Firm

Managerial theories focus on the divorce of ownership from control and its implications for the behaviour of firms. Behavioural theories examine the actual process of decision-taking in large corporations. In contrast, the important work of Coase (1937) raises much more fundamental issues about the very nature of firms as mechanisms for coordinating resources. These ideas, whilst comparatively neglected up to 1970, have been an important feature of more recent work in the theory of the firm and, notably, the work of Williamson (see Section 1.3.2).

The basic idea underlying Coase's work was clearly expressed in the earlier work of Dennis Robertson (1923, p. 85):

Here and there, it is true, we have found islands of conscious power in this ocean of unconscious co-operation, like lumps of butter coagulating in a pail of buttermilk. The factory system itself, while it involves endless specialization of the work of ordinary men involves also deliberate co-ordination of their diverse activities by the capitalist employer. But even these patches are still small and scattered in comparison with the whole field of economic life. In the main the co-ordination of the efforts of the isolated business leaders is left to the play of impalpable forces – news and knowledge and habit and faith, and those twin elements, the Laws of Supply and Demand.

Robertson, as later did Coase, contrasted the firm with the price (or market) system as alternative ways of allocating resources. The difference between these systems rests on the use of conscious authority in the direction of resources. In the market system specialized and diverse resources are coordinated by 'impalpable forces', in ways that make no use of conscious authority; in other words, as if by an 'invisible hand'. In contrast, the firm involves, in some way, the use of conscious authority or the 'visible hand' of an entrepreneur. The crucial question for Coase is why some economic activity is coordinated under the direction of an entrepreneur rather than the price mechanism? That is, why do firms exist?

Coase's answer, as is well known, is that there must be high costs of using the price mechanism in some situations. Hence 'firms arise voluntarily because they represent a more efficient method of organising production' (1937, p. 337, n.14). Coase suggests several reasons for this. First, costs arise from discovering what the relevant prices are. Second, there are costs of drawing up separate market contracts for a set of mutually dependent exchange transactions. Third, there are difficulties, in drawing up a long-term market contract, of completely specifying the details of transactions to be implemented in the future. And, finally, difficulties occur where governments treat a transaction differently according to whether it is arranged by a market or within a firm. With the exception of the last, costs of using the price mechanism arise, in Coase's view, from a common source: 'it seems improbable that a firm would emerge without the existence of uncertainty' (1937, p. 338). Whilst one might imagine some costs (e.g. costs of writing contracts) arising in a dynamic environment even with complete foresight, nevertheless it seems likely that *substantive* transaction costs are linked with uncertainty concerning the future.

Coase also seeks to explain the extent of a firm's activities:

'a firm becomes larger as additional transactions (which could be exchange transactions co-ordinated through the price mechanism) are organised by the entrepreneur and becomes smaller as he abandons the organisation of such transactions. The question which arises is whether it is possible to study the forces which determine the size of the firm. Why does the entrepreneur not organise one less transaction or one more?' (1937, p. 339)

Coase's answer is that the size of the firm will be determined such that the costs of internalizing an extra transaction will be equal to the costs of organizing that transaction in a market or in another firm. Factors such as costs of internal coordination, entrepreneurial mistakes and the supply price of factors of production will all be relevant. In so far as at least the first two of these increase with the size of the firm there would be a tendency to limit firm size. Also, Coase suggests that these factors will tend to increase *ceteris paribus* with the spatial distribution of transactions (e.g. in multinational transactions) and with the dissimilarity of transactions (e.g. with conglomerate transactions). On the other hand, improvements in managerial technique would lead to larger firms.

The importance of Coase's ideas is in his insights that firms are alternatives to markets in the resource allocation process, and that costs of organizing transactions are a crucial factor in the choice of organizational form. Firms replace price signals in the market with administrative decision and the key issue from this viewpoint is how economic activity is divided up between and within firms. This issue applies to a wide variety of firms, including vertical, conglomerate and multinational firms (see Chapters 5–7) in contrast to the traditional emphasis on single product firms.

The basic principle enunciated by Coase, that decisions to make or buy (and so on) will be determined by transaction cost-economizing motives is also of great importance. Whilst one may argue that cost economizing is not the only factor at work (there may be managerial, monopoly, or other reasons why firms develop in particular ways), it clearly is likely to be an important factor. As we shall see below, it forms the basic principle of Williamson's more recent attempts to formulate a general theory of organizational forms. Coase's own treatment of transaction costs, however, was, inevitably, only a first step, providing a framework rather than a detailed analysis. Clearly it is important for a theory to generate hypotheses capable of empirical refutation, and more recent work by Williamson and others can be seen as attempts to extend and fill out Coase's analysis, thereby moving in this direction.

1.3   More Recent Contributions

This section considers more recent (post-1970) contributions to the economics of the firm. Whilst a great deal of work has been done on the subject (both at a general and more applied level) we focus attention in the first half of this book on three general areas of development:

principals and agents, markets *versus* firms, and strategic firm behaviour. These topics can at least lay some claim to be the most active areas of recent research, and this justifies their special treatment in this book.

An important common attribute of these approaches is their attempt to incorporate modern economic analysis into the analysis of the firm.[4] In the case of principals and agents the concern is with problems of asymmetric information and the way this affects the incentives and behaviour of agents. In the case of markets *versus* firms emphasis is placed on economizing on transaction costs as a basic principle of organizational development. And, in the case of strategic firm behaviour, the role of credible commitments to strategic positions is considered in the context of oligopolistic interactions between firms.

Whilst the literatures in these three areas have developed largely independently, each recognizes that the analysis of the firm is complex and more subtle than had previously been thought. Since some of the ideas and topics may be new to the reader, we offer a brief introductory sketch of them here.

1.3.1   Principals and Agents

We begin with the analysis of principals and agents. This work has developed from initial theoretical contributions by Spence and Zeckhauser (1971) and Ross (1973) on problems of contracting with asymmetric information (see Jensen, 1983). Subsequent work has included the related work of Jensen and Meckling (1976) on agency cost[5] together with more formal analysis of the agency problem (see, for example, Shavell, 1979; Holmstrom, 1979; and Arrow, 1984). Since the actual analysis is quite complex, we concentrate here only on introducing basic ideas.

At a general level, a principal–agent problem arises when one party to a contract (the principal) engages another party (the agent) to take actions on his behalf in situations of asymmetric information. More specifically, it is assumed that the principal has less information concerning the agent's actions than the agent does himself so that the agent has some scope to pursue his own interests undetected by the principal. This may arise because the agent has greater expertise or knowledge than the principal or because the principal cannot directly observe the agent's actions. In either case, however, the key factor is that there is an asymmetric distribution of information which gives scope for an agency problem.

In principle, these ideas can be applied in a wide variety of circumstances, e.g. to a house seller and his agent; to a doctor and his patient; or to many other situations (see, for example, Arrow, 1984). They can, in particular, be applied to the analysis of the firm. Thus, as noted in Section 1.2.1, managers in a large corporation can be regarded as agents of shareholders if the latter, for example, have limited information on their actions. More generally, however, managers act as agents to all outside investors (including holders of debt) and, in some circumstances, can be viewed as agents of customers, suppliers, and so on. Also, as stressed by Strong and Waterson in Chapter 2, a variety of principal–agent relations exists within the firm, e.g. between top managers and middle managers, middle managers and workers, and so on. Potentially, therefore, the analysis has wide application to the theory of the firm both in the context of controlling managers and managers in control (see Chapter 2).

Analysis of the agency problem centres on the issue of asymmetric information. In the case of relations between shareholders and managers, for example, it is often assumed that shareholders cannot directly observe the actions of managers. Given that firms operate under conditions of uncertainty, moreover, shareholders are not able to infer managerial behaviour directly from the performance (profitability) of the firm.[6] In the principal–agent model this situation conforms to a problem of *hidden action* or *moral hazard.* Agents (managers) have scope to pursue their own interests (to put in less effort, pursue perquisites or growth or whatever) because shareholders cannot monitor (or, at least, costlessly monitor) their actions. The price shareholders pay for specialized management of their firm, therefore, is that some pursuit of managerial self-interest will exist.

The actual analysis of this problem draws on recent economic analysis of uncertainty (see, for example, Gravelle and Rees, 1981) and is left for illustration to Chapter 2. Here we may usefully make some more general points.

First, the analysis goes beyond the simple managerial models of the firm in looking explicitly at the constraints and incentives under which managers operate. Detailed discussion of these issues is given in Chapter 2. For illustration, we may note that scope for managerial discretion will depend on the ability of shareholders to *monitor* agents' actions and the *incentives* that managers can be given to pursue shareholders' interests. Questions of monitoring managers raise a number of organizational and institutional issues such as the role of auditors and the composition and size of the board of directors (see, for example, Jensen and Meckling, 1976; Fama and Jensen, 1983a,b). Questions of incentives raise issues of performance-related rewards for managers, e.g. via profit-related bonuses or stock options. Some of the more theoretical work in the area has been concerned, in particular, with these latter issues. In both cases, attention is focused on a detailed account of the constraints or incentives of managers.

Second, principal–agent analysis recognizes that *uncertainty* characterizes the agency problem. This, of course, applies in that principals lack full (or equal) knowledge of the behaviour of agents. In contrast to general references to uncertainty sometimes made in the economics literature, however, principal–agent analysis incorporates uncertainty formally into the analysis. In the hidden action (moral hazard) model, for example, agents (managers) can be given incentives only by being made to share in the risks of the firm. Their behaviour, moreover, will be influenced by their attitudes towards risks and their (interdependent) decisions over the incentives they are given. By explicitly considering uncertainty, therefore, a quite different perspective on managerial behaviour is given. Principal–agent models incorporate management attitudes to risks explicitly in the analysis, and examine effects of this risk on managerial behaviour.

Finally, we note again that principal–agent analysis can be applied much more widely than to simple shareholder–manager relations. Amongst other things it has been used to explore the conflicting interests of shareholders, debtholders and managers in the firm; to examine monitoring and incentives of workers; to consider organizational means of limiting agent discretion; and, more generally, to consider all aspects of the problem of asymmetric information. All of these issues cannot be considered in detail in this book, but some of the key issues pertinent to the analysis of the firm are considered further in Chapter 2.

1.3.2   Firms versus Markets

From the early 1970s, economic analysis of the firm has included specific attempts to develop Coase's (1937) ideas on the nature of the firm. As was pointed out earlier in this chapter, Coase regarded the firm as an alternative to the market as a way of organizing transactions, and suggested that firms would exist wherever their costs of organizing transactions were lower than those of markets. Starting from this general set of ideas, economists in the 1970s tried to develop more detailed analyses of transaction costs, with the aim of explaining which kind of transactions were more efficiently organized by markets and which by firms. The most notable contributions to these developments were probably the work of Alchian and Demsetz (1972) and Williamson (1975, 1981). This section is a brief introduction to these strands of thought whilst the analysis of Williamson is discussed in more detail in Chapter 3.

Alchian and Demsetz identified 'team production' as a crucial feature in the analysis of firms. Team production exists when it is not possible, by observing output, to identify the individual productivities of inputs combined in the production process. A simple example is the need for the joint effort of several people who together move a heavy object from one place to another. In these circumstances, it is difficult for a market to provide suitable incentives for individual members of the team. This is because market rewards are linked to the value of team output, and each individual knows he will not receive the full value of any extra efforts he might make. If markets are used to organize this kind of production process, shirking and low productivity can be expected.

The key to establishing a suitable incentive system is to observe input behaviour directly, using a person with a specialized monitoring role and with the authority to reduce the payments made to observed shirkers, in the extreme having the authority to fire them from the team and choose their replacements. Thus, team production is more efficiently organized in a way that corresponds to our general notion of a firm, in which authority is voluntarily ceded to someone who plays a central role in hiring, firing, and negotiating contracts with all members of the team.

The weakness of Alchian and Demsetz's argument, as Williamson (1981, p. 1565) notes, is that team production usually is found only in comparatively small work group activities. (Williamson cites the case of a symphony orchestra as possibly the largest conceivable example.) The activities typically found even in a single-plant firm (e.g. manufacturing and secretarial work) have outputs that are separable and so their joint administration cannot be explained in terms of team production. This argument applies even more strongly to multi-plant, multi-product, and multinational firms. Hence team production cannot offer *the* explanation of the existence of firms and, in particular, cannot explain why large firms exist.

For Williamson, the condition that gives rise to firms is 'asset specificity' in production; by which he means assets whose value in alternative uses (or to other users) is much lower than in their present use. Physical examples include machinery making components that will fit into the product of only one buyer (e.g. exhausts for Rolls-Royce cars), and dispensing machines that can handle pack-shapes peculiar to one brand, though the concept applies to human assets also (see Chapter 3). Williamson argues that transactions involving specific assets will eventually degenerate into a situation that involves bargaining among just a few people (in the extreme, the owner of the asset and the party on the other side of the transaction). In this situation, bargaining will be a costly process and, if the transaction is a recurring one, it will prove more efficient to have the process organized in a way that makes use of authority to resolve any prolonged disputes. In other words, asset specificity is a condition that makes the firm superior to the market as a way of organizing recurrent transactions.

This basic summary of Williamson's thesis does little justice to his detailed analysis of the nature and sources of transaction costs, and gives no indication of the wide range of organizational issues to which these ideas apply. Williamson's research programme includes not only the question of 'firms or markets?' but has the aim of explaining the much richer pattern of institutional arrangements that are observed in real life, including many non-standard commercial contracts that exhibit a mix of firm-like and market-like features. His theory of transaction costs is developed not just as an economic analysis of firms, but as an economics of organizational forms in general (see Williamson, 1979). Its comprehensiveness is the reason for its separate treatment in Chapter 3 of this book.

Both Alchian and Demsetz and Williamson, by arguing the importance of transactions costs and of the desire to economize on these along with more direct costs of production, have contributed to the revival of 'efficiency' explanations of institutions observed in the business world. The concluding chapter of this book identifies this as one of the main themes of modern economic analysis of the firm. However, it must be borne in mind that establishing the importance of transaction cost economizing does not imply that other (e.g. monopoly or managerial) motives can be ignored in analysing the structure and behaviour of firms. The later chapters of this book, particularly Chapters 5–7, clearly illustrate the role that other motives can play in the analysis of vertically integrated, diversified, and multinational firms. Moreover, as discussed in Chapter 3, Williamson's thesis has been highly controversial as an explanation of the way in which the modern business firm emerged and evolved, not least because of its neglect of the possible role of power in this process.

1.3.3   Strategic Firm Behaviour

A third important theme in recent economic theory has been its attempts to analyse strategic firm behaviour. This literature looks outside the firm and examines firm behaviour in situations of (actual or potential) oligopolistic interdependence. Much recent research has built on the important early contribution of Schelling (1960), and we consider some of the basic ideas deriving from Schelling's work here.

Economists' interest in oligopolistic interdependence is not new, but can be traced back to 1838 and the work of Cournot (1960). What is a new development, however, is the recognition that a firm's behaviour not only depends on the expectations it has about rivals' behaviour, but also may have the direct aim of influencing rivals' expectations about its own future behaviour.

Schelling's (1960, p. 160) definition of a 'strategic move' was an early identification of this important aspect of modern theory. 'A strategic move is one that influences the other person's choice, in a manner favourable to one's self, by affecting the other person's expectations on how one's self will behave.' The success of a strategic move will depend on one's ability to convince other people of how one would behave under particular future circumstances.[7] Success depends not just on communicating the intended behaviour, but doing so in a way that convinces others that it really would occur under specified future circumstances. If firm A threatens to react aggressively should firm B enter its market, will firm B believe the threat and so be dissuaded from entering?

Recent economic analysis of this question has developed a further insight of Schelling:

'Other people are more easily persuaded if one has already undertaken an irrevocable commitment which makes the threatened behaviour coincide with the action that best promotes one's own interest were the specified situation to occur. The essence of these tactics is some voluntary but irreversible sacrifice of freedom of choice. They rest on a paradox that the power to constrain an adversary may depend on the power to bind oneself; that, in bargaining, weakness is often a strength, freedom may be freedom to capitulate, and to burn bridges behind one may suffice to undo an opponent.' (1960, p. 22)

This paradox is highly subtle; an irrevocable pre-commitment leaves one with no other (rational) choice than to carry out one's own threat if the specified situation occurs; *even though given these circumstances* one might now regret having made the pre-commitment. One can imagine many social circumstances where it might apply; Schelling's book discusses a wide variety of economic and political applications. In our previous example, if firm B does enter the market, firm A's earlier commitment leaves it with no better choice than to respond aggressively. Made aware of this before entry, B might be dissuaded from entering.[8]

Several ways in which a firm might pre-commit itself have been analysed in the economic literature: investment in production capacity; advertising; brand proliferation; and product innovation. The details of these are discussed in Chapter 4. Their essential feature is that the firm invests in assets which, once installed, have low values in alternative uses and to other users. Any other firm that is planning to increase its share of the market can expect the pre-committed firm to allow returns to these assets to fall substantially before it considers retiring some of them from the market. The pre-commitment creates, therefore, the prospect of falling returns should any later attempt be made to enter the market. Moreover, it is possible for a 'first-mover' to find it profitable to invest in such assets beyond the level that, were there no possibility of later entry, would be in its best interest. The value, to the first-mover, of installing this 'excess capacity'[9] would be derived from its success in deterring later entry by other firms.

If it is to be successful in deterring later competition, strategic investment not only must be made but also communicated to other firms. There are advantages, then, if the assets involved are clearly visible to all parties. Mutually damaging competition can occur if rival firms are imperfectly informed about either the strategic investments made by a first-mover or what these would imply for profits if entry occurred at a later date. Economic analysis of both the nature of strategic investments and coordination among firms that they involve is in its early stages, but promises to provide important insights into the complex ways in which firms compete.

1.4   Summary and Plan of the Book

This chapter has considered developments in the economics of the firm since the 1930s. Section 1.2 considered developments up to 1970 focusing on managerial and behavioural theories of the firm and the contribution of Coase (1937). Section 1.3 then considered more recent (post-1970) work, concentrating on providing an introduction to developments discussed in more detail in Chapters 2–4 of the book. These developments (principals and agents, markets *versus* firms and strategic firm behaviour) were identified as areas of active research interest which are likely to have an important influence on the economic analysis of the firm.

The remainder of this book considers recent work in more detail. Chapters 2–4 deal with developments in the three general areas noted above. Chapters 5–7 then consider recent work on applications of the theory of the firm to vertical integration, and conglomerate and multinational firms.

Chapter 2, by Norman Strong and Mike Waterson, looks at ideas generated by the principal–agent model, focusing, in particular, on the incentive problems created by the existence of asymmetric information. *Inter alia*, they discuss the basic principles of the analysis and then move on to a detailed discussion of the constraints and incentives on the behaviour of agents (managers and/or employees) within the firm.

Chapter 3, by Tony McGuinness, discusses Oliver Williamson's theory of organizations. The theoretical framework has been used to explain a wide variety of organizational forms, ranging from classical market contracts to authoritarian hierarchies, and including hybrid, non-standard forms of contract. The focus in this chapter is in explaining when and why a market is replaced by an authority-based form of organization. Williamson's important work on hierarchy and hierarchical decomposition is also discussed.

Chapter 4 looks outside the firm and considers recent analysis of the strategic behaviour of firms. In this chapter, Bruce Lyons considers ideas concerning credible commitments developed from the initial work of Schelling (1960). Lyons develops ideas for the case of entry deterrence and strategic investment, and then goes on to show how the analysis can be extended both to other strategic situations and to multi-market operation.

In Chapter 5 Steve Davies discusses the main themes in the modern analysis of vertical integration. He shows that, despite several plausible arguments that vertical integration can improve efficiency, there are also circumstances in which it might have anti-competitive effects. There is a tension in the existing literature, between efficiency and market power considerations and Davies considers the various arguments on both sides.

In Chapter 6 Roger Clarke discusses the attempts that have been made to explain the appearance and growth of conglomerate firms. Again, recent work has emphasized that efficiency considerations play a role in the analysis. Other hypotheses (financial, managerial, and market (or political) power) are also discussed.

Chapter 7, by Mark Casson, deals with recent literature on the multinational firm. Though the literature is disparate, Casson identifies several underlying conceptual themes that give an overall coherence to the theory. He argues that the theory is highly relevant to explaining actual features of multinational firms.

Finally, in Chapter 8, the editors of this book discuss conclusions that one can reach about the modern economic analysis of the firm, and the prospects for its future development.

Further Reading

There is a vast literature on the economic analysis of the firm, though little that pulls together the variety of recent developments. Of the early contributions, Berle and Means (1932) is still worth looking at whilst Coase (1937) remains an important reference work. Managerial and behavioural models are discussed in several textbooks, including Koutsoyiannis (1979), Sawyer (1979) and Hay and Morris (1979).

Surveys of earlier contributions are provided by Caves (1980) and Marris and Mueller (1980). See also the Berle and Means Symposium (1983). Modern attempts to analyse the firm as part of a general economic theory of institutions are reflected in two Symposia (in 1984 and 1985) in the *Zeitschrift für die gesamte Staatswissenschaft*.

Detailed references to the material in Section 1.3 are given in Chapters 2–4 below. However, useful introductory references are Arrow (1984) and Jensen and Meckling (1976) on agency theory and Williamson (1981) on his own work. See also Alchian and Demsetz (1972) on team production and Schelling's important 1960 work on strategy.

For examples of recent approaches to the economics of the firm not discussed explicitly in this chapter, see Aoki (1983) and the work of Radner and others, cited in Radner (1986).

Notes

1   Berle and Means's work has recently undergone an interesting re-evaluation: see the papers contained in the symposium on their work (Symposium, 1983) 50 years on.
2   As noted by Stigler and Friedland (1983), Berle and Means (and indeed other pre-war writers) were concerned primarily to establish that the separation of ownership and control existed rather than to examine its implications for the behaviour of firms. Somewhat surprisingly, this latter development only really got under way 30 years after their book was published.
3   Managerial models are discussed extensively in standard textbooks on the economics of the firm (e.g. Hay and Morris, 1979) and are not considered explicitly in this book.
4   In the case of Williamson's analysis of markets and hierarchies emphasis is also placed on the incorporation of other ideas, notably those derived from organization theory (see Chapter 3).
5   Jensen (1983) distinguishes the 'positive' theory of agency deriving from Jensen and Meckling (1976) from the separate 'principal–agent' theory. Whilst some division of the literature clearly does exist, however, we do not emphasize this distinction here. See also the comments of Strong and Waterson in Chapter 2.
6   This is because many extraneous or random factors (e.g. exchange-rate movements, the success or otherwise of an advertising campaign, etc.) also influence firm performance.
7   The analysis applies both where the aim is to assure others of one's future cooperation and where the aim is to assure them of one's future non-

cooperation. We discuss the analysis only in the latter context; Williamson (1983) deals with the former.

8 This does not necessarily follow. It depends on B's expected post-entry rewards, given A's aggressive response. (See Chapter 4.)

9 That is, installing assets whose production capacity is bigger than would be optimal if later entry were assumed to be impossible. This will not always be profitable for a 'first-mover'. It depends on the indivisibility and purchase price of the assets and on the amount of excess capacity that is needed to give later entrants the prospect of a below-normal rate of return. (See Chapter 4.)

2 Principals, Agents and Information

NORMAN STRONG and MICHAEL WATERSON

In the standard textbook model of the firm, 'The firm is a "black box" operated so as to meet the relevant marginal conditions ... thereby maximizing profits' (Jensen and Meckling, 1976, pp. 306–7). In other words, that model contains no real discussion of the participants involved. The purpose of this chapter is to consider the actors explicitly, to explain their behaviour and to suggest partial solutions to some problems. We will be concerned with two groups of relationships – those between owners of the firm's capital (broadly interpreted) and the manager(s) of the firm, and those between manager and managed.

Many of these relationships can be thought of in terms of what is called the principal–agent model in which the principal commands the agent to take actions on the principal's behalf, motivated by a monetary reward. The environment in which all such actions are undertaken is one subject to uncertainties. In addition, the two actors, principal and agent, are likely to have differing information on aspects of this uncertain world.

In the section following, the concepts underlying the principal–agent (or agency) model are set out in more detail. They are then employed, first to examine the various influences upon the manager as agent in Section 2.2, then to consider the manager as principal delegating to agents within the firm's hierarchy, in Section 2.3. Some concluding remarks complete the chapter.

2.1   Basic Concepts

Explicit consideration of the effects of uncertainty and information are essential for an undertanding of the firm. The introduction of uncertainty means that outcomes are not linked in a deterministic way with inputs. Therefore knowledge concerning results does not unambiguously imply anything about effort or skill. If you win a game of 'Monopoly', that does not necessarily mean you were the best player. Similarly, if the firm you manage reports large increases in profits, this may be because of the strength of the dollar, over which you had no control. Should you then be rewarded with a bonus? These examples suggest that the introduction of uncertainty and information into the analysis of resource allocation within firms may allow a number of problematic features of the real world to be addressed. The features we concentrate upon here all arise fundamentally from asymmetric information – the fact that different economic actors do not share in common the same sets of information.

Informational asymmetry is basic to an understanding of the principal–agent model through which many aspects of the organization of the firm have been studied. Informational asymmetry is also the motivating factor behind models of screening and signalling which, although of subsidiary importance for our purposes, provide explanations of a number of facets of observed firm behaviour.

Agency theory and asymmetric information more generally therefore offer a means for better understanding (a) the internal organization of the firm, (b) the relationship between the top decision-makers in the firm and the firm's residual owners, and (c) the nexus of relationships between the firm and external parties.

2.1.1   The Principal–Agent Problem

The principal–agent problem characterizes a number of situations where self-interested individuals enter into an implicit or explicit contractual arrangement. Examples of agency relationships are pervasive. An obvious example is between employer and employee, but they extend to other relationships such as those between regulator and regulated, lender and borrower, client and adviser, insurer and insured, and government and governed (though here it is not clear who is principal and who is agent).

The simplest agency model assumes that the principal delegates to the agent the responsibility for selecting and implementing an action. The agent is compensated by the principal, with the principal being the residual claimant to the outcome of the agent's act, after payment of the compensation. The principal's problem is to negotiate a contract specifying the agent's remuneration, knowing that their interests are not in complete harmony. For example, the employer may design a form of wage contract which induces the employee to work hard.

In solving the problem, both principal and agent are assumed to be motivated by self-interest. This means that the agent selects an action, given his/her own information and the remuneration scheme, in order to maximize utility. Similarly, the principal selects a remuneration scheme to maximize utility in the light of the agent's self-interested behaviour.

In game-theoretic terms, the principal–agent problem is a two-person, non-cooperative (and non-constant sum) game. It is clearly non-constant sum since different actions can give rise to a different total outcome. The non-cooperative description arises from the assumption that principal and agent are driven by self-interest rather than communal interest. Some people (principally Aoki, 1983 and elsewhere) see the modern firm as a coalition of interests and therefore discuss relationships between the parties in terms of a *cooperative* bargaining game. This seemingly contrasts with the contractual viewpoint, though the idea that the firm encompasses a collection of interests is common to both. We would argue that it is not clear that the participants in these relationships see themselves as a community of interests.

Having developed the framework in outline, it might be useful to clarify an apparent divergence of approach in the literature to the theory of agency. One approach, originating with the writings of Jensen and Meckling (1976), has been labelled the 'positive theory of agency'. The second approach, originating in the analyses of Spence and Zeckhauser (1971) and Ross (1973), has sometimes been labelled *the* 'principal–agent' theory. In our view, Raviv (1985) has the correct perspective on the relationship between these two approaches in saying that they are essentially one. Both share the aim of developing a positive theory of how contracts are designed such that self-interested individuals act in the best interests of the party which is designing the contract. Both approaches look for contracts which minimize agency costs. In terms of the game-theory formulation, agency theory solves for the contract which minimizes the divergence between the non-cooperative equilibrium and the unconstrained Pareto-optimal or cooperative solution (which is unavailable because of an informational asymmetry). The so-called 'principal–agent' theory tends to be more formal and helps to clarify the precise informational assumptions required for any particular model, while the 'positive theory of agency' tends to be more intuitive, emphasizing the institutional details of contracting and control. But each approach has important contributions to make to agency theory and this chapter draws explicitly or implicitly on them both.

2.1.2 Numerical Examples

The remainder of this section discusses the basic problem of informational asymmetries underlying agency models. Though the argument and illustrations may seem stylized when compared with subsequent discussion, it is important to get a grasp of the problem first within a simple setting. The two phenomena we seek to elucidate are commonly called *moral hazard* and *adverse selection*.

Moral hazard arises when the principal and agent share the same information up to the point at which the agent selects an action, but thereafter the principal is only able to observe the outcome or payoff, not the action itself. For example a shareholder cannot hope to observe a manager's daily actions but does observe the outcome. However the payoff to shareholders depends in addition on exogenous factors.

The simplest form of adverse selection arises when the principal is not privy to some information which is relevant to the action, whereas the agent can make use of this information in selecting an action. Then, even if the agent's action and the outcome are jointly observed, the principal cannot know whether the action was optimal given the agent's private information. For example, an employer may not share a worker's information that a higher productivity outcome might have been attained with increased effort, in which case the worker has a strong incentive to suppress the information and economize on effort.

The first example we develop solves for the optimal contract where the only effect of informational asymmetry is to give rise to moral hazard.

Consider a simple setting in which uncertainty in the economy is represented by three mutually exclusive and exhaustive states of the world. Two actions are available to the agent with the following cash-flow outcomes contingent upon the state of the world which eventuates:

		State of the world		
		s_1	s_2	s_3
Actions	$a_1 = 6$	60,000	60,000	30,000
	$a_2 = 4$	30,000	60,000	30,000

We assume that both principal and agent agree that each state is equally likely to occur. The agent's action can be interpreted here as some form of effort, with the greater effort producing the higher *expected* cash flow but with the actual outcome depending also upon chance.

Both principal and agent are assumed to be expected utility maximizers. This assumption means that an individual acts as if s/he attaches utilities to each possible outcome associated with any action, weights these utilities by the corresponding subjective probability that they will occur (here $\frac{1}{3}$) and sums the result. The action which gives the maximum expected utility, so calculated, is chosen.

For this example, we assume that principal and agent have respective utility functions of the form:

$$u_p = f - z,$$
$$u_A = z^{\frac{1}{2}} - a^2,$$

where $f = f(s, a)$ denotes the cash outcome which is dependent upon the state and the action, and z denotes the monetary remuneration to the agent. These functional forms mean that the principal is risk-neutral while the agent is both risk- and effort-averse. To see the latter, first note that with remuneration constant, the agent's utility is decreasing in effort. Second, with effort constant, the agent would be indifferent between an equal chance of £9 or £25 and a certainty of £16 (either giving an expected utility of $4 - a^2$), though the average of £9 and £25 is £17. Thus, the agent is prepared to accept a certain payoff which is less than the expected value of the risky alternative, in order to avoid that risk. In contrast, the principal's utility function is linear in income.

We assume that the agent must be guaranteed a minimum level of expected utility in order that s/he be willing to provide a service at all. Such a reservation remuneration might be given by what is available in the market-place for these services, and we arbitrarily specify it here as $Eu_A = 114$. (The reader can check that for an effort level of 6, a salary of 10,000 with an incentive bonus of 20,625 if the 60,000 outcome results, is an example of a scheme which will meet this reservation remuneration – but there are superior schemes).

Now if, contrary to our asymmetric information assumption, the agent's action was jointly observed, it is easily shown that a constant remuneration schedule depending only on the action would be optimal and would achieve a first-best Pareto optimum. Thus, the principal would offer the agent a remuneration of 22,500 (i.e. $114 = 22,500^{\frac{1}{2}} - 6^2$) if a_1 is implemented and nothing otherwise, giving the principal an expected utility of 27,500.[1] That this so-called forcing contract achieves an optimum solution is readily explained by the fact that the agent, who is risk-averse, receives a fixed remuneration, leaving all of the risk of the variable cash flow with the principal who is risk-neutral. Relaxation of the assumption that the principal is risk-neutral would simply result in some optimal sharing of risks.

With the principal able to observe only the outcome of the agent's action, the previous solution is unattainable. Acting self-interestedly, the agent faced with a fixed remuneration would select a_2 and blame external factors if 30,000 was the observed outcome. This is the classic case of moral hazard where the agent's incentive to act is reduced because the principal can observe only an imperfect measure of the agent's action.

The principal must now design a remuneration scheme based only on the cash flow which makes it in the agent's own perceived self-interest to implement the principal's desired action. So, to ensure selection of a_1 not only must the agent be guaranteed remuneration corresponding to an expected utility of at least 114 but also, the expected utility from selecting a_1 must exceed that from selecting a_2. The best contract which achieves this is to offer a remuneration of 28,900 if 60,000 is observed and 12,100 if 30,000 is observed.[2] This can be interpreted as a basic remuneration of 12,100 with a bonus of 16,800 if 60,000 is the observed outcome. This leaves the principal with an expected utility of 26,700 (i.e. 2/3 [60,000 − 28,900] + 1/3 [30,000 − 12,100]).[3] Overall, this solution to the non-cooperative game, although better than others, is Pareto inferior to the first-best optimum since the agent is no better off and the principal is worse off. This arises because some risk must be transferred from the risk-neutral principal to the risk-averse agent in order to provide the correct incentives to the agent. Again, relaxation of the assumption that the principal is risk-neutral would change the quantitative but not the qualitative result. Only if the agent were risk-neutral would s/he bear all the risk; otherwise the risk is shared (Shavell, 1979).

The essence of the agency theory result on moral hazard is that the principal has inferior information to the agent. The agent knows the action chosen, but the principal is unable to tell from observing the outcome alone which combination of action and state of the world has occurred. The corollary is that (costless) information about effort is always of value to the principal (Holmstrom, 1979).

Let us now introduce the possibility of adverse-selection problems into the numerical illustration. To do this we assume that the agent receives perfect information regarding the state of the world prior to selecting the action. The optimal-action rule from the principal's standpoint is to choose a_1 if s_1 occurs and a_2 otherwise. If all information was shared, the agent would receive a fixed remuneration for agreeing to this. But, with only the outcome jointly observed, a fixed remuneration would cause the agent to maximize utility by always selecting a_2 and by misrepresenting information that s_1 had occurred. In the presence of the informational asymmetry, the agent must be promised a bonus, payable if 60,000 is the outcome, which is of sufficient size to ensure selection of a_1 when s_1 is revealed to the agent.

More complex cases of adverse selection occur when the informational asymmetry exists prior to the contract being agreed. This typically occurs where the principal is uninformed as to some exogenous characteristics of the agent, for example reliability.

This form of informational asymmetry also characterizes the literature on *screening* and *signalling* where there are two groups of economic agents (typically individuals or firms) one of which is uninformed as to the other's true type (for example, true firm profitability, true incumbent firm commitment, true worker productivity, etc.). In the signalling literature, the informed group members (putative agents) choose a decision variable which signals their true type to the uninformed group members (principals). In the screening literature, the uninformed group members offer contracts designed to distinguish between different types of informed group members. Apart from contexts involving firms, adverse-selection models have been applied to insurance settings in which the accident proneness or risk attitude of the applicant for insurance is unknown, to models of education in which the true productivity of the individual is unknown, and to the second-hand car market where the buyer cannot tell the true quality of the car.

2.2 Controlling Managers: the External Environment

Within the principal–agent framework, the firm's shareholders can be seen, collectively, as the principal delegating actions to the manager as agent. However, there are also other forces acting on the manager. In this section we examine the various influences impacting upon managers from outside the firm. These are of obvious importance to firm performance since it would seem natural to expect that the extent to which managers deviate from owners' interests is dependent (amongst other things) upon the scope available to them, thus upon the degree to which they are constrained from outside. Viewed from the other side of the contract, once we relax the assumption of homogeneous interests and introduce uncertainty and informational asymmetries we should expect to see measures being introduced by shareholders – and other external parties – to monitor and constrain the activities of management. In line with the traditional treatment of the separation of ownership and control, we consider these various influences in terms of the constraints they impose on managerial behaviour.

So, apart from the constraint imposed by the shareholders as (joint) principal upon the manager as agent, there are two other capital market constraints: the threat of takeover and the threat of bankruptcy. Additionally, there is a constraint that will probably be familiar – that imposed by competition in the product market; plus one which may not be – competition in the managerial labour market. Thus rather than one contract between principal and agent as in the examples of Section 2.1, control over managers in fact involves a nexus of (partly implicit) contracts between these various interest groups and management, involving multiple principals (Stiglitz, 1985) and perhaps multiple agents. Managerial behaviour is not determined by shareholders alone, but is conditioned by relationships with all suppliers of financial capital – banks, creditors, lessors, etc. In addition, monitoring of the corporate sector in general may be achieved through signalling and screening devices such as takeover bids and bankruptcies. The managerial labour market may also serve to assess the relative performance of different managers.

2.2.1 Shareholders

Berle and Means (1932) noted three significant points about the 'modern corporation'. First, no one person owns a substantial fraction of the shares of any one corporation; second, corporate officers' holdings are small; and third, their interests will often diverge from shareholders at large. Thus there is a separation between ownership and control.

Accepting this position for the moment, it is clear that in practice shareholders will be unable to exercise detailed control over managerial actions and equally that they will not be party to all the information on which managerial decisions are based. Hence the conditions are there for potential conflicts between principal and agent of the type that we encapsulated in our earlier examples. In fact Lambert and Larcker (1985) point to three conflicts which have attracted discussion.

First, executives may derive non-pecuniary benefits from their actions – arising for example from things as diverse as acquisitions of new companies and availability of executive limousines – and these may conflict with maximizing shareholders' returns. This is one of the oldest strands of the literature, and a number of models, of which the best known may be Williamson's (1963) managerial utility maximization model, have addressed the question of what managers might want to do if given some discretion. The second potential conflict relates to risk attitudes. It is commonly assumed that shareholders are able to maintain a diversified portfolio of assets. On the other hand, a large proportion of the manager's wealth will be tied to the performance of his/her own firm. Therefore, as regards any particular firm's investments, each of which involves some risk, it is likely that the manager will have a more risk-averse attitude than other shareholders because s/he holds a rather unbalanced portfolio and hence faces more personal risk. Third, the manager may be over-keen to take actions which have relatively short-run payoffs, in order to demonstrate success, whereas shareholder interests might be better served by longer time horizons in policy evaluation.

Berle and Means' first point is undoubtedly true. Most large firms' shareholdings are widely dispersed. To take just one example, in 1984 Grand Metropolitan had almost 730 million ordinary shares in issue with a share register showing over 104,000 shareholders, no one of whom owned more than 5 per cent. Therefore the shareholders do face a potentially serious problem. How can they act together so as to control management?

Essentially there are two main approaches to the management control problem, which should not be seen as mutually exclusive. Shareholders can threaten to remove management in order to replace them with others who will act more nearly in their interest. Alternatively, they can design an 'emoluments package' which attenuates management's incentives to move in different directions from those which are in shareholder interests. In discussing these two approaches, we shall draw on and develop the points made above. In practice though, solutions to the executive control problem are not straightforward.

To remove incumbent management, enough support must be gained for a motion at the annual meeting to command a majority among shareholders voting on the issue. This does not mean getting a majority of all shareholders in support because many will not vote (see Cubbin and Leech, 1983), but it is not an easy matter. Annual general meetings typically attract a very small fraction of shareholders, and while a proxy form is included with notices of AGMs, shareholders are usually asked to nominate a representative of the board as their proxy. Individual shareholders would want to act against management only if they could see that by doing so they would gain in increased share value/dividends more than the cost of an intervention. More likely perhaps, is that a small group of shareholders (maybe institutions) together would find it worthwhile. However, any coalition of shareholders faces a free-rider problem: why become a member when you can benefit from the result in any case? The costs of intervention are unlikely to be insignificant. Besides the basic costs of organizing a collusive arrangement, the coalition will have to incur costs of gathering information on management's performance (where there is a natural asymmetry) and costs of communicating information through the coalition. The free-rider problem means there is an incentive to let others bear these costs. Hence resources allocated to monitoring will be suboptimal.

This accepted, it is clear that if the executive's compensation is wholly independent of his/her performance, there will be substantial incentives to indulge in excess consumption of perquisites or non-pecuniary benefits. Therefore, to reduce this problem, managers are often paid partly in the form of bonuses. These are linked to financial performance in some way or other and an increasingly popular 'solution' is to relate them to stockmarket valuation. Such a scheme can be seen as an application of the principle uncovered in the example of Section 2.1 that, with actions unobservable, 'if the agent is risk-averse, his fee would always depend to some extent on the outcome, but it would never leave him bearing all the risk' (Shavell, 1979, p. 56).

It is sometimes said that by giving a manager shares in a firm, the incentive problem solves itself. Some rigorous support for this view comes from Diamond and Verrecchia (1982). According to their model, linking managerial reward to the price of the firm's shares alleviates not only the incentive problem of motivating management but also the free-rider problem due to there being multiple principals. In effect, shareholders exploit the information which is publicly available in share price to monitor management. Thus the manager becomes a shareholder, or has an interest in share price rising, presumably because of improved performance. But this form of monitoring is unlikely to remove managerial discretion entirely. If a manager is given a 1 per cent share option s/he will be more interested in negotiating a once-for-all £1001 p.a. increase in basic salary than in increasing profits once-for-all by £100,000 p.a. Or, to put it another way, there may be many other personal utility-creating activities which seem to the manager superior to seeking performance improvements in the firm. As the simple example developed in the previous section illustrates, careful design of emoluments' packages can improve firm performance, but there are no easy rules.

Employment contracts used in practice may induce other inefficiencies. The manager is likely to have a large proportion of human capital invested in the firm (some further implications of which we explore later). If the manager's non-human capital is also tied up with the firm's performance then this leads to a highly concentrated wealth portfolio. The typical shareholder will be well diversified and will be concerned only with risks which are common to other firms and investment media. But the manager with an undiversified portfolio is exposed to all sources of risk. Hence s/he may pass up investment projects with high expected returns but also large idiosyncratic risk components. Other results along these lines are discussed in Marcus (1982). For example, managers may pursue policies of diversification into 'safe' areas (see Chapter 6).

The upshot is that a well-balanced remuneration package requires more sophisticated incentive mechanisms than share price alone. One popular addition is the provision of share-option schemes. In a typical scheme, executives would be given the right to buy shares at some point (or by some time) in the future at a (striking or exercise) price fixed by reference to share price when the agreement was struck. The main benefit of these schemes is that if the shares do badly – share price is below the exercise price – the manager need not buy. Consequently, increasing the riskiness of the investment decisions made increases the expected return since the 'downside' risk is truncated at some point. This can offset the tendencies noted earlier. (However, the design of the executive share-option scheme is crucial here. Because executive share options cannot be traded, if the share price is well above the exercise price at some time before the option can be exercised, then the only means open to the manager to insure against subsequent losses on the option may be to reduce the risk of the firm.)

As an alternative or in addition to share incentive schemes, some internal performance measure might be used as a motivational device. Shareholders in any case receive annual and often interim financial statements designed to give a 'true and fair' view of the firm's performance. Indeed, the appointment of auditors to give an independent external check on the annual accounts may represent one form of monitoring by shareholders of management. Management salaries might then be linked to accounting earnings per share, for example. Management will have more direct control over this figure. But, at the same time, accounting earnings figures are notoriously subject to manipulation, for example by policies which boost earnings in the short run at the expense of current share value. Therefore it may be desirable to exclude strategic items such as advertising and R&D expenditure from the earnings figure on which management salaries or bonuses are based. The standard accounting treatment is to charge such items to profit as they accrue. But as they generate revenue into the future, they may suffer as management attention is focused on short-term earnings effects.

In sum, the compensation package will normally be somewhat complex in order to tackle the various dimensions of the constraints shareholders desire to impose on managers. Having said this, it is commonly observed in practice (Arrow, 1984, p. 20) that compensation packages have large discretionary components, to no obvious purpose. This may be evidence of management having the scope to award themselves a compensation package which does not serve shareholder interests.

2.2.2 Takeovers

Of greater empirical importance than shareholder usurpment of the manager is management change arising through new principals and agents taking over. Takeovers arise for all sorts of reasons, both economic and financial. Economic reasons include, for example: to gain additional product market power or efficiency (horizontal mergers), to gain vertical market advantages (vertical mergers) and to reduce risk (conglomerate mergers). As noted above, this latter reason may even be one manifestation of management's desire to reduce the volatility of earnings and share price, shareholders being able to achieve their diversification by owning separate holdings in the individual firms (again see Chapter 6).

However, we are not directly concerned at the moment with any of those reasons, but instead with the undervaluation of shares. From the shareholder's viewpoint, the alternative to arranging for the current management, believed inefficient, to be overthrown, is to sell out. In other words, in making their own portfolio choice shareholders use what information they have available. If the firm is widely believed to be inefficient and many people are selling out, the firm's share value will be low, compared to what it could be.

An astute outsider will see that the firm's assets are not being used efficiently, causing the undervaluation. This potential acquirer may wish either to develop the firm in combination with ones s/he already owns or simply to strip out profitable assets (office blocks, etc.) for sale. To a much greater extent than a shareholder arranging a coalition, this outsider may capture the externalities involved in replacing management by first purchasing the shares cheaply, then replacing the board. Therefore, although in this case also there are information costs, the takeover threat would seem necessarily superior to existing shareholder usurpment of management as a form of control. The efficiency of the takeover mechanism in signalling and correcting the mismanagement of firms' resources clearly warrants deeper consideration.

A natural informational asymmetry exists between the managers of the target firm and the bidding firm (Stiglitz, 1985). Major (institutional) shareholders may also be privy to superior information. Stiglitz argues that if a controlling interest in the firm accepts the offer and the bid succeeds, then this simply indicates that the bidding firm is paying too much. In effect there is an adverse selection problem here. Potential acquiring firms are unable to distinguish firms that are truly being run inefficiently but could be better managed, from firms that are performing poorly but are being managed as efficiently as possible in the circumstances.

Even before a bid occurs there may be a deterrent to a potential acquiring firm. The firm will in all likelihood have to expend considerable resources in order to screen and identify potential targets. The bid itself will signal a worthwhile target to other potential acquirers so that any competing potential acquirer may find initial search costs reduced. Also so-called 'white knights' who rescue the target from the original raider may have the further advantage of facing lower post-merger reorganization costs. Competition in the acquisitions market may discourage any firm from committing resources to identifying potential targets.

One reason why a bid, once made, may fail is due to the previously discussed shareholder free-rider problem spilling over onto the takeover mechanism. If the bid signals the inefficiency of current management to shareholders, they can reject the bid and retain their shareholding in anticipation of free-riding as a minority shareholder on the management reorganization when the takeover proceeds. As the argument applies to all shareholders, the takeover bid will fail. Yarrow (1985) has described two devices which may serve to overcome the free-rider problem. The first is the oppression of minority interests. By this device, the acquiring firm diverts some of the resources of the acquired firm to its own shareholders so that the minority shareholder who rejects the bid does not share in the improved performance. The second device is the compulsory acquisition of shares whereby the acquiring firm may compulsorily purchase the remaining minority interest once a certain proportion of the target's shares has been acquired. Yarrow argues cogently that while the first device has the capacity to give rise to undesirable takeovers (see also Stiglitz, 1985), the institutional control of takeovers in the UK approximates an efficient solution to the free-rider problem via the second device (although the Takeover Code – administered in the UK by the City Panel on Takeovers and Mergers with the support of the Stock Exchange – sets the critical equity stake which triggers the compulsory acquisition rights at 90 per cent).

Finally, Stiglitz points out that management may contest bids and even pre-empt them by taking strategic actions that make the takeover prohibitively costly. In the US, terms such as golden parachutes, poison pills, shark repellants, etc., have been coined to describe devices which may serve to deter takeover bids. In the UK, the Takeover Code serves to limit the ability of management to frustrate bids that would benefit shareholders, but only after the offer is made or is imminent.

Clearly, the efficacy of the takeover mechanism depends on the institutional and informational complexities of the process. Hence, it is worthwhile turning to the empirical evidence.

Most of the evidence on the efficiency of the takeover mechanism relates to the US. Summarizing much of this empirical literature, Jensen and Ruback (1983) conclude that the shareholders of target firms benefit while the shareholders of acquirers do not lose. They argue that 'the market for corporate control is best viewed as an arena in which managerial teams compete for the rights to manage corporate resources' (p. 5). In contrast to this view, Lev (1983), reviewing the same literature, finds evidence, particularly in more recent merger developments, that corporate management does not act in the best interests of shareholders. Thus he interprets management resistance to takeover bids and the expansion of firms through merger with at best no benefit to the shareholders of the acquiring firm, as consistent with managers pursuing their own self-interest. The evidence of Firth (1980) on the UK also supports the view that managerial motives rather than shareholder interests best explain the pursuit of takeovers.

2.2.3 Banks and Bankruptcy

Shareholders are not the only direct form of control over managers. They are also controlled by lenders, of whom the most important are banks, who will impose conditions for granting and maintaining loans. Hence it makes sense to think of a principal–agent relationship existing between the bank and the manager (Stiglitz, 1985).

There is one fundamental difference between the objective of the shareholders and that of the banks or other lenders. The former, we have argued, are interested in a high mean return on their assets, whilst the latter are concerned to minimize the probability of default. Hence banks, for example (assuming they have no equity interest), are unconcerned with how successful the firm is when it does well, but they will be concerned with the firm's prospects if things turn out badly. As a consequence, banks as principals are interested to constrain managers to avoid projects with high downside risk, and the constraints they impose may well be in partial conflict with shareholder interests.

From the manager's viewpoint, one important constraint at low-level performance is bankruptcy of the firm,[4] leading to its being liquidated or taken into receivership. Bankruptcy may be a much more powerful constraint than either of the previous two constraints, simply because its effect on management is likely to be more devastating. If it is difficult to distinguish whether a company failed because of or despite management, company insolvency is likely to be taken as a signal by prospective principals/shareholders of inept management. We shall return to this point below.

Suppose first that the only financial capital invested in the firm is through shareholdings. When is the firm likely to go bankrupt? This will occur when the shares are worthless. Such a situation presumably arises because the expected value of the profits stream (gross of any returns to shareholders) is negative into the foreseeable future.

Much more the norm is for a firm to raise finance through a mixture of debt and equity, that is for it to owe money on a contractual basis to banks and other lenders, as well as issuing shares. The key point about debt is that payments have to be paid whether the firm is doing badly or well. Hence the more debt the firm issues (the more highly geared or leveraged it is) the more likely it is to go bankrupt, since the more likely is poor performance to result in insufficient cash resources to meet debt obligations on time. Debt-holders will call in a receiver if they consider the firm to be insolvent. Nevertheless, the use of a mixed financial package is readily explainable.

One explanation uses the concept of 'bonding'. By issuing debt, managers can bond or pre-commit themselves to the firm. Hence they, as agents, can signal that they are committed to the firm's good performance, in the sense that they are willing to take on the risk of partial debt finance which manifests itself as an increased probability of bankruptcy. In other words, it will be costly for them personally to take things easy.

But why should a manager create a weakness in his/her own position? The answer is that by issuing debt, the market sees the manager has an incentive to perform well and the share valuation is thereby raised. The manager will benefit directly from this if s/he holds shares. Benefits will also accrue indirectly from increased share value if managerial salaries depend upon market value, if the threat of shareholder intervention or of takeover is thereby reduced, or if the corresponding fall in the costs of raising capital allow management to increase their perquisites. The effect is modelled formally by Grossman and Hart (1982).

Of course, debt-holders (banks, etc.) have costs of monitoring and controlling the loan. Expected losses through default will increase with the probability of insolvency and hence with the amount of gearing. In addition, as we have said, shareholders and debt-holders have divergent interests, particularly when insolvency threatens. For example, given limited liability, shareholders may have little to lose and much to gain by taking on very risky investments. Because of this and also because those firms willing to borrow heavily may be the most inherently risky anyway, firms may be unable to increase debt beyond a certain point even if they are willing to pay higher interest rates. Credit rationing rather than market clearing characterizes the equilibrium (Weiss and Stiglitz, 1981).

It has been suggested (Easterbrook, 1984; Diamond, 1984) that debt-holders, and banks in particular, may yet perform a useful policing role for shareholders. Thus banks may be in a better position than a diverse set of shareholders to monitor the information provided by management and so periodically vet management performance. Some support for this view comes from Cable (1985). In an empirical analysis of banks' involvement in firms' behaviour in West Germany, he concludes that 'there is a significant positive relationship between the degree of bank involvement in leading industrial companies and their financial performance' (1985, p. 130).

This monitoring role for banks may also be important in another way. In order to support a request for new finance from the stockmarket, a firm might have to give away information to investors which is useful to competitors, whereas the bank would not have to disclose such information to outsiders. On the other hand, the bank may face a conflict of interest if it also finances competitors of the firm in question.

2.2.4   The Product Market

It is a longstanding view that imperfect competition in the product market allows distortion away from identity with the shareholders' interests by management (and allows the workforce to enjoy some of the benefits also). This can be traced back to Leibenstein's 'X inefficiency' theory of the firm, for example (see Crew, Jones-Lee and Rowley, 1971). The basic idea is very simple. Under perfect competition, long-run economic profit is zero. Hence inefficient firms earn negative profits and must exit. Under monopoly or some form of oligopoly, even inefficient firms may earn positive profits and hence can survive in the long run. Thus if the product market is sufficiently competitive, management will be constrained to act in accordance with shareholders' interests, or eventually face bankruptcy.

Critics of the importance of product market conditions attack the 'straw man' nature of perfect competition assumed here. To quote Smirlock and Marshall (1983), who have focused many of the arguments: 'The realities of imperfect information and costly monitoring and enforcement of contracts may result in managerial discretion within the firms that populate competitive product markets ... optimal contracting arrangements will not fully eliminate discretionary behaviour' (p. 168). The point illustrates something which comes out in our example of Section 2.1 where the first-best optimum is not available because the agent's action cannot be observed, or at least cannot be observed without very substantial expenditure.

Therefore the argument of the first paragraph does not suffice; what has to be shown is that monopoly power makes the imperfections in the other management controls worse. This could be true under some conditions and it has been formalized in a particular way by Hart (1983). The basic idea of his example is quite simple. Suppose there is an exogenous fall in a firm's total and marginal costs. If this firm competes with no others (is a monopolist) the manager may choose to take all of the benefits in the form of increased managerial slack. However, if the firm is in competition with others who have experienced similar cost falls, and at least some of whom are profit-maximizing, then product price will fall and the manager of the non-profit-maximizing firm forced to compete will be unable to take all of the benefits as increased slack. Hence under competition there will be a lesser amount of managerial slack.

Whether examples such as this reveal important truths is essentially an empirical matter, though testing it is not easy. Smirlock and Marshall (1983) claim their findings do not lend support to the idea of the product market being of any importance in constraining managers.

2.2.5   Markets for Managerial Labour

Finally we come to a factor which has been implicitly underpinning many of the earlier subsections. Why, for example, does the manager dislike bankruptcy in the case where s/he holds no share interest? Presumably because the fact that the firm has gone bankrupt is a bad signal to future employers. Similarly, the fact that the firm has been taken over provides others with a bad signal regarding management's efficiency.

Thus, there is a market for managers: the salary a potential manager can command is assumed to reflect performance to date. Indeed, Fama (1980), one of the foremost proponents of this view, would go further. A manager's present salary (or remuneration package) will reflect that manager's current worth to the firm, for if it did not, that firm would be in danger of losing the person in question. Moreover, as well as top-level managers monitoring their subordinates, Fama claims that managers below the top level, because they have aspirations to move on, have an interest in seeing that the top-level management provides the correct signals to the managerial labour market by choosing appropriate policies for the firm. Fama argues that constraints provided by the managerial labour market are more likely to be potent in disciplining managers than is the shareholder constraint, since most shareholders maintain diversified portfolios, whereas managers must use all (or a large part) of their human capital in one firm.

The problem with these arguments is that they proceed very largely by assertion. They assume managers have monetary considerations very much to the fore, and they assume managerial labour markets operate efficiently in raising future managerial wages. More fundamentally still, they beg the question, which we discussed in the previous section, of whether managerial actions can actually be observed. Fama claims that in effect they can be, through *ex post* settling up. However, these are essentially untested assertions and until evidence has accumulated about them (for a study bearing on this, see Walkling and Long, 1984) the managerial labour market constraint should not be regarded as necessarily more important than those previously discussed.

Nevertheless, there is one *potential* difference between the effects of a managerial labour-market constraint and the other constraints we have discussed. Managerial reward structures in the firm arguably do not act so as to focus sufficient managerial attention on the long-term consequences of their decisions. The interests of banks and other short- to medium-term lenders, may serve to reinforce this neglect of the longer term. Takeover raiders also often are interested in swift returns. However, it is *possible* that, perhaps ten years afterwards, once the influence of a particular manager has been recognized in the firm, the managerial labour market will also take cognizance. At the same time, recognizing the influence of a single manager may be difficult, particularly if managers move jobs at all frequently, so inheriting the legacy of previous managers and leaving behind a legacy for successive managers.

2.3   Managers in Control: the Internal Organization

As well as managers acting as agents of shareholders, managers can be viewed in turn as taking on the role of principal in their relations with lower-level managers and operatives. A complete and rigorous analysis would obviously require a full specification of the hierarchy of successive principal–agent relationships. But restricting attention to the immediate relationships between management and subordinates still helps to explain a number of features of the internal organization of the firm as adaptations to information problems.

The evolution of the modern firm has seen an increasing degree of delegation of decision-making, and as a consequence innovations have taken place (over the last 60 years) in firms' hierarchical forms. This process of decentralization and organizational innovation, the major features of which are discussed in Chapter 3, can be attributed to three factors which are experienced as the firm grows in size: (a) the increasing complexity of the environment; (b) the limited calculating ability of top management; and (c) constraints on the ability of top management to assimilate information. In sum, it is said that the manager is only boundedly rational; no one has the ability to take all decisions optimally. Thus by delegating some decisions, the firm is better able to take advantage of specialization in information and knowledge about particular aspects of the production process.

Arguably though, these very same factors which lead to decentralization and principal–agency relationships in the first place, simultaneously make detailed monitoring of subordinates infeasible. This means that top management will not be able to verify the private information received by subordinate decision-makers, or to validate their courses of action. As was illustrated in the stylized example of Section 2.1, the opportunity then arises for lower-level decision-makers to exploit informational asymmetries resulting in a divergence between self-interested and cooperative behaviour. In response to this, we should expect to observe top management initiating schemes to deal with these problems in an attempt to minimize this divergence. In the remainder of this section we consider such issues.

2.3.1   Controlling Divisional Managers

One measure that the firm might introduce to control divisional managers is suggested by our simple illustration of moral hazard. Inability to observe application and effort may result in the use of output-related remuneration schemes. Salaries may be linked to divisional profitability thereby imposing some risk on divisional management via a variable reward. Such a scheme may in turn induce inefficiencies. Besides the possibility of being able to manipulate accounting-based earnings figures, divisional managers may be reluctant to undertake investment projects which are viewed as risky at the divisional level, despite much of the risk of these projects being diversified away at the corporate level. Salaries linked to accounting earnings might also induce a narrow focus on the short term with advertising, research and development, and other long-term investment suffering as a result. Further difficulties are then encountered in assessing the performance of new divisional managers. These are essentially the problems referred to earlier being encountered again, one rung down the firm's hierarchical ladder.

Recent results in agency theory and game theory suggest that rivalry between divisional managers can be profitably exploited. There are two main reasons for this. First, in assessing an agent's performance, all available sources of information should be used. To be precise, if common environmental factors affect the outcomes from different divisions in similar ways, then top management should link a divisional manager's reward not only to the absolute outcome level of the division, but also to the differences in outcomes between 'competing' divisions. This is partly because in comparing relative performance under these assumptions, much of the general risk which is not a result of the manager's actions is excluded: the relative outcome depends, to a far greater extent than absolute outcome does, on actions. Also, by making comparisons, the weaker can be encouraged to emulate the stronger, along the lines of Hart's (1983) paper discussed in the previous section. For example, a firm divisionalized on a geographical basis might exert greater control over production costs by this means. However, multi-period considerations could temper this result because divisional managers may have incentives to coordinate decisions over matters such as interdivisional transfers of goods and services, at the expense of the firm's overall profits.

Second, it is often the case that for strategic reasons a principal would want an agent acting on his/her behalf to have preferences differing from the principal's. The principal desires a good overall performance from the firm, whereas the agents want their divisions to do well. Yet agents acting with divisional objectives can improve the overall performance of the firm in some circumstances. This happens because the rivalrous actions over competing brands, say, within the firm have the effect of reducing output of rival firms, an effect which would not come about if the brands were to be managed jointly. Vickers (1985), who analyses a number of general examples of this type, draws the parallel with merger between a subset of firms in a Cournot oligopoly group, explored by Salant, Switzer and Reynolds (1983), where the subset can often find itself worse off after the merger as a result of actions of the firms not in the subset.

Finally, top management may find that monitoring devices for divisional management are more effectively designed if they reward superior performance rather than penalize inferior performance. This occurs because divisional managers, perhaps on the way to more principal-like roles, are characterized by a high degree of risk-tolerance. It may then be more efficient to exploit this risk-tolerance rather than to attempt to overcome it (Baiman and Demski, 1980).

2.3.2 Management of Operatives

Moving on to consider lower-level employees, output-related salary schemes may again be introduced in order to create incentives for agents to supply effort, where this is hard to measure directly. Thus we might expect to see piece-rate wage schemes used in some firms in preference to time-rate schemes. Stiglitz (1975) has suggested that greater reliance may be placed on piece-rates when workers are more tolerant of risk or when their responsiveness to monetary incentives is greater. At the same time, piece-rates can allow employees greater freedom over work–leisure trade-offs. Their use is widespread in clothing industries where there is a tradition of outwork (there are similarities between the 'putting-out' system and sharecropping (Stiglitz, 1974)), although piecework is also linked to high levels of female employment, as well as to tradition. Piece-rates may also prove useful in screening worker types if abilities to perform the job vary across workers. Of course, piece-rates are not confined to manual workers. The payment of marketing and sales personnel partly on a commission basis can be seen as an attempt to motivate by imposing some risk on the employee.

On the other hand, where quality or profitability and not just quantity of output is important, piece-rates may provide incorrect incentives. Time-rates may then be preferred, or more rigorous standards of quality control may be introduced. Piece-rates are not at all common in advanced technology industries. It is also interesting to note that in the UK motor vehicle industry piece-rates were largely abandoned in the 1970s in favour of schemes such as 'measured daywork' by which employees contract for a fixed rate to be paid in exchange for an accepted output level. More recently though, collective bonus schemes have been introduced into this industry, that is, bonuses for performance above a norm rather than penalties for low output, perhaps because the latter involves too much general risk.

In fact, the use of bonuses related to the joint outcome of a group of employees or even to the firm's overall performance has become increasingly popular throughout industry in the UK. These bonus schemes can be viewed as attempts to exploit the (increasing?) team production problem described by Alchian and Demsetz (1972), in situations where perfect *ex post* monitoring of workers by management is impossible. It seems reasonable to assume that workers themselves will be better placed to monitor each other than will top management. If this is the case, and if some form of peer-group pressure exists, then incentives may be improved by linking rewards to the performance of a group of workers rather than a series of individual contracts being negotiated or flat-rate schemes imposed. Group bonuses are important in the coal-mining industry where peer-group pressures might be considered important. General results pertaining to the subgame between (multiple) agents involved here await further research. Nevertheless, the results of a recent survey in Britain by M. White (1981) show a 'clear and unequivocal ... trend towards "collective" bonus schemes, accompanied by a movement to harmonize the treatment of direct and indirect production workers' (p. 133). Of particular interest is their widespread use for maintenance as well as production workers in industrial plants.

At the same time, and alongside bonus schemes, more rigorous methods of job evaluation have been employed in many industries in an attempt to monitor effort more closely. One means of controlling workers which is employed extensively in practice is the use of variance investigation policies. By these procedures, standards are set for performing various tasks and significant departures or 'variances' from standards are investigated. It has been found that if workers are sufficiently risk-averse, then a policy which calls for investigation of outcomes below a certain level will result in greater effort being applied in an attempt to avoid outcomes which trigger the investigation (see again Baiman and Demski, 1980).

One characteristic of the internal organization of the firm which has received a lot of attention in the academic literature is the prevalence of internal labour markets: 'markets' for labour within the firm. These can be readily explained as attempts to overcome informational asymmetries between employer and employees. For example, top management may be unable to distinguish between (to screen) workers of differing abilities when they are first employed, or between workers with different intentions about length of employment with the firm. If employees must be given on-the-job training or if there are other costs of hiring and firing workers, then employment contracts may be designed to take these factors into account. Some firms operate 'attendance bonus schemes' as part of their pay structure. White-collar employees' salaries are often linked to subsequent review procedures when further information about the employee may be available, or more simply to length of service with the firm (Salop and Salop, 1976). The design of pension schemes which penalize worker mobility might also be interpreted as an attempt to screen workers.

Multi-period considerations may alter some of the previous results. Radner (1982) has shown that in a multi-period setting, the divergence between cooperative and non-cooperative behaviour may disappear as parties enter into long-term arrangements. But here again, general results are elusive. For example, if multiple agents are included in a multi-period setting then the increased scope for coordinating activities by teams of workers in collusion against top-management must be considered.

Finally, consideration of one of the rationales for decentralization cited earlier suggests a further set of arrangements designed to ameliorate informational asymmetries. Decentralization facilitates specialization in information gathering. Moving down the hierarchical ladder, divisional managers, foremen and operatives will increasingly have superior local information. While there are obvious benefits to this specialization, there are also costs caused by differences in information. Lower-level workers need to be given the correct incentives to use local information optimally (from the firm's viewpoint) in decision-making and, if necessary, to report information truthfully to superiors. One means of benefiting from the superior local information of subordinates is to encourage participation in setting standards for work tasks.

More radically, worker representation on the board of directors may be encouraged and employee shareholding schemes may be introduced (see also Stiglitz, 1985, pp. 149–50). In the same way that giving a manager a shareholding or share option provides the manager with an incentive, so too will giving shares to employees provide them with an incentive to act in the common interest.

2.4   Concluding Remarks

We have attempted to analyse the relationships between managers, shareholders and other capital owners, also between managers and employees, within the modern firm. In doing this, we have discussed the various institutions controlling managers in rather more detail than the institutions for managerial control. This is a deliberate difference in emphasis, for the hierarchy within the firm is the subject of the next chapter.

Throughout, we have focused upon the importance of information, of uncertainty, and of the principal–agent model where it is relevant. As information technology improves, it may be thought that the problem we have discussed will be ameliorated. However this is true only to a limited extent. It is not only that those in control do not have information, or that they are unable to evaluate it (problems improved information technology may assist with) but also that the information provides only an imperfect or indirect measure of what would be optimal from the point of view of control.

Further Reading

Useful references to some of the basic results of agency theory applicable to this chapter include Arrow (1984) and Shavell (1979). Unfortunately, textbooks tend not to cover these aspects of the theory of the firm well, and many sources on the principal–agent model are rather technical.

Stiglitz (1985) provides a good modern overview of the many-principal–agent model of constraints on managers discussed in Section 2.2, and Lambert and Larcker (1985) give a good non-technical discussion, focusing on design of executive compensation packages. See also Lawriwsky (1984, particularly Chapter 3) and, for an unusual but interesting approach, Aoki (1984). Yarrow (1976) relates constraints to the more traditional 'managerial' models of the firm.

Concerning the internal organization material, again little of the agency-theory approach has filtered through to the textbooks. This is partly because of the technical nature of the material but also because the material is at a very formative stage. The journal literature is very diverse, encompassing both the economics and the management-accounting areas. For a survey emphasizing applications in management accounting, from which further references can be sampled, try Baiman (1982).

Acknowledgements

In addition to the editors, we would like to thank Trevor Buck and Kevin Keasey of the University of Nottingham for helpful comments.

Notes

1 The best contract to achieve implementation of a_2 would be to give the agent an unconditional payment of 16,900 (i.e. $114 = 16,900^{\frac{1}{2}} - 4^2$) which would leave the principal with an expected utility of only 23,100.
2 This can be computed by solving the two simultaneous equations:

$$2/3 \ z^{\frac{1}{2}}_{60} + 1/3 \ z^{\frac{1}{2}}_{30} - 36 = 114$$

$$2/3 \ z^{\frac{1}{2}}_{60} + 1/3 \ z^{\frac{1}{2}}_{30} - 36 = 2/3 \ z^{\frac{1}{2}}_{30} + 1/3 \ z^{\frac{1}{2}}_{60} - 16$$

where the first gives the agent the minimum remuneration, and the second ensures that the expected utility from selecting a_1 is no less than that from selecting a_2. Strictly speaking, the agent is now indifferent between the two actions but we assume that in such an instance the action preferred by the principal is implemented.
3 The contract in Note 1 would still achieve selection of a_2 but is clearly inferior to the present contract.
4 Actually, in the UK only individuals go bankrupt, not corporate bodies, but the terminology is well established and otherwise meaningful.

3 Markets and Managerial Hierarchies

TONY McGUINNESS

3.1 Introduction

The aim of this chapter is to present and evaluate Oliver Williamson's theory of the firm. Before launching into the details of his explanation, however, it will be useful to state clearly what it is that is to be explained. This will help also to put Williamson's work in perspective in relation to past and contemporary ideas about the firm.

Chapter 1 of this book introduced the idea, usually attributed to Coase (1937), that firms and markets are alternative methods of coordinating resource allocation. Though firms in the real world, like markets, involve a subtle mixture of control mechanisms, this chapter assumes that the essence of firm-type organization is the use made of authority to direct and coordinate resources. The object of the analysis is then to identify and explain in what circumstances the authoritarian direction of resources has advantage over market-type alternatives.

This definition of the essential nature of firm-type organization must not be confused with the idea that only authority is used to direct resources within firms that exist in the real world. The internal operations of real-world firms are controlled by a blend of authority and market-like mechanisms. This fact of life is reflected in recent economic analysis of the firm, which addresses the limits of authority and the options available *within* firms when direct supervision of a subordinate by a superior is difficult, perhaps because of information asymmetry.

The principal–agent relationship discussed in Chapter 2 is such a within-firm, market-type alternative to a supervisor–subordinate relationship. In passing, it should be noted that the conceptual framework developed by Williamson claims to provide an explanation of organizational forms in general, in that it seeks to explain the circumstances in which a variety of institutional forms – including classical market contracts, non-standard market contracts, government regulatory agencies, and trades unions, have, in turn, a comparative advantage in the organization of resources.

Despite recognizing the need for theory to explain market-type control mechanisms within real-world firms, this chapter accepts that some use of direct, non-delegated authority is the necessary, defining feature of a firm, and turns to Williamson's work for an explanation of the circumstances in which it has a comparative advantage over other control mechanisms. Section 3.2 presents the general concepts used by him. Section 3.3 uses these concepts to explain when and why a market is replaced by an authority-based form of organization; why authority might be distributed and used in a hierarchical way; and when the authority to make certain kinds of decisions might be delegated within a hierarchy (these latter circumstances involve limits to the centralization of authority, and give rise to the need for principal–agent contracts of the kind discussed in Chapter 2).

Before proceeding with the details, it is worth pointing out that at least one influential modern article on the theory of the firm denies that authority is the essence of the firm. Alchian and Demsetz (1972, p. 777) state unequivocally: 'It is common to see the firm characterized by fiat, by authority, or by disciplinary action superior to that available in the conventional market. This is a delusion.'

From what has been said, this is not the view of this chapter. Nor is it consistent with Coase's (1937, p. 37) attempt to define the abstract nature of the firm (author's emphasis):

'... owing to the difficulty of forecasting ... the less possible, and indeed, the less desirable it is for the person purchasing to specify what the other contracting party is expected to do ... Therefore, the service which is being provided is expressed in general terms, the exact details being left until a later date ... The details of what the supplier is expected to do is not stated in the contract but is decided later *by the purchaser*. When the direction of resources (within the limits of the contract) becomes dependent *on the buyer* in this way, the relationship which I term a 'firm' may be obtained.'

The interpretation of this statement here is that the contractual arrangements that define the firm are left open-ended, with the details of resource direction to be decided later by a member (or members) of the firm in whom authority is voluntarily vested. What is involved is the direct exercise of authority, not merely the design of an incentive system through which the 'agent's' interests are harnessed to serve the purposes of the 'principal'. This (authority) view of the firm is endorsed by Fitzroy and Mueller (1984, p. 37), who flatly reject the Alchian and Demsetz view. It is perhaps no coincidence that only when one is prepared to recognize that the firm is based on authority do issues of power come to the fore in the theory of the firm.

3.2 Concepts

This section discusses the concepts used by Williamson in his analysis of the firm. The problems and costs of organizing transactions depend on both their nature and the assumed characteristics of decision-makers in the model. In addition, the way in which they are organized is determined, at least in a competitive environment, by the principle of economizing on transaction costs. The aim of the analysis is to explain, and possibly to predict, the institutional arrangements by which transactions are negotiated, enforced, and adjusted. To serve this purpose, Williamson uses a model of human nature based on three behavioural attributes: bounded rationality, opportunism, and dignity. (See, for example, Williamson, 1984, pp. 196–202).

Bounded rationality is a weak form of rationality. People are assumed to try to make rational decisions but their ability to do so is constrained by limits on their capacity to receive, process, store and retrieve information. The importance of bounded rationality is stressed in the work of Herbert Simon (1957 and 1978). One implication is that people are unable to take full account of, or possibly even imagine, all future situations that might require changes in the terms of a transaction. Transactions that are more than just once-only exchanges cannot be organized, therefore, by a long-term market contract, agreed at the outset, specifying terms appropriate to any future state of the world. Complete, contingent-claims contracts of the type discussed by Radner (1968) are just not feasible, and some other institutional arrangement must be used.

Opportunism is a devious kind of self-interested behaviour. Williamson assumes that at least some people might behave in strategic, guileful ways, if they can do so undetected and thereby promote their own interest. This might involve representing their position (abilities, preferences, intentions) in a way that is less than completely honest, or even, perhaps, downright dishonest. An example inspired by Akerlof (1970) is the seller of a second-hand car who is much more knowledgeable about its true quality than any potential buyer. It is in the seller's interest to be selective in the information he gives the buyer, emphasizing the car's good points and down-playing its defects, since this would raise the price he will receive.[1] The opportunistic seller will selectively reveal and distort information, even provide false information, if he can do so without later penalty. The implication is that, even though gains from trade are potentially available, the transaction might not take place unless some means can be found to protect one party from the opportunistic representations of the other. The kind of institution that can best provide the protection depends on the nature of the transaction, an issue discussed later. If the assumption of opportunism is something you regard as an unnecessarily cynical view of human nature, note that its importance requires only that some, not all, people behave in this way and that it is difficult to tell who is opportunistic and who is not.[2]

The third human attribute in Williamson's model is dignity, though it is one of the least-developed concepts. It captures the idea that humanity should be respected for its own sake, so that people should not be treated in organizations solely as the means in an economizing process. However, taking account of dignity requires the acceptance of any necessary tradeoffs between it and other valued objectives. For example, if society believes workers should be democratically represented on firms' boards of directors, it also should be recognized that additional costs of democracy are to be borne by someone: shareholders who get lower profits, workers who get lower wages, customers who pay higher prices, or taxpayers. The need for tradeoffs should be recognized clearly, so as to avoid the implicit assumption that dignity is to be pursued at all costs. The economic approach to issues posed by dignity is the same as to more familiar externality problems such as environmental pollution: the optimum level of pollution is not zero, but can be determined only after due consideration of all the costs and benefits associated with the polluting activity. The integration of dignity into an analysis of the firm is at an early stage of development but might help to reduce barriers between economics and other approaches to the study of human behaviour.

3.2.1   Nature of Transactions

Transactions differ in the strains they place on decision-making ability, the scope they give for opportunism, and the degree to which they involve human dignity. Consequently, the best institutional arrangement to use depends on the nature of the transaction. There are three relevant dimensions along which transactions can differ: asset specificity uncertainty; and frequency (Williamson, 1984, pp. 202–7).

Asset-specificity refers to the extent to which the resources used in a transaction have a value therein that is higher than in any other use or to any other user. Highly specific assets are ones whose values elsewhere are comparatively low and, consequently, whose owners have a strong interest in continuing the transaction because of the high quasi-rents they receive. One expects durability to be a hallmark of highly specific assets, for quasi-rents are then available over many periods. However, this does not imply that transaction-specificity is confined to physical durable assets: human investment in individual or team knowledge that is not fully transferrable is also transaction-specific. Physical examples include equipment designed to make components that will fit into the product of only one buyer (e.g. exhausts for Rolls-Royce cars) or dispensing machines that can handle pack-sizes peculiar to one supplier. Human capital examples include a manager's knowledge of the idiosyncrasies of his firm's administrative system, or a team's knowledge of the comparative advantages of its members and thus of how tasks can be allocated most efficiently within the team. Site-specificity occurs where, for example, separable stages of production are placed in close proximity to economize on transport costs, and their relocation costs are high. Finally, 'dedicated' asset-specificity refers to resources which, in principle, are usable elsewhere but for which no effective demand exists outside the present transaction;[3] their installation was conditional on continuing demand from a particular buyer (see Williamson, 1983, p. 526).

The distinction between specific and non-specific assets does not coincide with the familiar distinction between fixed and variable inputs. Some fixed assets are equally valuable in other uses (e.g. general office space) whilst some variable inputs have relatively low values elsewhere (e.g. transaction-specific labour).[4] Outlays incurred in producing specific assets are 'sunk' in that they are not recoverable if the assets are redeployed.

Asset specificity has implications for organization because of the reluctance of parties to terminate transactions to which they have committed specific assets. Owners are aware of the capital losses they must incur if they redeploy their assets, and people with whom they are transacting know that nowhere else can they find assets as suitable to their needs as those already committed.[5] In other words, both parties are to some extent 'locked into' a transaction to which highly specific assets have been assigned. Such a situation offers great scope for opportunism when occasion arises for changing the original terms of the contract. Bargaining is then confined within a small group, and there are no pressures from a large number of competing sources or bidders to oblige people to present their positions in a fully honest way. Some institutional arrangement other than large-numbers competition needs to be found to safeguard the transaction from excessive opportunistic wrangling, which could siphon off the available gains from trade. The importance of these considerations is underlined by what Williamson (1984, pp. 207–8) calls the 'fundamental transformation', by which a transaction whose original terms were negotiated in an environment of large-numbers competition is transformed during its implementation to one where small-numbers bargaining is inevitable at the stage of contract renewal. This would occur if the winner of the initial contract benefited from learning-by-doing during its execution and was able to appropriate those benefits, enabling him to compete advantageously when terms are renegotiated.[6]

The second relevant attribute of a transaction is uncertainty about the environment in which it is to be executed. Where there are very many known alternatives, or there are known to be currently unimaginable possibilities, the ability of people to make detailed plans for the future is limited, given bounded rationality. Under these circumstances the future details of a transaction can be settled only when uncertainty is resolved by the passage of time. If time also gives advantages to the initial winners of a contract, arrangements for the final settlement of terms must not only be flexible, but also able to deal with opportunistic behaviour at the final settlement date. In these circumstances, coping with greater uncertainty requires a form of organization that is both adaptive and able to control opportunism in small groups.

Frequency is the third relevant attribute. If the original parties to a transaction effectively have no other outlet or source once the original contract has been awarded, and they are highly uncertain about the contemporary environment at the time when terms must be renegotiated,[7] an organizational form (e.g. a monitoring and control system) that is tailor-made for that transaction might substantially reduce bargaining costs on each occasion when renegotiation takes place. However, governance structures differ in terms of their set-up and running costs. Whether or not it is sensible to invest in a tailor-made structure depends on the capitalized value of the savings derived from it in relation to the present value of its costs. The greater the frequency of a transaction, the more justifiable is a (relatively) expensive governance structure that brings about (relatively) large savings in transaction costs.

3.2.2   Economizing

The hallmark of economic analysis is how to make best ('efficient') use of resources that are in scarce supply. In situations that involve uncertainty, bounded rationality and opportunism it is important to economize on resources used in negotiating, implementing and adapting contracts as well as on those used for more narrowly defined productive tasks. The efficient objective is to minimize the sum of production and transaction costs for the tasks required.

Williamson's advice to the organizational designer is to operate in a discriminating way, i.e. only after making a comparative assessment of the costs of using one organizational form rather than another. This advice is offered to designers in any field where resources are scarce: government departments, non-profit bureaucracies and families, in addition to profit-oriented businesses. But beyond this normative use of the analysis, Williamson claims that the economizing principle actually operates in the commercial world; that here, transactions do get organized, sooner or later, in efficient ways. This proposition amounts to an efficiency explanation of both the variety of organizational forms that exists at any one time and the way in which the pattern of organizations in the commercial world evolves over time.

The efficiency explanation contrasts sharply with attempts to explain organizational forms in terms of power, drawing on political and sociological concepts. A comparative evaluation of the alternative approaches should be based not on ideological issues, but on their ability to make sense of empirical observations. Williamson and Ouchi (1983, pp. 29–30) admit the relevance of power to the analysis of organizations but submit that

'... power considerations will usually give way to efficiency – at least in profit-making enterprises, if observations are taken at sufficiently long intervals ... This does not imply that power has no role to play, but we think it invites confusion to explain organisational results that are predicted by the efficiency hypothesis in terms of power. Rather power explains results when the organisation sacrifices efficiency to serve special interests. We concede that this occurs. But we do not believe that major organisational changes in the commercial sector are explained in these terms. The evidence is all to the contrary.'

The efficiency thesis should also be contrasted with the 'inhospitality tradition' of attempting to explain non-conventional institutions in the commercial world in terms of efforts to enhance monopoly power (Williamson, 1981, p. 1542). The 'efficiency' *versus* 'monopoly' debate has dominated theoretical and applied work in the field of industrial

economics. Williamson argues that giving due recognition to the importance of transaction costs serves to redress the balance towards efficiency
explanations, particularly if one accepts that rather stringent structural
preconditions must be satisfied before anti-competitive behaviour is
plausibly successful (1983, p. 537, n. 38).

A critical evaluation of Williamson's analysis is given later in the
chapter. At this stage, two points are worth making. Firstly, a purely
'efficiency' view of how organizations develop ignores the possibility
that the nature of transactions is not completely exogenous: the development of technology and the kinds of production techniques used
might depend on whose interests they promote. It is possible that
efficiency considerations dominate once the nature of transactions is
given, but that power is important in explaining their nature. Secondly,
one might accept the view that efficiency should not be ignored in
analysing the firm, without believing that monopoly issues are relevant
in only a few situations. Some organizational developments might occur
because they are more efficient ways of extracting consumer surplus.

3.3 Internal Organization

The concepts outlined in Section 3.2 are relevant to the design of
markets, the replacement of markets by some internal form of governance (the 'internalization' issue) and the design of internal forms of
organization. The design of markets involves the organization of non-
standard market transactions, such as those involving franchising or
reciprocal trading. A detailed consideration of these issues is outside
the scope of this book, whose subject is the firm rather than markets.[8]
The rest of this section deals with internalization, and with two aspects
of the design of internal forms of organization: hierarchy and hierarchical decomposition.

3.3.1 Internalization

A transaction is said to be internalized when its administration involves
the use of authority rather than voluntary bargaining between people
in a market. As discussed in Chapter 1, Coase (1937) argued that
familiar tools of economic analysis could be used to explain why one
system of organizing transactions would prevail over another. Williamson (1971) pursued Coase's line of inquiry by using the concepts
of Section 3.2 to explain the 'failure' of markets to organize transactions
between vertically related, technologically separable stages of
production.[9] Later, the internalization of financial and international

transactions within conglomerate and multinational firms were also analysed within the same framework. These specific forms of internalization are discussed, respectively, in Chapters 5, 6 and 7 below. This section deals with the general features of Williamson's analysis.

Markets and internal organization are two alternative types of 'governance structure' analysed by Williamson.[10] The type of transaction to which each is most suited can be explained after describing their characteristics.

In a market, bargaining is constrained by threats of imminent termination of any existing or proposed contracts; opportunism is controlled by the readiness of people to sever their dealings with other resource owners; and continuity of an agreement between people is not valued for its own sake: transactions are administered in an impersonal way, typified by the 'faceless' bargaining of competitive market models. The costs of using a market to organize transactions will be lowest when the threat to terminate a contract is an effective control mechanism.

Such a threat is credible only if carrying it out would impose little loss on the person terminating the contract. This requires the availability of other potential contractors, prepared to offer terms no worse than those available from the original parties to the contract. But these conditions do not exist where the original parties have invested in transaction-specific assets. As discussed in Section 3.2, any later re-negotiation of terms[11] would then be confined to parties to the initial contract. If this small group tried to draw up a new market contract, bargaining would be protracted because of the known absence of alternative partners. The costs of using a market, therefore, will be high for the organization of transactions that involve highly specific assets.[12]

In comparison, internal organization[13] is a more attractive way of administering such transactions. Bounds on rationality are eased by adjusting terms within the small group of people in an adaptive way, as time reveals new circumstances. Protracted bargaining, Williamson argues, is less likely for three reasons: people feel part of a unified organization, and so are less inclined to argue; management has the right to demand information from workers in the organization, and therefore can restrict opportunism; and, ultimately, management can use its authority to guillotine any dispute that threatens to be prolonged.

In Williamson's framework, therefore, an internal form of organization is an effective way of economizing on bounded rationality and controlling opportunism in the context of recurring transactions that involve specific assets. A market would be a relatively costly way of adjusting the uses made of specific assets in response to unforeseen changes revealed over time.

Two general aspects of Williamson's analysis of organizational forms are seen in this explanation of internalization. Firstly, the question of the best form to use hinges on efficiency in the use of decision-making resources. Secondly, the advantage that internal organization possesses in certain circumstances turns on its recourse to authority as a means of eliminating information asymmetry or terminating any prolonged wrangling between employees. There can be little doubt that this explanation of internal organization is an explanation of those authoritative aspects of management in real-world firms that, earlier in this chapter, were taken to be the *sine qua non* of Coase's (1937) definition of a firm.

One obvious example of internalization is the integration of vertically related, technologically separable stages of production. This is dealt with in depth in Chapter 5, but two comments are worth making here. Firstly, even if vertical integration leads to savings on decision-making resources it may, at the same time, so alter market structure that there is a shift of economic power in the relevant markets. The possible 'efficiency' consequences of vertical integration should not be assessed, therefore, in isolation from its possible effect on market power. Secondly, vertical integration between the production and distribution stages of supply can be explained easily within Williamson's framework. In fact, he himself (1981, pp. 1553-4) highlights its ability to make sense of the observed, selective pattern of forward integration by US manufacturers into distribution, in the late nineteenth century. The framework has claims, then, also to explain the marketing motives discussed in Chapter 7 (Section 7.5) as reasons for the forward integration of manufacturing firms into overseas distribution.

3.3.2   Hierarchy

Issues of institutional design don't disappear once a decision has been made to adopt internal organization. The details of its form influence organizational behaviour and performance just as structure influences conduct and performance within a market system. An important feature to explain is why a hierarchical system is invariably found in organizations such as firms.[14]

The debate on the rationale of hierarchy has been a heated one. It is an important focus of the conflict between 'efficiency' (economic) and 'power' (political/sociological) explanations of organizational forms. Williamson's views are hardly equivocal:

'... it is no accident that hierarchy is ubiquitous within all organisations of any size. This holds not merely within the private-for-profit sector but among non-profits and government bureaus as well. It likewise holds across national boundaries and is independent of political systems. In short, inveighing against hierarchy is rhetoric: both the logic of efficiency and the historical evidence disclose that non-hierarchical modes are mainly of ephemeral duration.' (1980, p. 35)

His efficiency arguments for hierarchy are connected with both bounded rationality and opportunism. First, let us define what we mean by hierarchy. Internal organization is a class of governance whose distinguishing feature is that a resource owner accepts restrictions on his sole rights to use his resources in whatever way he might choose. Within the bounds of some agreed domain, he allows his resources to be controlled by an authorized decision-making unit to which he might or might not belong. How might one define an increase in hierarchy across governance structures within the class? Williamson (1980) discusses both contractual and decision-making bases for defining hierarchy, and chooses the latter as the most relevant to organizational performance. On this basis the degree of hierarchy could be said to increase, *ceteris paribus*, with increases in the domain delegated to authorized control, and with reductions in the extent to which resource owners are involved in making decisions about the deployment of their resources. In other words, holding constant the controlled domain, hierarchy increases as authorized decision-making becomes more concentrated amongst people in an organization.[15]

In assessing the comparative efficiency of non-hierarchical and hierarchical forms of internal organization, it is instructive to contrast the peer group with a simple hierarchy (see Williamson, 1975, Chapter 3). The peer group makes decisions in a democratic way, with all owners having a say in the final decision. This might be achieved either by having all owners involved in all decisions, or having people take turns to make the decisions. A simple hierarchy puts decision-making authority permanently in the hands of a few people.[16] Williamson argues that, compared to simple hierarchy, the peer group is inefficient in both making and implementing decisions.

If all input owners have a say in all decisions, decision-making is a costly process: the greater the number of decision-makers, the more resources are used up in sending out the information needed to make the decision; and the more time is needed, in total, to give each person the opportunity to argue his preferred solution to any problem. One way round this, that remains consistent with the democratic spirit of the peer group, is to have a central decision-making unit comprising, at any one time, only a few people, but to rotate membership of this unit, each person taking a turn. However, this solution prevents the group achieving any gains from assigning people to tasks according to their comparative advantage. People can be expected to differ in their abilities[17] and this inevitably gives some people a comparative advantage in processing information, making decisions, and communicating them to others. Failure to exploit this involves efficiency losses. But making permanent appointments to a group that has the authority to make decisions creates an elite, and effectively transforms the peer group into a hierarchy.

Opportunism is claimed to be particularly relevant to the implementation of decisions. If it were absent, all transactors could be relied on to keep a promise to implement any decision to the best of their ability. With opportunism, a central monitoring unit is a possible way of controlling shirking, by monitoring input performance and adjusting compensation accordingly over time. Again, the fundamental principles of the peer group would not be compromised if monitoring roles were rotated. But rotation involves efficiency losses if (as seems likely) some people have a comparative advantage in monitoring. In the case of both decision-making and monitoring, therefore, Williamson argues that realizing gains from comparative advantage requires forming an elite, and therefore a hierarchy.

One possible situation in which a peer group would not cause a loss of efficiency is where democracy acts as a spur to individual effort and productivity. Whether or not this is a common occurrence is a matter for empirical investigation. Ben-Ner (1984, p. 248), for example, cites, among explanations for the high incidence of liquidations of producer co-operatives, 'their inability to settle personal disputes, their lack of discipline in the absence of a central monitor (and) their low motivation caused by excessive egalitarianism'. This would seem to suggest that a high price, in terms of efficiency, is paid for democracy. However, more empirical evidence on this is needed.

Criticisms of Williamson's efficiency rationale of hierarchy have the same basis as criticisms of his approach in general, and are dealt with in Section 3.4 below. It should be noted at this stage, however, that democracy might be a 'desirable output' of an organization, in which case its production at the expense of other outputs would not necessarily involve inefficiency.

3.3.3 Hierarchical Decomposition

Within hierarchical organizations of any size, more complex structures are observed than the simple (two-level) system discussed in the last section. In assessing the relative efficiency of alternative forms of hierarchy, the extent to which they economize on bounded rationality and control opportunism is of some importance. In this section, two forms of complex hierarchy are compared: the unitary form ('U-form') and the multidivisional structure ('M-form'). Williamson argues that the M-form is a more efficient way of administering certain types of transactions. He claims, therefore, that one of this century's most important innovations in business organization is explained by his approach.

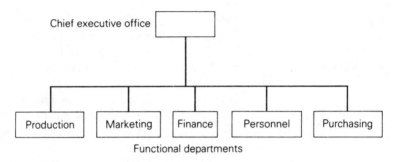

Figure 3.1   U-form organization

The U-form, illustrated in Figure 3.1, is a hierarchy organized on functional lines in which the chief executive office (CEO) has responsibility for both long-run ('strategic') planning of the organization as a whole and day-to-day ('operational') coordination of the functional departments (production, marketing, purchasing, personnel, finance). Each functional department is hierarchically organized, and is in the charge of a middle manager responsible for coordinating activities within his department. By 1917, vertical integration was a common feature of large US industrial firms, many of whom had adopted the U-form to administer their activities (see Chandler, 1976, p. 29). Some of these firms (typically, ones that possessed marketing or technological knowledge that could find application in new product lines: see Chandler, 1962) next tried to grow by diversifying, a strategy which revealed that the U-form had weaknesses when used to administer activities in several different markets. If a firm operates in several different markets the occasion more frequently arises for adjustments to be made in coordinating operational activities between functional areas. With a U-form structure, in which the functional basis of decomposition is preserved all the way up the hierarchy, more of top management's time is devoted to these operational matters, whose pressing need for resolution gives them an urgency not usually attached to issues of a more long-run, strategic kind. Because of cognitive limits within top management (i.e. bounded rationality), the effect that diversification has, therefore, in the U-form firm is for strategic planning to be 'crowded-out' by operational decisions. As Simon (1960) pointed out, one of the main tasks in designing a hierarchy is to decide the appropriate level of authority for each class of decision that has to be made. To economize on top management's bounded rationality there is an obvious need within the diversified firm for operating decisions to be decentralized. This would not be possible in a U-form because middle management has only functional responsibility: no one below the CEO has responsibility for overall operating performance in a given market.

Strategic planning with a diversified U-form organization is difficult not only because top management's limited attention is more frequently diverted to operational matters. Problems are caused also by the absence of information on overall operating performance in each separate market. Firstly, this makes it difficult to decide where best to expand or contract the firm's resources. Secondly, without such information, the performance of each department within the U-form is assessed by the CEO on the basis of criteria specific to that department, rather than by aggregating its contributions to overall performance in the separate markets. This severely distorts the incentive system within the organization: since their efforts are judged and rewarded on the basis of functional criteria, middle managers have the incentive to pursue functional (sub-global) goals beyond levels that are optimal from the corporate (global) point of view. This is an example of opportunism by middle managers, due to their superiors' inability to check their claims about what is actually in the best interests of the firm.

Williamson argues that the M-form, illustrated in Figure 3.2, avoids these weaknesses in administering the diversified firm, by economizing on bounded rationality and improving control of opportunism. In the M-form, below the top level of management, the hierarchy is organized on an operating rather than on a functional basis. Each division controls the operations of a fairly self-contained part of the organization's activities (for example, a particular product line, or a geographical area). The aim is to place in one division activities which interact strongly, and put weakly interacting parts in different divisions. The head of each division is responsible for its operating performance, which is judged by indicators of overall success in its markets (for example, by operating profits, sales growth, or market share). Divisional heads therefore have incentives that, compared to the U-form, are aligned more closely with corporate (global) goals and which discourage over-pursuit of functional (sub-global) goals. Each division is itself organized on U-form lines.

The M-form economizes on the bounded rationality of top management by decentralizing operational decisions to the divisional level. Strategic planning for the organization as a whole is the responsibility of top management in a 'General Office'. People here are not functional

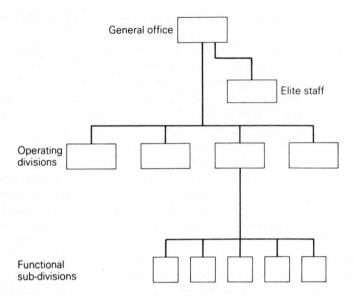

Figure 3.2 M-form organization

specialists and, therefore, are less likely to advocate policies that promote functional at the expense of corporate interests. The General
Office chooses organizational goals, monitors the performance of the
separate operating divisions, and allocates the organization's resources
among these divisions. In doing these things, it is supported by an 'elite
staff', again comprising people with no functional interests, whose roles
are to audit the operating divisions and advise the General Office.

The M-form was independently developed by several US corporations (Du Pont, General Motors, Standard Oil of New Jersey,
Sears) in the 1920s and 1930s, in response to management problems
that emerged from their attempts to diversify. However, its efficiency
advantages in these circumstances should not be used to infer that it is
a panacea of organizational design. The general principle is that net
gains can be made by identifying and giving effect to decomposability
amongst the organization's activities. The M-form is not appropriate if
divisions are formed between which there are strong links on either
the supply or the demand side (see Williamson, 1970, Chapter 8). Steer
and Cable (1978) found, among large UK companies, evidence that
profitability was increased by having the form of internal organization
appropriate to the firm's environment. The M-form is suitable only in
some environments. As markets and technology evolve, one would
expect the nature of transactions to change and present new con-
figurations of administrative problems. The emergence of the 'matrix'

form has been interpreted (Knight, 1976) as a structural response to increasing environmental complexity. However, little work has been done, as yet, on analysing its appearance in terms of Williamson's framework.

3.4   Critique

Williamson's theory of the firm, presented in Section 3.3, is an explanation of why some resources are managed, rather than allocated by markets, and why managerial functions are divided into several different, specialized roles within the firm. This section briefly reviews the essential features of Williamson's theory, then presents two types of criticisms: firstly, that the theory is a confusing mixture of static and dynamic elements, analysed in a loose way that does not make clear which things are endogenous and which are exogenous; secondly, that the approach is too sanguine about the desirability of the organizational forms that are explained.

That transaction-specific assets are organized by management rather than markets, is explained by savings on the resources used to decide how to adjust to changes unanticipated at the start of the contract. Given that resources are managed, hierarchy is explained by gains from allowing people to specialize according to their comparative advantage: in particular, those with a comparative advantage in deciding how to coordinate the diverse resources used in the firm and how to adjust this coordination in response to unforeseen changes, are assigned specialist managerial roles. Finally, the decomposition of managerial hierarchies allows some managers to specialize in strategic decision-making and for this task to be performed by people who not only possess a relevant comparative advantage but also whose corporate loyalties are not compromised by undue devotion to narrow functional goals. In essence, therefore, Williamson's theory of the firm explains the existence, division, and specialization of management in terms of economizing on resources used to make decisions. In addition, allocative efficiency may be improved if the shift to an M-form of internal organization leads to behaviour that is more profit-oriented.

It is a strength of Williamson's theory that attention is drawn to the need for decision-making resources and to the importance of economizing on these. A further attraction of the approach is its discussion of the role of such resources in deciding how to respond to changes unanticipated at the start of a contract: it is this feature that adds a fundamentally dynamic element to the theory. A major weakness, however, is that this element is fitted only roughly into the discussion, in a way that makes it difficult to integrate the dynamic with the static features of the analysis. In particular, given the importance attached by Williamson to efficiency, there is no clear treatment of the trade-offs that might be necessary between short-term and long-term efficiency. One example of the inadequacies that arise from such informal presentation of the theory is the absence of a clear analysis of the interdependence between production technique and organizational form. Instead of focusing on this interdependence, as one would expect of a truly dynamic theory, Williamson discusses the efficient resolution of contractual problems that are associated with given techniques of production. The techniques themselves, it would seem, are regarded by him as exogenous to his analysis. If so, only limited claims, if any, should be made for the theory as an explanation of the historical evolution of the firm, and of industrial organization. A second example of this type of criticism is found in Putterman (1982, p. 149) who, in arguing against Williamson's explanation of management hierarchy, points out (1982, p. 149, original emphasis)

'... that while static *economizing on scarce decision-making capabilities*, which characterizes hierarchical organizations, may be advantageous in the short-run, this same characteristic may have an associated property of retarding such multiplication of capabilities as might be brought about by a more participatory system, and which might, in fact, prove widely beneficial.'

This type of criticism stems from the lack of formal analysis in Williamson's theory. Until such analysis is developed, and the various elements of the theory are integrated in a consistent way, no convincing claims can be made about having explained the historical pattern and evolution of organizational forms.

The second type of criticism made of Williamson's analysis is its emphasis on efficiency at the expense of distribution. Malcomson (1984, p. 126) argues that 'an essential feature of the world Williamson is interested in ... is not one in which one can simply *assume* that economic efficiency will win out in the end'.

The reason is that the organizational changes discussed by Williamson influence the distribution of power both within and between firms, and one cannot presume that power is used to produce efficient outcomes. Within firms, the existence of a specialized managerial hierarchy inevitably sacrifices equality in the distribution of power, and raises the issue of whether workers are adequately compensated for their loss of autonomy in controlling the work process. Marglin (1975) argues that the development of the factory system was not in the interest of workers who, being left with no alternative but the freedom to starve, were forced to comply. Putterman (1984), whilst accepting the necessity for hierarchy in a complex organization, questions whether this needs to be associated with the domination of capital over labour.

There is also the possibility that organizational changes might alter the distribution of market power between firms. Williamson's expressed aim is to redress the balance, in industrial organization theory, between arguments that emphasize the consequences of organizational changes for monopoly power, and those that focus on their efficiency consequences. Nevertheless, as discussed in Chapters 5 and 7 below, the monopoly power effects of decisions such as vertical integration and multinational production should not be ignored. If read in isolation, Williamson's analysis is far too sanguine about the efficiency effects of the organizational forms it explains.

3.5   Summary

Williamson's theory of the firm is an attempt, following Coase, to explain the existence and internal structure of firms rather than to take them for granted. In doing so, it rightly emphasizes the need for an economic analysis of decision-making resources. Despite introducing some dynamic elements into the discussion, these are not treated in a formal way. This lack of formal analysis leaves the dynamic features of the theory inadequately specified, and thereby limits the relevance of claims it makes to explain the historical evolution of the firm. In isolation, Williamson's discussion neglects the effects of organizational changes on distribution and monopoly power.

Further Reading

The most comprehensive statement of Williamson's theory is his book, *Markets and Hierarchies* (1975). Summaries of his framework and its applications are given in his articles (1981) and (1984). Criticisms of his analysis are presented by Fitzroy and Mueller (1984), Malcomson (1984) and Putterman (1982). Attempts to find empirical support for Williamson's ideas are Masten (1984), Monteverde and Teece (1982a) and Palay (1984).

Notes

1   This assumes the potential buyer has no low-cost way of redressing his initial relative lack of knowledge, and that the seller's interests are not

threatened by any unfortunate experience the buyer might have with the car after purchase.

2   Adverse selection and moral hazard, long recognized as behavioural features of insurance markets, are nothing more than examples of opportunistic behaviour. Adverse selection occurs prior to the writing of insurance contracts, moral hazard afterwards, representing, respectively, examples of *ex ante* and *ex post* opportunism (see Williamson, 1975, pp. 13–16).

3   For example because sufficient capacity already exists elsewhere.

4   Strictly speaking, labour should be treated as a multi-attribute input, some of the attributes being specific and others not.

5   By definition, transaction-specific assets are not generally available elsewhere in the economy. A person who terminates a transaction that has involved someone else investing in such assets faces the prospect either of turning to non-specific assets or of persuading others to invest in specific assets. The latter might prove difficult if others know he has reneged on the original contract.

6   More generally, people who have already invested in transaction-specific assets have advantages when terms are renegotiated because they need be offered only the transfer earnings of their assets. Bargaining is then about the distribution of quasi-rents among the parties to the original contract.

7   Because different people inevitably learn different things with the passage of time, opportunism might involve people giving a distorted report of what they have learned privately. There would then be an imperfect view of the contemporary world as a whole, even though every part of it might be known to someone. Even the contemporary environment is uncertain, therefore, though in a different sense than is the future.

8   The organization of non-standard market transactions is discussed in Williamson (1983).

9   The term 'market failure' is somewhat misleading in this context because the same ideas are used to explain the circumstances in which markets will be used to organize transactions. The real issue is about which form of organization has the lowest transaction costs.

10   Arbitration and obligational contracting are the others, but are not discussed in this chapter. What is said about 'markets' in the text relates, strictly, to Williamson's (1979, pp. 248–9) notion of 'classical contracting'.

11   We are here analysing a transaction that recurs over time.

12   The argument in the text relates to the costs of using a series of short-term market contracts to organize the transaction. Bounded rationality prevents the anticipation of all disputes that might arise, and thus rules out a long-term market contract, drawn up before investment in specific assets takes place, containing details of an agreed resolution for every dispute that might occur.

13   A 'unified' governance structure, in Williamson's terminology.

14   Hierarchical decision-making is also commonplace in other social organizations that are based on authority, for example, government bureaucracies and charities. The same principles can be applied in these contexts,

though presumably the pressure for efficiency is not as great as in commercial firms.

15 In practice, of course, different decisions in a firm will differ in the degree to which they are hierarchically controlled.

16 In other words, is defined so as to exclude democracy-via-rotation (see Williamson, 1975, p. 45, Footnote 4).

17 Following Simon (1959) some attempts have been made to develop bounded rationality as an alternative to the mainstream approach to rationality found in economics (i.e. an approach that recently has encapsulated expected utility maximization and rational expectations). Little recognition has yet been given to the likelihood that people differ in the way in which their rationality is bounded, and to the analysis of what this implies. Haltiwanger and Waldman (1985) have made a recent attempt to take up the issue.

4 Strategic Behaviour by Firms

BRUCE LYONS

4.1 Introduction

'If a man knocks at a door and says that he will stab himself on the porch unless given $10, he is more likely to get the $10 if his eyes are bloodshot' (Schelling, 1960, p. 22). Why? Because the bloodshot eyes are a signal that the poor wretch has been drinking enough or is sufficiently depressed or insane to carry out his threat. A sober and mentally healthy man would be much less likely to get the $10 because it is improbable that he would carry out his threat. A threat only becomes convincing if the recipient believes it to be true, and the simple but crucial point is that it is easier to prove the truth of something that is true than of something that is false.

This does not mean that it is not feasible for a healthy man to put himself into a position such that his threat appears to be credible. For instance, he may be able to drink himself into such a state of despair that the threat becomes convincing. Note, however, that if the householder is aware of this potentially embarrassing situation arising, he may be able to negate the threat by, say, being out when the man knocks. Unfortunately, this alternative commitment will be of little use in averting the self-mutilation unless it can be effectively communicated *before* the drinking starts. Thus, the timing and sequence of strategic moves is usually crucial.

These actions of 'deliberate drunkenness' and 'being out' are examples of strategic moves. For the most part, we shall follow Schelling in defining a strategic move as an action 'that influences the other person's choice, in a manner favourable to one's self, by affecting the other person's expectations on how one's self will behave' (Schelling, 1960, p. 160). On occasions, however, a slightly more general definition may be used to include actions which directly affect the other person's utility without necessarily affecting their expectations on how one's self will behave. A strategic move in the latter class would be a punch on the nose. Thus, for the most part, and in the context of the theory of the firm, we shall be concerned with actions that are more subtle than burning down a rival's factory.

This chapter is about the ability of firms to act strategically in order to gain the same sort of advantage over actual or potential rivals as the man on the doorstep hopes to achieve in the above example. It will be seen that the main lessons of strategic behaviour carry over to such business variables as capital investment, advertising, R&D, and product choice. For instance, an irreversible commitment (e.g. drunkenness or a fully paid-up advertising campaign) is far more effective than an unsubstantiated threat; also the one who is able to make the first commitment (e.g. to get drunk or be out, or the first one to enter the industry) will usually gain the advantage.

4.2   The Theory of Strategic Behaviour

In order to bring out most clearly the underlying logic behind strategic behaviour, it is useful to analyse a simplified theoretical model in some depth. This has the added advantage of, at the same time, presenting the reader with an introduction to modern game theory. The following presentation closely follows Dixit (1982); indeed, this section is effectively an annotated version of Dixit's excellent, but very condensed, exposition. The example of entry deterrence is used because it brings out the theory of strategic behaviour most clearly. Direct applications to the theory of the firm are left to later sections.

A monopolist is currently earning profits with a present value of V_m, but is threatened with the possibility of entry. Since we shall be comparing profit outcomes with and without actual entry, it is convenient to call the monopolist 'the incumbent' and the single potential entrant 'the entrant' whether she enters or not.[1] If entry occurs, both entrant and monopolist earn $V_d > 0$ if they 'share' the market but $V_w < 0$ if the incumbent decides to 'fight' the entrant. Sharing implies reluctant acquiescence rather than collusive agreement.

Although this model is capable of many interpretations, it may help if the reader bears the following reference case in mind. Both firms have the same constant marginal costs and small overheads. V_d is the outcome of a Cournot duopoly with 'low' advertising and V_w is the result of a price war and/or aggressive advertising with the result that losses are made.

Returning to the general model, the entrant earns exactly zero profits if she does not enter. The pattern of payoffs is therefore $V_m > V_d$

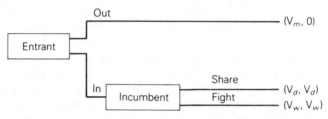

Figure 4.1   Game tree showing value of incumbent and entrant profits (in that order)

$> 0 > V_w$, and is illustrated in the form of a game tree in Figure 4.1. Formally, we have a two-stage game with the decision to enter or not being made in the first stage and the decision to fight or not being made at a second, later stage.[2] The central question to ask of this model is: which of the three possible outcomes (monopoly, entry with sharing, and warfare) will result?

In order to narrow down the field, we require a solution concept, which is to say a set of rules that imposes certain constraints on the abilities and rationality of the participants in the game. Firstly, we rule out collusion and examine non-cooperative behaviour, in particular a Nash equilibrium. This is not because we believe that collusion is unusual or improbable, but because much can be learnt by focusing on an interesting set of tractable problems. A Nash equilibrium is defined as a situation in which each firm is optimizing given the strategy being pursued by his or her rival.

Next, and most central to the question of strategic behaviour, we must decide what actions it is reasonable to expect that the incumbent can take and what threats the entrant might reasonably believe. The most straightforward case arises when simple, unsubstantiated threats are believed.[3] If the incumbent claims he would fight a price or advertising war if there was entry and the entrant stays out, then this is a Nash equilibrium. Given each firm's declared strategy, the other is doing the best it can. Entry deterrence is easy for the incumbent who can costlessly plan the most horrendous retaliation against the smallest incursion into his market.[4] This is at the same time one of the simplest and one of the least convincing examples of strategic behaviour that we shall come across.

The main problem with the argument behind this solution to the game is that were the entrant to ignore the threat and actually enter, then there would remain no incentive for the incumbent to actually carry out his threat.[5] The entrant is therefore being unduly naïve in believing an empty threat.

An attractive alternative way of deciding which outcome in Figure 4.1 is most likely is to argue that at each point in time, whatever situation might arise, each firm will act on the assumption that its rival will act rationally from that point on. This stronger form of rationality, which rules out empty threats, leads to what is known as a perfect equilibrium.[6] In the present example, the entrant observes that since $V_d > V_w$, were she to enter, the incumbent's best response would be to share. Therefore, entry implies profits of V_d for both firms. Since staying out gives only zero profits to the entrant, and $V_d > 0$, she will choose to enter. The perfect equilibrium is entry and sharing.

Thus, as the model currently stands, unless we are satisfied with a very weak form of rationality, there is nothing the incumbent can do to prevent entry. However, this model is excessively simplistic and restrictive because the incumbent is given no means by which the entrant can be influenced prior to entry. In other words, he is unable to act strategically. Two extensions will suffice to illustrate the power of strategic behaviour even in the presence of the strong rationality implied by a perfect equilibrium. Firstly, we look at what happens when the threat of entry is repeated many times and there is more than one potential entrant (so firms may wish to establish a reputation). Secondly, we allow the incumbent to invest in certain commitments that leave the entrant in no doubt that she is better off out of the industry than in it.

In a one-off game, the incumbent has no incentive to establish a reputation for aggressively responding to entry. However, if a passive response is interpreted by other potential entrants as a sign of weakness, the industry may be swamped by new firms in search of easy profits until the original incumbent is left with none for himself. An early price war may then be a very good strategic move as long as it is interpreted as a signal that all future incursions would be similarly treated.[7] Unfortunately for the incumbent, such predatory price wars are often frowned upon by anti-trust authorities and are sometimes illegal[8] (which is not to say that they never happen).

The second, and more subtle, strategic move that the incumbent might try is to make some commitment, prior to the entry decision, that alters his own expected profits and so the entrant's expectation of his reaction to entry. This idea is best illustrated by directly extending the earlier example to allow the incumbent to invest C in resources that would only be useful in the event that a price war actually takes place. Thus, the incumbent's payoffs are reduced to $V_m - C$ or $V_d - C$ in the event of monopoly or sharing, and remain at V_w in the event of a price war. It may be helpful to bear in mind the example of productive capacity that is in excess of monopoly requirements but which would be necessary to sustain a price war. Another effective commitment might be heavy advertising which has an effect on goodwill that persists long enough to be valuable if entry should occur. Other examples which may have similar characteristics include R&D expenditures and brand proliferation. The crucial assumption is that such commitments would become necessary expenditures in the event of a fight with the entrant.

It turns out to be important that the investment be a commitment, by which we mean that it is both irreversible and visible to the entrant. If C is visible but can be sold off at its full value at any time, the entrant can expect the incumbent to sell C whenever this would give him greater profits. The threat to use C in a price war is then empty. Similarly, if C is irreversible yet not observed by the entrant, then she would not realize that the game had changed from that given by Figure 4.1 and she would still enter. As will become clear, such entry due to imperfect information can lead to actual (as opposed to threatened or expected) price wars.

The new set of possible profit outcomes is given in extensive form in Figure 4.2. Since the incumbent can always choose not to be commit-

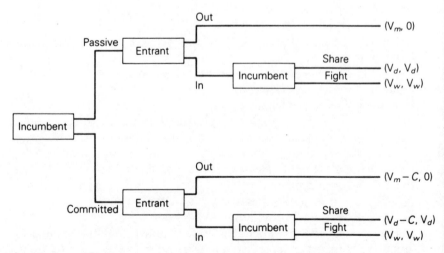

Figure 4.2   Game tree when incumbent can choose to pre-commit resources

ted, the top half of the game tree is exactly the same as Figure 4.1. The new game has three stages. First, the incumbent chooses whether or not to invest C. Second, the entrant decides whether or not to enter. Third, the incumbent decides whether to share or fight. We can now search for the perfect equilibrium.

We have already deduced that entry followed by sharing is the outcome if the incumbent has not committed himself. He can therefore expect V_d if the top branch of the game is followed. If the incumbent commits by spending C, and the entrant stays out, he can expect $V_m - C$. On the other hand, if there is entry despite commitment, the incumbent will now choose to fight as long as $V_w > V_d - C$. Realizing this, the incumbent will stay out rather than end up with $V_w < 0$. Thus, as long as the incumbent can find some commitment which satisfies $0 > V_w > V_d - C$, or, put another way, some positive $C > V_d - V_w$, he will be able to deter the rational entrant and earn $V_m - C$.

Note that in a one-shot game this will not necessarily be the perfect equilibrium because this payoff must be compared with that from no commitment, V_d. It is only if $V_m - C > V_d$ and $V_w > V_d - C$ or, rearranging, $V_m - V_d > C > V_d - V_w$ that it is both more profitable to deter entry and feasible to do so.[9] What this formal example suggests is that provided potential commitments exist, strategic entry-deterring behaviour is more likely when the value of monopoly is high relative to sharing and the cost of a fight is not so great as to put warfare out of the question.

The model discussed at length in this section has the great attribute of clearly bringing to the surface the structure of the argument behind the modelling of strategic behaviour. Unfortunately, this may appear to be rather divorced from real economic problems. It will be the task of the later sections of this chapter to convince the reader otherwise, but in the meantime we provide a political example that exactly matches the parameters of the present model. *Of course*, any resemblance to actual political events is entirely coincidental.

The nation of Thaka is in possession of the territory of Falvina, but ownership of the land is bitterly disputed by neighbouring Galta. Galta, however, is unwilling to press its claims by force because Thaka maintains a small but significant defence force which would put up a costly fight. This is the perfect equilibrium predicted in the Figure 4.2 game.

Time passes and domestic stringencies lead to Thaka withdrawing its military commitment to Falvina, leaving it poorly defended. Galta now reassesses the situation and finds that because Thaka now has less to lose (there will be no military casualties and less loss of face), a military takeover of Falvina should not provoke any military retaliation. Galta consequently occupies Falvina, leaving Thaka with the option of either accepting the new status quo or fighting a mutually ruinous war with the militarily committed Galta.

Actual war will only result from either irrational behaviour or, more interestingly, because the two countries have mistaken the parameters of the game. For instance, Thaka may think that an apparently irrational war in Falvina is a good investment to gain a reputation and deter incursions into other disputed territories it possesses. On this interpretation, Galta is mistaking a repeated game for a one-off game, and Thaka has failed to realize that it would do so. Alternatively, one country may be committed to Falvina in some non-military way that the other has not fully appreciated (e.g. through a domestic promise that the other country's intelligence services have failed to pick up). In this case, the problem is that the commitment is not being made visible enough. Note that in either case, if war actually happens, one or both countries will have had to have made serious errors concerning each's knowledge of the other's commitments (i.e. there is incomplete information). Finally, it is possible that Thaka is deliberately trying to cultivate a reputation for irrational aggression in order to frighten future disputants. Such strategies are not investigated in this chapter.

In what follows, it should always be borne in mind that firms are also likely to make mistakes and, because of the inherent uncertainties in the world, strategic behaviour may not always have the desired outcome. Mutually ruinous price wars may be uncommon, but human frailty ensures that they do exist. Nevertheless, economic models set in a world of certainty, where destructive fights are threatened but never occur, are very useful in improving our understanding of business behaviour, and it is such models that are explored in this chapter.

4.3   Strategic Investment: an Example

We have so far looked only at cases of dichotomous behaviour. Choices have been to commit or not commit and to be passive or fight. Few economic examples present such stark alternatives and this section investigates a problem which has continuous choice in both dimensions. The question of strategic investment to deter entry is also one of the most written about topics in the recent industrial organization literature.

Is it possible for an incumbent monopolist to choose his productive capacity such that a potential entrant is put at a disadvantage? The basic idea is simple but there are many complexities, particularly when the share/fight decision is replaced by a continuous post-entry pricing game. Throughout this section, we assume that the entrant would make an identical product to the incumbent's, that both firms have access to identical cost curves, and that there are economies of scale.

The first answer to the above question was given by the famous Bain–Sylos-Labini–Modigliani model of limit pricing. Essentially, the incumbent adopts the position of a Stackelberg leader[10] while the entrant passively accepts the incumbent's current output as what he would produce post-entry. The implication is that any output supplied to the market by the entrant would reduce industry price and, given economies of scale, the incumbent may be able to earn positive profits while a potential entrant believes she could not. The details of this model are well treated in the standard industrial economics textbooks,

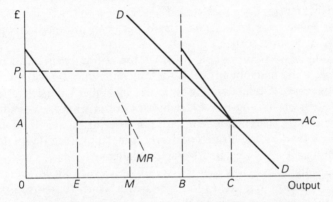

Figure 4.3   The traditional limit-pricing model

but a simplified diagram may aid understanding (see Figure 4.3). The long-run average cost curve is, for simplicity only, drawn as steeper than the demand curve. At output levels greater than $0E$, average costs are constant at A. By choosing an output rate $0B$ and charging P_l, the monopolist is making a profit of P_lA multiplied by $0B$. However, the entrant does not expect to find entry profitable because her extra output reduces price along the residual demand curve to the right of B and $BC < 0E$. At no output can costs be covered.

Many criticisms have been levelled at this model but in the present context we need explore only one. Limit pricing is clearly an example of strategic behaviour. The incumbent is choosing current output at a higher level than the monopoly output, $0M$, in order to influence the expectations that potential entrants hold with respect to what output would be post-entry. This influence on expectations depends on a simple belief that current output will be sustained. As it stands, however, the model has no explicit means of commitment by the incumbent. Why, then, should the entrant expect him to maintain output rate $0B$? The real problem is that there is no explicit model of what happens in the event of entry (the final stage in the game tree) so we do not know if the incumbent's threat is empty or not. Put more formally, is limit pricing a perfect equilibrium?

Once an explicit treatment of commitment is introduced, it soon becomes clear that the benefits of strategic entry deterrence become strongly dependent on the expected pricing behaviour of the firms (i.e. the post-entry game). In the following paragraphs a number of possibilities are explored. The reader should not expect to find one 'right' model, but rather a series that may apply in differing circumstances. Commitment is introduced by allowing for sunk costs. Sunk costs are costs which once spent are no longer recoverable. An example is specialist machinery which costs K_n when new, but which has a resale or scrap value of only K_r as soon as it has been installed. In this case $K_n - K_r$ is a sunk cost.

Consider a post-entry game in which the entrant expects to be able to undercut the incumbent's price for long enough to be able to recover her sunk costs. Understanding this, the incumbent must live in continuous fear of 'hit-and-run' entry by an entrant who could snatch any positive profits. The incumbent dare not price at greater than average cost. Such markets are termed perfectly contestable (see Baumol, 1982) and they leave no room for strategic behaviour.

Contestability requires that the speed with which incumbents match price cuts is slow relative to the speed with which the entrant sets up production and gathers market share. This is a patently unrealistic assumption when applied to most industrial markets. This might not matter were it not for the fact that even a small change in the conditions required for contestability completely reverses the competitive conclusion. For instance, if both firms can set price freely and rapidly, and do so competitively (so a Bertrand–Nash equilibrium in prices is expected to develop), then the entrant must expect price equal to marginal cost post-entry. In this case, even a very small, sunk, overhead cost would be sufficient to deter entry. This is because, with constant marginal costs, there would be no surplus to cover overheads. While in the contestability case strategic behaviour is not feasible, in the competitive pricing case it is not necessary. In fact, the incumbent can price as a safe monopolist happy in the knowledge that no one would be fool enough to attempt entry into such a *potentially* competitive industry. The entrant has to take note of her own sunk costs in both cases, but the incumbent's costs matter in neither.

In attempting to add strategy back into the model, Spence (1977) distinguishes the incumbent's choice of capacity from his choice of current output. In terms of Figure 4.3, it is argued that a capacity of

0B is necessary in order for the incumbent to be able to expand output whenever entry is threatened. Given that capacity is selected in this entry-forestalling manner, pre-entry price and output can be chosen so as to maximize short-run profits. Spence argues that sunk costs are a crucial element to this strategy since prior commitment is 'a way to issue a credible threat'. Thus, the Spence model improves on the profitability of limit pricing by replacing low prices with excess capacity. Unfortunately, the Spence model still fails to explain why potential entrants should expect the incumbent to produce at full capacity post-entry. Without an explanation of how firms would behave in the event of entry, we do not know if Spence's incumbent does have a credible threat or not.

It was the major contribution of Dixit's (1980) paper that he explicitly modelled the post-entry game, and argued 'that the role of an irrevocable commitment of investment in entry-deterrence is to alter the initial conditions of the post-entry game to the advantage of the established firm, for any fixed rule under which that game is to be played'.[11] If the post-entry game is such that the incumbent is expected to reduce his output, then there is no point in investing in excess capacity that will not be used under any circumstances.

This is usually the case with, for example, Cournot oligopoly and also collusion. Only if the post-entry game is so competitive that the incumbent is expected to actually increase output will excess capacity be a sensible strategy. This does *not*, however, mean that there remains no room for strategic behaviour in the former cases. By means of irreversible investments, the incumbent can usually 'sink' some of his *marginal* costs prior to an entry threat, and so reduce his effective marginal costs relative to an entrant's. By paying such costs in advance (i.e. by commitment), he is able to create an asymmetry with respect to the entrant. Since in most oligopoly models firms with lower marginal costs end up with higher market shares, the ability to act strategically is a distinct advantage. Dixit demonstrates that this advantage can be sufficient to deter entry.

The basic idea can be illustrated by means of a reaction curve diagram based on a post-entry game that is expected to be Cournot duopoly. A reaction curve shows the most profitable output for each firm given any output chosen by the other (see Figure 4.4). The arrows show the direction of increasingly profitable outcomes for each firm (e.g. if the entrant produces nothing, then the incumbent's most profitable output is 0M). Unlike in the usual textbook treatment, each curve is discontinuous. This is because economies of scale mean that, for instance, if the incumbent produces any more than 0B the entrant's expected profits drop below zero. Thus output rates 0B and 0M are exactly the

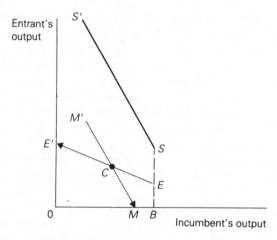

Figure 4.4   Over-investment to deter entry

same as in Figure 4.3. In the absence of sunk costs, limit pricing is ineffective because the entrant will rightly expect a profitable Cournot equilibrium to develop at C. Entry is not deterred. However, if the incumbent is able to commit himself such that his effective marginal costs post-entry are lowered, he can push his reaction curve out to $S'S$. The intuition behind this shift is that for any given expected marginal revenue, the lower marginal cost encourages a higher output. Now if the incumbent chooses capacity $0B$, so that his reaction function becomes $S'SB$ instead of $M'M$, the entrant will no longer expect a profitable post-entry game to develop. Entry is effectively deterred. As argued before, because he never envisages having to raise output competitively, the incumbent will also choose to produce at full capacity, $0B$.

It can be seen that there have been many refinements as to what is and what is not a credible threat since the early limit-pricing literature. The tools of game theory, particularly the idea of a perfect equilibrium, are a powerful way to impose rationality on a firm's actions. Only in Dixit's example is a perfect equilibrium involving strategic behaviour fully defined. However, we close this section with one word of warning. Although it may not appear so to the reader delving into this literature for the first time, these models are terribly simplified. In particular, there is no uncertainty with respect to, say, rival's costs, demand conditions, or the post-entry game. All firms are assumed to know these exactly. Whilst one would expect many of the main conclusions to carry through to a more complex world, confidence in understanding the way the economy works should be muted by massive modesty when it comes to making predictions and prescriptions.

4.4 A Menagerie of Strategic Moves

The strategic moves discussed so far emphasize over-investment as compared with that which would take place were the incumbent to take the entrant's actions as given and not try to influence her through his choice of pre-entry investment. However, this need not always be the case. In other circumstances, using the same benchmark of the optimal investment level in the absence of an entry threat, under-investment may be preferable. Fudenberg and Tirole (1984) explain the various options by means of zoological analogy.

Top-Dog Trick.   The example of strategic investment in capacity is a case in which it is an advantage to be the 'top dog'. Over-investment makes the incumbent tougher in the post-entry game, reducing the potential entrant's expected payoff and so reducing the entry threat. The top dog is always willing to fight to defend his market position.

Puppy-Dog Ploy.   Consider next what happens if there is no way that entry can be prevented. In the Section 4.3 example, it remains an advantage to over-invest in order to reduce the entrant's post-entry output. Bulow, Geanakoplos and Klemperer (1985a) call such forms of rivalry, where an increase in one firm's output has the strategic effect of reducing the other's, 'strategic substitutes'. Put another way, the reaction curves of Figure 4.4 slope downwards. However, other forms of rivalry, such as some forms of price competition, lead to quite the opposite reaction such that, for instance, a lower price by one firm induces rivals to also lower their prices. With such 'strategic complements', reaction curves slope upwards and high investment by the incumbent would lead to an aggressive response by the entrant to their mutual disadvantage.[12] With strategic complements, over-investment remains the best strategy to deter entry since it still reduces the entrant's expected profits. However, *under-investment* may help to reduce the vigour of post-entry competition if entry is inevitable.

This situation is illustrated in Figure 4.5 where under-investment is shown to reduce the output of both firms nearer to the joint profit-maximizing level. Both firms consequently earn higher profits. To be convincing, such under-investment must be credible in the sense that it must not be easy to increase investment at a later date and so get drawn into a price war. This strategy of minimizing the damage of

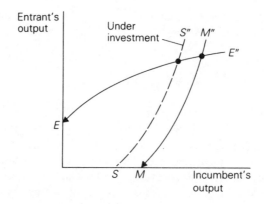

Figure 4.5   Under-investment with strategic complements

entry by turning the incumbent into a 'small, friendly, nonaggressive puppy dog [can be] desirable if investment makes the incumbent tougher, and the second-period reaction curves slope up' (Fudenberg and Tirole, 1984, p. 365). The puppy dog understands the dangers of a fight and prefers to minimize the potential damage. Returning to the military analogy, if war is inevitable, it is better to keep it non-nuclear by unilateral disarmament; even though the nuclear threat may on other occasions prevent war in the first place.

Lean and Hungry Look.   In all the examples discussed so far, investment makes the incumbent tough, which is to say that high productive capacity makes the incumbent more likely to act competitively post-entry, and low capacity leads to less competition. However, there are other types of investment, such as advertising (and possibly R&D), which make the incumbent soft. By 'soft' we mean that high advertising can make the incumbent less likely to act vigorously post-entry, while low (or lean) advertising may make him hungrier for competition.

Consider the feasibility of advertising to deter entry. Assume that consumers are ill informed, and advertising is necessary in order to make sales. Once informed, at least some consumers will not trouble to look at further adverts and so continue to buy from the incumbent. Without the threat of entry, the incumbent sets the marginal return to informing consumers equal to the marginal cost. Advertising less than this has the direct effect of reducing market size and profits. However, it also has an indirect strategic effect on the entrant's expected profits. The larger is the incumbent's market share, the greater is the cost to him of price competition. Thus, low advertising can increase the credibility of a price war and so help to deter entry. Schmalensee (1983) shows that, in quite plausible examples, the strategic effect of low advertising raising the threat of a price war can outweigh the direct effect of low advertising increasing the entrant's expected market share. Overall, the entrant's expected profitability is reduced by the incumbent remaining 'lean and hungry'. At the same time, this strategy raises the incumbent's profits compared with permitting entry and sharing the market. Thus, the 'lean and hungry' look of under-investment in advertising can lead to credible entry deterrence.[13]

Fat-Cat Effect.   Continuing with the advertising example, what happens if entry is inevitable? The incumbent no longer has a strategic incentive to posture that price competition will be fierce. Quite the opposite, there is every incentive to signal that he is a cuddly, pacifistic 'fat cat' who does not want to fight a price war. Thus, both the direct effect of reducing the entrant's market share, and the strategic effect of reducing the incentive for a price war argue for over-investment in advertising in order to soften the blow of entry.

This menagerie of strategic moves illustrates some of the complexities of economic life. In particular, it should highlight three important factors. First, it can make a very significant difference to a firm's behaviour whether or not it believes that a rival can be deterred from entering the market. Second, the expected reaction of rivals already in the market is critical. With strategic substitutes, one firm's aggression leads to accommodation by the other, but with strategic complements, aggression inspires retaliatory aggression. Third, certain types of investment (e.g. physical capacity) make a firm tough (more aggressive) when it comes to price competition, whilst other investments (e.g. advertising) can make a firm soft (less aggressive). The subtleties of strategic behaviour are manifold.

4.5   Applications to Multi-Market Firms

Later chapters in this book are about the decisions a firm takes to enter more than one market. The previous two chapters provide a framework to understand such decisions which is based on the efficiency of the internal control systems within the firm. This chapter takes an alternative complementary view looking outside the firm, into the market. Using the tools developed in the earlier sections, we emphasize the strategic advantages and disadvantages of vertical integration, diversification and multinational enterprise. Finally, we provide a connecting link between the two views by discussing the strategic appointment of managers. Because the nature of multi-market activity is linked primarily with physical investment, most of the strategic moves to be discussed fall into the class of the top-dog trick.

4.5.1   Vertical Integration

The most common modes of strategic behaviour associated with vertical integration are of a blunter kind than that of the Schelling definition given in the introduction. Nevertheless, we must not scorn them just because they lack subtlety.

Consider an incumbent with market power in industry A and selling significant quantities of his output to a more competitive industry B. If the incumbent vertically integrates, he can significantly narrow the market that an entrant into A would have for her output. The entrant is then left with the alternatives of either entering only into A in the hope that a sufficiently large market can be found in industry B; or entering at both stages and so incurring the higher costs of large capital borrowings and inexperienced production; or not entering at all. An identical argument applies to backward vertical integration from A into a competitive input market in order to shrink a potential entrant's sources of supply. This strategy of narrowing an entrant's options is analysed in more detail in Chapter 5.

More subtly, the incumbent in A may be threatened by the prospect of an aggressive entrant who rightly believes that he is insufficiently committed to the industry to resist a significant incursion. Lacking the means to commit in industry A, perhaps because the technology does not allow irreversible investment decisions, or lacking the desire to commit too heavily in A because rivalry is in strategic substitutes so if there *is* to be entry he would rather be a puppy dog, the incumbent may still be able credibly to signal his commitment by making some irrevocable investment in the vertical market B. This may be sufficient either to deter entry or to reduce the aggression of the entrant who now realizes that she has no chance of forcing the incumbent out of the market. An example might be the airline (industry A) which invests heavily in a local marketing network (industry B) and commits funds to promote his own name. Without this, a marginally more efficient or aggressive airline would have had a much better chance of dislodging him from the air-carrier market where physical commitments to a particular route do not exist. A related example of vertical integration in the brewing industry in order to exploit entry barriers (as opposed to the more subtle commitment possibilities just described) is given in Chapter 5.

4.5.2   Diversification

We have space to briefly discuss one strategic reason for diversifying and one strategic reason for not diversifying. The first reason involves an overlapping product range and so involves a strong element of horizontal integration.

It is easiest to get the first point across using an example involving an extremely limited form of diversification. Consider the reasons for setting up a chain of retail pharmacies diversified across localities rather than specialized in one. Assume away any economies of bulk purchasing and concentrate on the advantages of optimal location. The closer pharmacies are located together, the fewer customers each will attract and the lower will be their profits. By locating further apart, profits can be increased; but if too large a gap in the market is left, an entrant can step in with the result that profits fall again. (We assume that there are some pharmacy-specific economies of scale or else every potential customer could have her own tiny pharmacy next door!) The trick for the chain is to spread out its shops far enough to make handsome profits yet close enough such that there are no gaps in the market which are profitable enough to attract entry.[14] It *may* be sufficient that individual proprietors recognize the possibilities and locate independently so as to earn profits whilst deterring entry. However, coordination would be much easier within a chain of shops under joint ownership. The organizational advantages of within-firm organization are discussed in Chapter 3.

Of particular interest to the present chapter is an implicit assumption contained in the above argument. This is brought out by questioning why potential entrants do not try to enter next door to an existing shop in the expectation that the latter will feel crowded and shift itself further away, thus making entry profitable *ex post*. Such an expectation might be quite reasonable if moving shop was as easy as moving an ice-cream van further along the beach. However, with a chemist's shop there will be more location-specific sunk costs such as fitted shelving and a dispensary as well as knowledge of the exact address by potential customers. Such sunk costs are not recoverable if a pharmacy has to move locations. It is exactly the non-salvageable nature of these assets that makes the 'threat' not to move so credible.

This very narrow example of strategic diversification generalizes to much wider cases. The essential preconditions remain the same. It must be possible to represent consumer tastes along some sort of spectrum, there need only be a minimum of scale economies, and there must be product-specific sunk costs such that incumbents would not find it profitable to change product specifications were entry to occur (i.e. the threat not to accommodate entry must be credible). Schmalensee (1978) suggests that the ready-to-eat breakfast-cereal market appears to meet exactly these criteria.

The strategic reason for not diversifying sounds deceptively simple. It can leave a firm vulnerable in its primary market. Thus, there may be a profitable opportunity in market B, but if the incumbent tries to diversify, this may stretch his capacity to respond to entry or expansion by rivals in A, and so leave him with lower overall profits. It is better to stay out because what the firm does in market B changes the expectation of how he will react in A.

Another wrinkle to this argument arises if both A and B are monopolies. Assume that B does not expect entry into A's market to be profitable while A does see the potential for profits in B's market. However, if A actually enters B's market, there are two reasons why retaliation by B entering A's market may be a credible threat because it becomes profitable. First, as just discussed, A might become overstretched. Alternatively, B might be left with excess capacity (physical or managerial) which could be turned towards A's market. Either way, mutual forbearance in staying out of each other's markets may be a powerful force.[15]

Of course, in other circumstances, entry into a second market can make a firm *stronger* in its primary market (as in the vertical integration example or when there are economies of scope; see Chapter 6). In such circumstances, the above arguments can be reversed to provide a force encouraging strategic diversification even when projects are independently unprofitable.

4.5.3 Multinational Enterprise

Multinational enterprises (MNEs) may, in part, be the result of strategic behaviour with respect to other firms, governments, and/or labour unions.

The arguments regarding other firms are logical extensions of those for diversification and vertical integration.[16] These need not be repeated here, except to suggest that local production makes a firm's commitment to a market much stronger than mere exporting because more costs have to be sunk in productive capacity. This enables the use of credible top-dog and fat-cat strategies.

Because of the unique political situation of MNEs, strategic interdependence with respect to governments and unions is particularly interesting. Multinationality affects the way these institutions expect the firm to behave and this can be exploited for strategic gain. A single-nation firm in search of government grants and favours may use the threat not to invest as a bargaining ploy. Unfortunately for the firm, this is not a credible threat unless the investment is truly marginal. If the firm can make £1 million from the project, it will go ahead with or without a £5 million grant. However, the MNE which is already operating in two similar countries (say Ireland and France) *can* credibly threaten to not invest in one particular country because the decision to invest in one rather than the other *is* truly marginal. If the MNE can make £1 million by producing in either country, the country offering the higher grant will get the investment and the MNE can play one country off against the other. The same argument can be extended to include influence on tariff setting, labour law, taxation and any other legislation that interests the MNE. Once this game has been appreciated by governments, no explicit threats need take place. As long as there is an excess demand for local investment, governments will competitively set subsidies so high as to lose nearly all the surplus from attracting new investment. Note that if the government has a basic preference for home-based firms, it is domestically based multinationals that have the greatest grant-pulling power, followed by foreign-based MNEs and domestic single-nationals, with importers bringing up the rear.

The argument with respect to bargaining strength *vis-à-vis* the unions follows exactly the same lines. The explicit or implicit threat to transfer production or new investment to an overseas subsidiary can be used to reduce wages, intensify work rates, speed the introduction of new technology, or otherwise modify working conditions to the benefit of the MNE.

Finally, it is interesting to note how governments and unions could circumvent the MNE's strategic power. This would require the international coordination of regional grants, wage bargaining, etc., with a view to switching the bargaining boot away from the MNE's foot. This prospect is just beginning to enter the arena of international relations but it remains, for the present at least, firmly at the speculative stage.

4.6 Owners, Managers and Strategic Behaviour

All the economic examples so far examined have been attempts to directly influence a rival's behaviour by means of investment policy. If the ownership of the firm is divorced from its management, the appointment of managers or their remuneration packages may also be chosen to give a similar strategic advantage. The following analysis adds a new strategic dimension to the discussion of the principal–agent problem in Chapter 2. Adding the analysis in Section 4.3, the basic idea is that the owners are able to employ managers who do not *directly* try to maximize profits, in order to shift their firm's reaction function and so increase realized profits.

For instance, suppose it is known that the mode of competition in the market is Cournot duopoly. If the reaction curves slope down then it is advantageous for the firm to be able to shift its curve outwards (as in Figure 4.4). It is able to do this by appointing a manager who has a preference for sales as well as profits, because such a person will always choose a higher output than would a profit-maximizer for any given output by rivals. On the other hand, if the mode of competition is such that there is strategic complementarity (as opposed to strategic substitution), then a different type of manager, one who has a positive aversion to size, will lead to greater profits (as in Figure 4.5). Thus, sometimes it is better to appoint a go-getting, top-dog manager, while on other occasions it is better to settle for a meek puppy dog.

Finally, there may be other tactics that owners (or directors) can use with similar effect. The efficiency reasons for organizing the firm into independent divisions have already been discussed in Chapter 3. However, a strategic reason for divisionalization exists if this can be manipulated so as to lower rivals' output. This could be the case if independent profit-maximizing divisions produce similar products but are prevented from colluding, and rivalry with outside firms is such that there is strategic substitution (Vickers, 1985).

4.7 Summary and Conclusions

Strategic behaviour is about committing resources in order to influence rivals' expectations of how one will react. Such investments would be wasted if they were seen as an empty threat. An important development of modern game theory has been to develop the concept of a perfect equilibrium, which formalizes the idea that threats are credible only if it is in a firm's own best interests to actually carry them out. This idea was developed in Section 4.2 and an example of investment to credibly deter entry was investigated in Section 4.3. A full zoological classification of various strategies was suggested in Section 4.4 and the last two sections applied the concepts to the economic phenomena discussed elsewhere, particularly in later chapters, in this book.

Although the title of this book requires our emphasis on applications to the theory of the firm, the underlying concepts are of much wider relevance. For instance, a government may credibly commit to a monetarist economic policy by promising 'no U-turns' so vehemently that it would lose more in terms of lost political face by not controlling the money supply than it would gain in terms of improved employment prospects were it to relax control. One advantage of such a commitment may be to make trades unions less aggressive in their wage demands and firms more resolute in resisting them. This is because neither can rely on general inflation to accommodate an individual firm's higher prices. Of course, this is not to say that there does not exist another, better policy to control inflation. Nevertheless, a sound understanding of the theory of strategic behaviour undoubtedly leads to a clearer perspective on, amongst other matters, the behaviour of firms, government economic policy, arms control talks ('we must bargain from strength'), and why parents get angry when their daughter is only five minutes late home on a Saturday night.

Further Reading

Once more, this topic is not well covered in the current stock of textbooks. Fortunately, an excellent and accessible review of some related issues is to be found in the *Oxford Review of Economic Policy* (Vol. 1, No. 3, Autumn 1985). See especially the articles by Mayer (on commitments), Vickers (introducing game theory), and Yarrow (on strategic issues in industrial policy). Williamson (1983) provides a stimulating discussion of how firms make strategic commitments to each other.

The basic approach of this chapter has followed Schelling (1960), Dixit (1982), Fudenberg and Tirole (1984), and Bulow, Geanakoplos and Klemperer (1985a). Of these, the classic work by Schelling is replete with fascinating examples and remains the most entertaining and approachable. Chapters 2 and 5 have been particularly influential and are absolutely convincing on the importance of strategic behaviour to economics, politics, warfare, and everyday life. Finally, Salop (1979) gives a very neat and brief (three-page) summary of the main ideas behind binding commitments and self-enforcing threats.

Notes

1   As an aid to clarity, the incumbent is sexed as male, while the entrant is always female.
2   As will become clear, the ordering of the two stages can be critical.
3   More formally, it is assumed that the incumbent can credibly commit himself to any set of conditional strategies during the first stage of the game (i.e. before the entry decision).
4   Observe now how critical is the temporal ordering of strategic moves. If the entrant can commit to entry before the incumbent can commit to

fighting, then the equilibrium is entry and sharing. The reader should be able to reason why.

5   This criticism forms the basis of the now famous rebuttals of predatory pricing as an anti-competitive strategy. Such warfare hurts incumbents at least as much as entrants (see Scherer, 1980, Chapter 12).

6   Sequential equilibrium is, in the present context, an alternative name for the perfect equilibrium solution concept.

7   In fact, it is surprisingly difficult to show that such a strategy could be part of a perfect equilibrium (see Dixit, 1982). It is necessary that either the game be repeated infinitely many times or that the entrant be uncertain as to the incumbent's response (perhaps because she is unsure about the incumbent's payoffs, or she may doubt his rationality).

8   Predatory pricing is not *per se* illegal in the UK, but it can be investigated by the Monopolies and Mergers Commission under the terms of the 1980 Competition Act.

9   Incidentally, the argument in the text shows how strategic games are solved backwards, first determining the payoffs to sharing, fighting, etc., then determining the entry decision conditional on these payoffs, and only then deciding whether or not the incumbent decides to become committed. This follows the same methodology as dynamic programming.

10   In fact, a Stackelberg leader may prefer to permit limited entry in order to maintain industry price even at the expense of market share. The limit-pricing model implicitly assumes away this possibility.

11   Dixit proceeds by means of example. Some of the underlying ideas have been clarified by Bulow, Geanakoplos and Klemperer (1985b).

12   The examples used in the text should not be generalized to imply that Cournot quantity competition leads inevitably to strategic substitutes, nor that price competition is invariably associated with strategic complements. For many demand and cost conditions, this will be the case, but Bulow, Geanakoplos and Klemperer (1985a, b) point out quite clearly that there are other familiar examples for which the reverse is true.

13   Fudenberg and Tirole (1984) show that a similar strategy may be advisable with technological competition.

14   See Hay (1976) and Schmalensee (1978) for formal models and Davies and Lyons (in press) for an excellent textbook treatment!

15   This argument is given in greater detail in Bulow, Geanakoplos and Klemperer (1985a). As they point out, the mutual forbearance argument is an old one, but as usually phrased it implies that retaliation is an expensive disciplinary device which may not provide a credible threat.

16   For instance, consider a development of the strategic product spacing argument. If there are two similar countries between which trade incurs tariff or transport costs then it can be shown that the optimal (in the sense that profits are maximized while entry is deterred) distribution of products internationally is for each country to produce alternate products along the spectrum of tastes. As in the example of chemist's shops, the internal organization provided by an MNE may be necessary to exploit this (see Lyons, 1984).

5   Vertical Integration

STEVE DAVIES

5.1   Introductory Remarks and Definitions

Nearly all finished goods involve a method of production with many
different stages: consider, for instance, the various stages involved in
transforming the raw materials of this book (including wood and the
creative genius of the authors) into its finished form. Even the production of the humble building brick entails a number of stages, including clay winning, shaping and baking (Davies, 1971).

Typically at least some of these stages are *technologically separable*:
they could be performed separately in different plants or firms. Vertical
integration involves the joint administration of two or more such stages
within a single firm. Given fine enough definitions of different stages,
it follows that virtually all firms are integrated to some extent. It is for
precisely this reason that an understanding of the reasons for vertical
integration helps to illuminate one of the fundamental questions of
micro-economics: why do firms exist? Equally, however, a discussion
of vertical integration inevitably bears on various more down-to-earth
policy issues. Within the firm, the decision on whether or not to extend
integration, perhaps through vertical merger, is often an important one
when developing a corporate strategy. Similarly, government anti-trust
agencies must often form an opinion on whether or not such mergers
are in the public interest.

To illustrate, we shall change examples to a more familiar (at least
for the author) consumer good: beer. Using first a broad definition of
stages, we might identify four: (a) production of raw materials, mainly
in the agricultural sector, e.g. barley and hops, (b) malting, (c) brewing,

and (d) distribution of the beer. Within the British brewing industry, we observe a variety of firm structures. On the one hand, the big brewers typically undertake their own malt production and run their own retail outlets (public houses) as well as producing beer. On the other hand, there are other, usually smaller, firms specializing in one or other of the stages: independent maltsters, breweries with few, if any, 'tied' public houses, and independent 'free house' pubs who buy their beer from whichever brewery they choose. Given this diversity, it is natural to ask why some firms are highly integrated while others are specialized.[1]

At this point let us introduce some definitions to be carried right through the chapter. We shall talk of *backward (or upstream) integration* when a firm located at one stage moves into the production of its raw materials and/or other inputs. Thus a brewer setting up his own malting facilities or merging with a maltster is integrating backwards. *Forward (or downstream) integration* occurs when a firm moves into the subsequent stage of the process. So, for example, a brewery with its own pubs is said to be integrated forwards. In principle then each firm faces the decisions of whether to 'buy or make' and whether to 'use or sell'. These decisions will form the cornerstone of its corporate strategy. From the point of view of society, as represented in the UK context, for example, by the Monopolies and Mergers Commission, is integration in the making and selling of beer to be encouraged, or does it have anti-competitive, price-raising consequences?

Two other preliminary definitional remarks are necessary. We have already referred to 'specialized' firms. But specialized is a relative term defined with respect to the stages we have (to some extent arbitrarily) chosen to identify. For example, within the malting stage, there are in fact three steps: steeping, germination and drying and curing. In principle at least, each of these steps could be conducted by separate entities; similarly, the various ancillary activities involved, such as buying and selling, secretarial, factory floor sweeping, etc., might be undertaken by the maltster's own employees or by buying in such services from specialist firms or individuals. As we suggested at the outset, virtually all firms are integrated to some extent, given a fine enough definition of stages, and to understand why this is so we need to know why all firms opt to replace the market, but to varying extents.

Finally, the term 'vertical integration' also requires an important qualification. It is tempting to characterize the choice faced by a firm as a dichotomous one, with the merits of undertaking transactions on the open market to be compared with those of outright merging of two stages within a single firm. In fact, as Richardson (1972) has argued, the choice is not so simple. There is a range of other alternatives lying between these two extremes, in which firms at successive stages in the production process are linked and where operations are coordinated, yet where the firms remain under independent ownership. These intermediate cases invariably involve specialized contracts, and are known variously by terms such as 'quasi-integration' or 'non-standard commercial market contracts' (Williamson, 1983). Examples which come readily to mind are long-term contracts to supply; reciprocal sales arrangements; cooperation on technology and design. Their fairly widespread incidence in the real world demands more of economic theory than merely an answer to the question 'to integrate or not to integrate?'; we must also examine whether quasi-integration can achieve all of the benefits of full-fledged integration, but at lower costs.

Most of the remainder of this chapter explores the possible motives for integration. As in many areas of economics, there is no single unified theory of integration but rather a collection of contributions from different economists. Some offer general, wide-ranging frameworks or approaches within which various aspects of the subject can be interpreted: others are much more specific, suggesting particular motives for integration which may apply under certain conditions. We shall not attempt to provide a completely comprehensive survey of the literature but instead try to draw out main themes. As a start, the following section is devoted to establishing the three foundations of the literature: firstly, the view that vertical integration can be interpreted as a response to *market failure*; secondly, the undoubted importance of *technological interdependence* – in many circumstances there are sound technological reasons for grouping adjacent stages of the production process under one roof; and thirdly, the prediction of traditional intermediate price theory that *vertical integration has no anti-competitive consequences*, thus unlike horizontal mergers, for example, integration does not imply price-raising behaviour.

Section 5.3 builds on this groundwork by describing a selection of alternative specific motives for integration; some of these flow quite clearly from the market failures framework, but others question the third of our foundations, suggesting that there may be circumstances when integration can have objectives which might be defined as monopolistic exploitation.

Section 5.4 provides a brief summary of other parts of the literature including empirical research findings.

5.2   Three Foundations to the Literature

One undoubted reason why the economic literature on vertical integration can appear disjointed and apparently lacking a 'core', is that its roots lie in three different traditions.

At present the most dominant is probably the market failures framework popularized by Coase and Williamson. Here the emphasis is on the comparative merits of markets and firms as institutions for coordinating production decisions. The world described differs significantly from that of basic neoclassical micro theory, with emphasis placed on uncertainty and limited rationality of economic agents. Moreover, in recent years, this approach has led increasingly to the interface between economics, organization theory and the law. This is a result of the significance attached to contractual problems (see Williamson, 1984, especially pp. 195–6).

A second ingredient is the technical dimension. A key reason why in many instances successive stages of the production process are undertaken jointly within a single plant is that there are important cost savings which derive from the technological interdependence between the stages. This is well understood by economists but is a subject which rarely attracts much interest in economic discussions of integration. This is unsurprising since it is a subject in which economists do not have a comparative advantage. Nevertheless, it would be wrong to attribute this lack of attention to a view that such economies are unimportant.

The third type of input into the literature lies more comfortably in the tradition of intermediate neoclassical micro theory. At its simplest this involves comparative static analysis of the consequences for final price of integration between two vertically linked industries under different forms of market structure. The main contributors in this area tend to be economists working under the umbrella of applied oligopoly theory, and often within the structure–conduct–performance paradigm.

Having identified these three roots, we hasten to add that they are not necessarily mutually exclusive, indeed to the extent that an economic theory of vertical integration is now evolving, this can be seen as drawing on each of these traditions.

5.2.1   The Market-Failure Approach

As described in Chapter 1, Coase explained the firm as an institution which displaces the market when market failure occurs due to high transaction costs. The sorts of costs he had in mind include the costs of discovering market prices and negotiation costs in arriving at the contracts (either implicit or explicit) which characterize exchange on the market. To put it another way, entrepreneurial coordination would displace market coordination wherever the costs of using the price system exceed the costs of internalizing those transactions within a firm. This is not only an explanation of why firms exist, but also of why they choose to integrate. He argued that the firm will expand (and integrate) up to the point where 'the costs of organizing an extra transaction within the firm become equal to the costs of carrying out the same transactions by means of an exchange in the open market or the costs of organizing in another firm' (1937, p. 341).[2] It is at this point, Coase argues, that an equilibrium level of vertical integration is achieved, a level which entails the most efficient organization of production and distribution, given competitive conditions.

More recently, Williamson has taken the argument further by attempting to specify the circumstances under which market transaction costs will tend to be high, and where integration is therefore more likely. The details of Williamson's framework are described in Chapter 3 of this book, and are only summarized briefly here as follows. Vertical integration is more likely in circumstances where, given bounded rationality and opportunism, the assets required are highly specific to the transaction, there is a high degree of uncertainty involved and, to justify the costs of setting up a system of internal organization, the transaction recurs frequently.

In such circumstances, an integrated firm can deal with future changes in the environment in a sequential, adaptive way. Where adaptation is required, it is less likely to involve costly haggling for three reasons. Firstly, both parties are now within the same firm and are less likely to benefit from gains made at the other's expense. Opportunistic behaviour is also therefore less likely. Secondly, where disputes do arise, they can be settled more quickly by the ultimate authority of top management. In addition, by organizing adjacent activities within a single administrative unit, one is more likely to develop 'convergent expectations'; that is, the risk is reduced that the parties to the transaction will make incompatible plans for an uncertain future. Thirdly, administrative control might further reduce haggling costs because a single management has easier access to relevant information (Williamson, 1981, p. 1549).

There is little doubt that this framework of Williamson's has been a major influence on current thinking on the theory of the firm. (It has been applied, by Buckley and Casson (1976) for example, to produce an interesting explanation of why multinational enterprises exist.) There are, however, criticisms which have been made in our present context.

It is argued, with some justification, that this framework is difficult to test because the transaction costs associated with uncertainty and small numbers are difficult to measure.[3] This makes it almost impossible in any specific real-world example to assess how important transaction costs have been, as opposed to other motives, for vertical integration.

5.2.2   Technological Interdependence

Most textbook surveys of vertical integration pay lip service to technological interdependence as a cause of integration, citing thermal economies in the steel industry as an example, and then pass on quickly to other academically more interesting reasons. We shall not break with this tradition save to underline the significance of this factor.

The specific example just mentioned refers to the fact that, by siting various stages of the steel-making process in the same plant, major fuel economies are available since cooling and reheating of the product is avoided as it passes through the various stages; similarly, transport costs of moving the product from one location to another are eradicated. In fact technological interdependencies of this sort probably exist in most industries. Most obviously, similar thermal economies exist in the other metal industries, and economies in handling costs exist in all the process industries. More generally even the more technologically simple industries usually exhibit thermal, handling and/or transport-cost reasons for various stages being grouped under a single roof. Our earlier example of the malting industry is a case in point.

Two other comments are in order. Firstly, and this may account for the usual neglect of this motive, technological interdependence is probably more important as a determinant of the degree of integration built into the plant or firm from its outset, than as a motive for changes say through vertical merger. In established technologies, interdependencies will be well understood and recognized as new plants are built; yet where technologies are undergoing radical changes, new interdependencies might arise, thus encouraging vertical merger or internal expansion into adjacent stages. Given that there has been a post-war trend, away from intermittent, towards continuous technologies, this should account for a corresponding increase in integration (for examples, see Nabseth and Ray, 1974). Secondly, stimulated by the discussion of Section 5.2.1, we should ask why technological interdependence leads to integration within a single firm, rather than, say, different firms (or even individuals) conducting the different stages in the same plant which might be jointly owned? The answer must presumably lie in the difficulty of drawing up contracts which cater for the interdependencies. It is probably more flexible and cost effective to leave day-to-day coordination decisions, such as speed of throughput and breakdowns, to works management than to contingent contracts. In fact, most instances of technological interdependence are examples of what Williamson would call 'site specificity' (1984, p. 214), where the immobility of durable assets leads to transacting problems which are invariably resolved by common ownership.

5.2.3   Monopolistic Motives for Integration

We suggested in the introductory section that vertical mergers should interest government anti-trust agencies, the guardians of the public interest in matters of competition, or the lack thereof. The possibility that integration might be motivated by less respectable concerns than efficiency is not a new one. It is somewhat surprising to find therefore that, until recently, the formal neoclassical analysis of integration came down strongly in favour of vertical integration. Even ignoring any beneficial cost savings, it suggested that integration between a monopoly at one stage and another industry at the next vertically related stage will at the worst leave the final product price unchanged (if the other industry is originally perfectly competitive) and at the best actually reduce price, and perhaps costs (if the other industry is originally monopolistic). Indeed, even as late as 1979, a leading text in industrial economics (Hay and Morris, 1979, p. 61) could suggest, 'All the arguments based on the idea that integration will permit the capture of monopoly profits can be shown to falter'.

In fact this question is by no means cut and dried, and as will be seen in the next section, this comforting conclusion can be overturned once certain key assumptions are relaxed. Nevertheless the traditional analysis retains an important role in our understanding of vertical integration and merits a description here. We assume there are two vertical stages in the production process, with a downstream industry B selling its output, X, to final consumers whose demand curve is described by DD in Figure 5.1. Amongst the inputs used by this industry there is one, A, supplied by an upstream industry which is monopolized. The point of the analysis is to explore the consequences if the monopolist in A integrates downstream, say by taking over the entire B industry.

A crucial assumption is that the *various inputs must be combined in fixed proportions* in the product of the downstream industry. In fact to simplify we shall assume that one unit of the input from A is required for each unit of B output (this is not critical to the analysis but merely allows us to denote the output levels of the two industries by X). To focus attention on the relationship between A and B, all other inputs

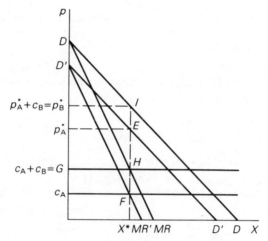

Figure 5.1   Vertical integration: Case 1

are relegated to a minor role and we assume that they cost a fixed amount, c_B, per unit of B output.[4] In other words, if the monopolist in A sets price p_A for his input, marginal costs in B are $p_A + c_B$. We now consider two cases in turn, with the downstream industry being perfectly competitive or monopolistic, pre-integration.

Case 1.   If, pre-integration, B is a perfectly competitive industry it will produce where price, p_B, equals marginal cost, $p_A + c_B$. In turn this means that the upstream monopolist will face a *derived demand curve*: the higher he sets p_A, the higher are downstream marginal costs and thus price, and the lower is demand for the final product and thus the A input. The derived demand curve is easily identified graphically as $D'D'$, displacing the final demand curve downwards vertically by a distance c_B: in other words, the demand for the A input at price p_A is equal to demand for the finished product at price $p_A + c_B$. In order to maximize profits, the monopolist equates the marginal revenue associated with this derived demand curve, shown here as $D'MR'$ to his own marginal costs, c_A, which we assume to be constant at all scales of output. This yields an optimal input price of p_A^* at which X^* is demanded, providing the monopolist with profits of $p_A^* E F c_A$ and resulting in a final product price of $p_B^* = c_B + p_A^*$.

Now suppose that the A monopolist integrates (merges) with the downstream industry. The integrated monopolist has direct access to the final demand curve but also incurs combined costs of $c_A + c_B$, setting the latter equal to the marginal revenue curve associated with final demand, i.e. *DMR*, optimal output remains at X^* and final product price at p_B^*. Profits also remain at their pre-integration level because price received by and unit costs of the monopolist are both raised by c_B. (Graphically, $p_B^*IHG = p_A^*EFc_A$ since $HF = IE = c_B$). This gives us the first conclusion of the traditional analysis: vertical integration between an upstream monopolist and a perfectly competitive downstream industry has no effect on either profits or final product price.[5] There is no monopolistic motive for integration because monopoly profits have already been extracted in full in the pre-integration state.

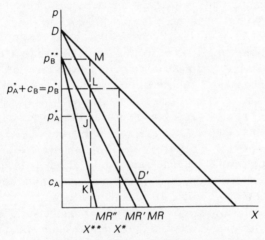

Figure 5.2   Vertical integration: Case 2

Case 2.   We now repeat the analysis but with the downstream industry also monopolized, by a separate firm (see Figure 5.2). Assuming the two monopolists act myopically (treating each other's action as given) then the monopolist in B will presume his marginal costs to be constant at $p_A + c_B$ and choose output where these equal his marginal revenue. This in turn presents the monopolist in A with a derived demand curve which is a vertical displacement of B's marginal revenue: $p_A = MR - c_B$ shown by $D'MR'$ in Figure 5.2. The optimal price and output for A are then described by the point where his marginal revenue $D'MR''$ equates to his marginal costs. This yields X^{**} and p_A^*. To derive final product price we read off p_B^{**} from the final demand curve associated with X^{**}. At this solution, the A monopolist earns only $p_A^*JKc_A$ profits and the B monopolist, $p_B^*LMp_B^{**}$.

Upon integration between the two, the single integrated monopolist will act as already explained in Case 1; thus integration will lead to a fall in price from p_B^{**} to p_B^* and an increase in output from X^{**} to X^*.

Moreover the profits of the integrated monopolist must exceed the sum of the profits of the two independent monopolists prior to integration.[6] Thus we have the second conclusion of the traditional analysis: integration between successive monopolists leads to a reduction in price, and, although it also raises aggregate profits, this does not reflect an extension of market power, but rather a realization of interdependence between existing monopolists.

Bilateral Monopoly.   In one important respect our description of the pre-integration state in the second case is incomplete. If the B monopolist is an important, or perhaps the only, customer of the A monopolist, he may be unwilling to accept price p_A^* in the first place. As can be seen, his profits are considerably lower than A's, and his monopsony power may encourage him to negotiate better terms. But equally, A also has a strong card to play: he can threaten to withdraw supply. In short, and assuming for simplicity that B is A's only customer, we have the classic case of bilateral monopoly.

A conflict of interests arises: while it is in the upstream monopolist's interest that the value of p_A be as shown in Figure 5.2, the downstream monopolist's interest is better served if p_A is lowered towards c_A, at which extreme case A tends to zero profits and B tends to the profit level of an integrated monopolist. Now to the extent that some compromise price between p_A^* and c_A *is* negotiated, then the gross profit gain from integration is reduced. On the other hand, such a bargaining process will itself entail costs and raises the possibility of Williamsonian opportunistic behaviour. These would be avoided by integration.[7] But allowing the successive monopolists to negotiate does not materially affect the main conclusion of this strand to the literature: there is no *monopolistic* motive for integration and a vertical merger would, at worst, leave product price unchanged, and, at best, reduce price.[8]

It is now time to take stock of the assumptions required to generate this warming picture of benevolent monopolists. First we recall that the analysis rests on the initial assumption of fixed coefficients of production in the manufacture of the final product. Thus we have excluded the possibility that the downstream producer will economize on the A input as its price rises. Second, almost by default, we have assumed that an upstream monopolist is able to extract full monopoly profit without integration. Implicitly then, we ignore the possibility that he may be constrained in some way, either by the fear of new entry or by exercise of government controls. These are matters to which we return to Section 5.3.4; to anticipate, the conclusion that integration is free of anti-competitive consequences is, in fact, by no means universally held.

5.3 Specific Motives for Integration

A multitude of specific motives for vertical integration has been suggested in the economic literature and in this section we shall discuss a sample of them. Our main criterion for inclusion is that they develop or question the themes described in the previous section.

5.3.1 Opportunistic Re-contracting

This is a motive for integration which follows immediately from Williamson's analysis and which he discusses in detail in a recent paper (Williamson, 1983). Opportunistic re-contracting is said to occur if one party to a (market) contract changes the terms of the contract once the other party has already committed himself in some way. For example, firm A makes a contract with firm B for the latter to provide him with a certain specific input, whereupon B buys and installs specialized capital equipment in order to produce that input. If there is no other readily available customer for the input, A may try to re-negotiate terms, safe in the knowledge that his supplier B is 'locked in'. Indeed so long as B is offered enough to cover his operating costs plus a premium to make it just worthwhile to continue supplying rather than selling the equipment for scrap, in the final event he will (presumably reluctantly) agree to the re-negotiated terms. It is not necessary that such re-contracting should occur, only that it is a possibility, for integration to be an attractive proposition.

One apparent way of guarding against such behaviour is to invoke the law: B has the option of suing A for breach of contract. Recall, however, that opportunism is self-seeking *with guile*; in our hypothetical example, A might ask for revised terms, pleading a downturn in his own business and claiming that unless he is able to cut costs he may go out of business. If B believes this – and this depends on how readily he can gather information about his client – it must make economic sense to accede to the new revised contract.

The broad conclusion to emerge is that opportunistic re-contracting is most likely the more specific are the capital assets employed to fulfil the contract (see Williamson, 1983, for the concept of 'dedicated specificity') and thus the fewer the alternative suppliers or buyers. In turn, it is in these circumstances that vertical integration is more likely to emerge as preferable to the market contract. As an empirical test of the alternative case with a buyer fearing opportunistic suppliers, Monteverde and Teece (1982a) collected data for 133 car components used by General Motors and Ford in 1976. For each component they estimated (a) a proxy for the extent of engineering investment required to develop it, and (b) the extent of vertical integration (ranging from zero, if independent component manufacturers were totally responsible, to 100 per cent, if GM or Ford developed the component themselves). They found a positive and strongly significant correlation between the two and concluded that this was consistent with integration to avoid re-contracting. In other words, with components that are technologically complex and expensive to develop, there is a greater risk that the supplier can turn round at the last moment and ask for better terms, safe in the knowledge that the car manufacturer has no alternative supplier to turn to.

This particular example has been contested by Silver (1984, Chapter 9) who has also questioned the presumption that fears of re-contracting will necessarily lead to full-blown integration. The crux of Silver's and others' criticism is that there will usually be other forms of vertical links which will guard against opportunism but which fall short of vertical integration and which may be less expensive. He cites as examples (a) exclusive dealer contracts between car makers and retailers, whereby the former guarantees the latter refunds in the event of changes in new model prices, and notice of the decision to withdraw a franchise, (b) agreements by car manufacturers to own the specialized equipment required by suppliers, and (c) agreements whereby the customer firm conducts the development itself, then providing the supplier with the results of the development in order for it to produce the input or component. Equally important, however, is the implied threat that the buyer (supplier) will not use the same supplier (buyer) in future, but this depends, of course, on there being alternative suppliers (buyers) and the ability to detect cheating (itself dependent on access to information).

There is little doubt that quasi-integration, rather than full integration, may often be a preferred solution to this problem,[9] although especially when one party is significantly smaller, he may resist in an attempt to retain independence.

5.3.2   Integration necessitated by innovation

Silver (1984) has recently suggested a motive for integration which stems from informational problems associated with innovations. As an illustration, he describes the following scenario (ibid., pp. 13–17). An entrepreneur perceives that a new product (maybe his own invention) is potentially profitable, but to produce it he needs specialized and uncommon or novel intermediate inputs or operations in which he has no particular expertise. Very often these operations would be most efficiently undertaken by other independent producers who already have the relevant skills.[10] However, because the product (and often the entrepreneur) is new and untried, these firms have no way of knowing whether it will be a viable proposition and they are therefore loath to commit the necessary resources and investment to supply him. In Williamson's terms, the entrepreneur is faced with a problem of *information impactedness*. That is, one of the parties (here, the supplier) to a potential contract has significantly less information than the other, and it would be costly for him to achieve parity, i.e. the supplier would perhaps have to undertake market research to establish that a market for the entrepreneur's new product will exist, and/or examine carefully the entrepreneur's blueprints for the innovation, perhaps employing the services of a technical expert to do so.

Faced with this reluctance on the part of potential suppliers (and possibly similar reluctance by potential distributors to sell his new product) the entrepreneur must make a choice between (a) offering potential suppliers a premium to cover what they see as the excessive uncertainty involved, or (b) writing a detailed and costly contract specifying in detail how he will react in various conceivable contingencies, or (c) purchasing or renting the capital equipment and labour services of the suppliers and then using them within his own firm. Depending on the relative costs of the alternatives, and these depend in turn on how risky suppliers view his new venture to be, fully-fledged vertical integration, or at least quasi-integration may be the best option.

Silver goes on in his book to cite various case studies to which he believes this model can be applied. One might argue that he describes what is only a special case (albeit a very interesting one) of a more general phenomenon, i.e. that of asymmetric information;[11] opportunistic re-contracting might be described as another special case. In our opinion, however, his thesis merits a separate discussion; not least because it bears on an important issue mentioned briefly in our final section, namely the analysis and prediction of long-run trends in vertical integration within a capitalist economy.[12]

5.3.3 Other Aspects of Uncertainty

By now it should be clear that the desire to avoid or ameliorate uncertainty lies at the heart of many motives for integration. In this subsection we consider briefly three other dimensions; these correspond very obviously to the reasons often cited by businessmen for backward (and to a lesser extent) forward integration.

In some cases the *quality* of an intermediate product from an upstream supplier may be, by its nature, uncertain. Where the monitoring of quality is costly or possible only *ex-post*, it may be preferable for the user to integrate, keeping a closer check on quality by producing the input itself. Extreme examples are farmers buying seed from seed merchants (quality only becomes apparent too late) and inputs whose quality characteristics can be tested by applying only sample checks which involve destruction of the units tested.

Often contractual solutions falling far short of integration may be adequate: the buying firm might install its own inspectors in the supplier's factory, penalty clauses for supplying defective units can be included in the contract, and insurance policies might be employed. On the other hand, such devices are less practicable where, for instance, the supplier wishes to protect trade secrets or where failure of inputs may also be due to their misuse by the buying firm. Particularly in instances of supplying industries characterized by pronounced scale economies, and thus with small numbers of firms, competition cannot be relied upon as an external check on quality, and vertical integration may be the most efficient alternative. Casson (1982a) and Silver (1984, Chapter 10) pursue this motive in more detail, using specific cases.[13]

One of the seminal papers in the area of integration and uncertainty is by Arrow (1975). Loosely, this concerns *uncertainty about input prices*. More specifically, he constructs a model in which there is information asymmetry between the downstream and upstream industries: in particular, downstream firms have only limited information on the likely price of the input, and this restricts their ability to make efficient decisions on input proportions in their own production. Upstream firms, on the other hand, are better informed since they will have more immediate knowledge of their own ability to supply in a given time period. Hence downstream firms have an obvious incentive to integrate backwards and acquire upstream firms in order to be better able to forecast input prices. Since, in this model, it is assumed that ability to forecast prices increases as more and more intermediate producers are acquired, the logical conclusion is that all upstream firms will eventually be grouped together with a single monopolist downstream firm. To put it another way, where this sort of asymmetry exists, there will be a natural tendency for even competitive down- and upstream industries to be displaced by a single overall monopolist. Not surprisingly, the assumptions of this model have not been received uncritically. For instance, it is unclear why downstream firms should necessarily be less able than upstream firms to anticipate changes in the external environment which will lead to changed conditions of supply. Alternatively, a market response might be the emergence of specialist marketing firms selling information about supply conditions to buyers (and, for that matter, about demand conditions to sellers).

Carlton (1979) focuses attention, alternatively, on the consequences of *uncertain demand* for the product of the downstream industry. This combines with rigidities in the upstream industry's supply, to generate a motive for backward integration to reduce costs. The rigidity arises from the assumption that firms in the upstream industry must make their own pricing decisions before the downstream demand, and thus also the derived demand for their product, are known. This means that upstream producers must run the risk of having unsold stock and must therefore set price in excess of marginal production costs. In these circumstances there is an incentive for downstream producers to integrate and thus obtain the input at cost. But this must be weighed against the disadvantage that it is now *they* who run the risk of having unused stocks of the input. On the face of it then, there appears to be no incentive – risk would be merely transferred downstream. This need not be so however if the downstream producer settles for a relatively 'low' production of the input, i.e. one which is almost certain to be required, and then simply enters the market to purchase extra supplies as and when demand dictates.

5.3.4 Monopolistic Motives Revisited

We now turn to a group of motives which call into question the earlier conclusion that integration is free of anti-competitive consequences.

(a) Forward Integration by a Monopolist to Avoid Downstream Substitution. First recall the model of Section 5.2.3, Case 1 which showed there to be no monopolistic incentive for an upstream producer of A to integrate with a perfectly competitive downstream industry B. This rested on the assumption that the A input could only be used in fixed proportions with all other inputs, represented for simplicity hereafter as a single input C, to produce the downstream product. We now replace this with the more usual neoclassical assumption that substitution is possible, and is described by the traditional isoquant shown in Figure 5.3 which is downward sloping with a diminishing marginal rate of substitution.[14]

In these new circumstances a motive for integration now emerges. It derives from the fact that, without integration, the A monopolist is unable to extract the full monopoly profit, since raising p_A leads to downstream substitution of the other input C for A.

The analysis can be explained more formally in terms of Figure 5.3 (taken from Vernon and Graham, 1971). The isoquant depicts the pre-integration position, with the A monopolist charging its profit-maximizing price p_A, X_1 being the optimal level of output in the

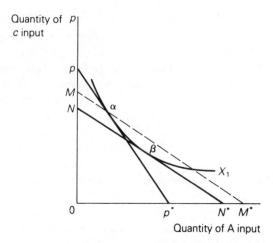

Figure 5.3   Vertical integration: downstream substitution possibilities

downstream industry. The optimal factor combination, chosen by the latter, is at point α where an isocost line PP^* is tangential to the isoquant. The slope of PP^* reflects the relative prices of A and C and its intercept ($0P$) the level of B's costs (in terms of the C input) associated with this output. If however, the A input were supplied at marginal cost, c_A, the isocost line would be flatter as shown by NN^* and factor combination β would now be optimal, leading to greater use of the A input. In fact this depicts the outcome following integration between A and B, *assuming that the post-integration level of output is unchanged*. (Following integration, factor intensities are decided on the *cost* of producing A rather than its previous (distorted) market price.) It follows that costs in the downstream industry have now declined to $0N$ (in terms of B). Since it is easily shown that pre-integration upstream profits are depicted by PM,[15] there is also a net increase in monopoly profits of MN.

Note however that this is conditional on integration leading to no change in final output, i.e. no change in p_B. In general there is no reason why this should be so. On the one hand, it could now be profitable to increase output since the cost of producing any given output has fallen; on the other hand, the monopolist has now extended his monopoly power, previously constrained by the substitution possibilities, and it may be more profitable to raise price, p_B. In other words, profits must rise by at least MN, and more if it is optimal for the monopolist to change output.

Since Vernon and Graham first established this result, considerable research activity has centred on the question of whether or not product price will rise and, if it does, whether this leads to a loss in consumer surplus which exceeds the increase in producer surplus, i.e. whether such integration is in society's interests. Unfortunately, this is a subject which refuses to generate simple conclusions. Perhaps the most striking, but in no sense general, result has been established by Schmalensee (1973), Hay (1973) and Warren-Boulton (1974) who show that, with a Cobb–Douglas production function and constant elasticity demand function in B, it is optimal for the monopolist to *raise* price post-integration. In fact Warren-Boulton, using simulation techniques, suggested that this result usually extends to all forms of constant elasticity of substitution production functions.[16] Whether or not these price rises are sufficiently high to generate losses in consumer surplus exceeding the gains in producer surplus is even less certain. But again in the special case just mentioned Warren-Boulton uses simulation techniques to suggest that this is generally so.

On the basis of known research findings to date it would be foolish to conclude that there are now strong reasons for *outright rejection* of traditional analysis. Nevertheless, the extension of the model to this more realistic variable proportions case *does* establish a monopolistic motive for forward integration into a competitive industry; moreover, this integration quite clearly *can* raise price and diminish aggregate welfare in some cases.[17]

(b) Integration as an Entry Barrier.   The suggestion that vertical integration may raise barriers to entry is perhaps the most controversial of all the potential motives considered in this chapter.

As a preliminary to our discussion we should first ask perhaps how any potential role for integration as an entry-deterrent would square with the traditional analysis of Section 5.2 or, for that matter, the revision just described. The answer is, quite simply, that it is irrelevant – by assumption. In all cases thus far considered, monopolists have been able to act without any constraint on the exercise of monopoly power within their own industries. By implication, therefore, potential entry is impossible or, using Bain's term, 'blockaded'. In these circumstances it is of course irrelevant whether integration raises entry barriers as there are already (assumed to be) sufficient barriers to entry to protect monopoly power. Once this rather unrealistic assumption is dropped, however, any entry-deterring potential for integration becomes of considerable anti-trust policy interest.

Assuming then that there will be many instances where incumbent firms in industry X wish to raise or erect barriers to entry into their industry, can vertical integration into a related upstream or downstream industry Y serve this purpose? Fairly obviously, unless all firms in X have integrated into Y the answer must be no; so long as independent suppliers to, or buyers from, X still exist, then there is no necessity for new entrants to be integrated themselves.[18] The controversy arises, rather, in the case where all incumbents are already integrated. Here it is difficult to envisage how any prospective entrant would contemplate entry into X without also entering Y. The alternatives are to hope that an independent firm enters Y and agrees to buy or sell from X, or to hope to be able to buy or sell from one of the incumbent's operations in Y. The former option seems highly unlikely, although just possible given a contractual agreement to simultaneous entry; the latter option leaves the entrant prone to predatory price tactics, unsatisfactory service or even subsequent refusal to supply or purchase.

We shall suppose then that in many instances an entrant is forced to enter in an integrated form. The most common suggestion as to why this makes entry more difficult is that it raises the *capital requirement* of the entrant. Whether or not this constitutes an increased barrier to entry is contested by two schools of thought. Those who believe it does tend to be adherents to the structure–conduct–performance framework (e.g. Comanor, 1967). The argument rests on the fact that the cost of raising finance on the capital market typically rises the greater the sum involved (because of greater perceived risk). Indeed, in extreme cases, the capital requirement of setting up a new integrated firm may be so large that finance is unavailable at *any* price. There are three responses to this. Firstly, whilst accepting that this may constitute a barrier for entirely new firms, it should not apply to large firms diversifying from an existing base in other industries (assuming that such diversifying firms will already have 'established a name' and will be viewed as no more or less risky than integrated firms already operating in X). Secondly, and again accepting that new entrants may indeed face a higher cost of capital, some argue that this is indicative of an imperfection in the capital market, rather than an entry-deterring consequence of vertical integration *per se*. To some extent this is a matter of semantics, but, more substantively, it is unclear why the capital market should be accused of imperfection when assessing unknown new firms as inherently more risky than others. Thirdly, and the most extreme opposition to the barrier hypothesis, is the view, most persuasively articulated by Bork (1978), that if indeed vertical integration does permit higher profits for incumbents in the short run, this will constitute a signal to other firms and the capital market which will inexorably attract new entry. In other words, capital is more likely to be available for such uses than in other areas when the prospect is of more moderate (normal) returns. In fact this controversy is not peculiar to vertical integration and arises in many different instances where the actions of incumbent firms raise the capital requirements of potential entrants.[19]

Other writers have suggested other ways in which integration may raise entry barriers. Comanor (1967), for instance, argues that integration may increase the product differentiation barrier: since integrated firms manufacture their own inputs, they have increased opportunities to vary the specification of inputs which may be necessary to offering a range of differentiated products in the final goods market. Sullivan (1977) points to instances where, although profits may be high enough to attract entry into one part of the integrated industry were it separate, these do not compensate for losses or lower profits which must be incurred at other stages. Bain (1956) suggests a number of reasons why new entrants might be at a serious cost disadvantage; for instance, where incumbents control strategic plants, markets or supplies, forcing new entrants to use inferior facilities. None of these arguments is particularly persuasive: Why shouldn't entrants also be able to differentiate their products? Is it rational for incumbents to subsidize loss-making stages from profit-making stages in the long run? Won't the greater profit potential of Bain's strategic plants be reflected in correspondingly higher rents and therefore costs?

Two other arguments are rather more convincing (at least for the author). The first (Buzzell, 1983) concerns a case where the minimum efficient scale of production at one stage far exceeds that in another. If the potential entrant is forced to enter both, this clearly raises the scale of entry. This is not dissimilar to the increased capital requirement argument; but additionally it suggests that integration may raise the scale economy barrier. The second can be illustrated by referring back to our earlier example of the beer industry. It is often argued that by integrating downstream into public houses, brewers not only assure themselves of a certain market, but also restrict potential entrants at the distribution stage. The normal option for new brewers, i.e. to open their own retail outlets, is effectively denied them by the generally strict British public controls on the number of licensed premises allowed in each locality. Whatever beneficial social or medical returns this public policy may have, it undoubtedly helps existing brewers to restrict entry into their own industry by tying up outlets at the next stage down.[20] Generalizing from this particular case, it can be seen that an artificial governmentally imposed barrier to entry in one industry can be used to the advantage of firms in a related industry by vertical integration. Having said this we should beware of accepting this argument uncritically: the barrier to entry is not integration *per se*, but, rather, government restriction. Integration only becomes questionable if it increases the chances that the barrier concerned will be exploited. While this may be true in the beer case[21] this need not always be so.

(c) Other Motives.   The previous paragraphs described the potential utilization of integration to deter new competition. Relatedly, *'foreclosure'* refers to the use of integration to remove existing competition: it can be defined as the practice of acquiring an upstream source of supply and then denying its product to one's existing downstream rivals. This motive is also hotly contested however. Firstly, such an action might involve serious cutbacks in the output of the acquired upstream firm, and secondly, the unintegrated downstream firm should have little difficulty in locating alternative sources of supply from new entrants to the upstream industry. Nevertheless it is often argued that *fears* of potential foreclosure by others motivates firms to integrate themselves. In this case it is not the *actual* consequences of such foreclosure which should concern us, but firms' *perceptions* thereof (see Bain, 1968, p. 827).

An alternative motive which is analytically similar to the earlier barriers argument, is the use of integration to *circumvent government regulation*. In the US in particular, firms with a natural monopoly are often controlled by government limiting the rate of return they can earn (and indirectly the price charged). Dayan (1975) argues that where such regulation applies to a downstream firm, by integrating upstream it can so distort the transfer price of the now internally supplied input as to transfer excess profits to the unregulated upstream stage. It is perhaps a little unkind of us to comment that this presupposes a fairly gullible government agency!

Finally, it is sometimes argued (e.g. Williamson, 1979) that integration is undertaken to *facilitate price discrimination*. A necessary condition for this is that an upstream firm sells to a number of downstream markets which exhibit different price elasticities of demand. In order to maximize profits s/he should then sell in each at a different price, with the most inelastic-demand consumers charged the most. In many instances, however, 'arbitrage' (the low-price markets re-selling to the high-price markets) precludes such discriminatory practices. In this context, downstream integration into some of the downstream markets may be a means by which arbitrage can be prevented. For instance, suppose an upstream producer of an intermediate good selling to downstream firms for some of whom the input is essential but for others not so essential. Without integration it may be impossible to charge the former more and the latter less; but by integrating with the latter group and continuing to sell to the unintegrated group the supplier successfully separates the market.

Although it is usually argued that price discrimination leads to a higher output and thus greater aggregate surplus, the re-distribution of that surplus towards the upstream supplier may be considered sufficient grounds for viewing this alleged motive with concern.

5.4 Conclusions

It would be wrong to impose too rigid a structure on even the sample of motives for integration we have considered here. It is not however forcing things to point to a tension which runs through much of the literature: that between efficiency considerations on the one hand and market power considerations on the other. Without in any way wishing to downplay the possibility that vertical integration sometimes may have unsavoury monopoly implications, it is the work of Coase and Williamson that raises the subject beyond being just another battle-ground for the protagonists on competition policy. We have already mentioned the close affinity of the question 'why integration?' to the more fundamental issue 'why firms?'. But in addition, the transaction-costs approach offers the real possibility of a coherent framework in which to examine other lofty issues such as the long-run evolution of corporate form in the capitalist economy (see Williamson, 1981). But once we turn to issues of that nature we encounter a different battle-ground. Is the drive towards efficiency really the explanation of chang-ing organizational forms or is it more the result of considerations of power (say of capital and/or managers over labour). It is currently argued (by Cowling, 1984, for example) that the de-industrialization of the UK economy is due in part to the deliberate disintegration by multinational companies of some of their operations so as to avoid the growth of labour power in the UK relative to that in other parts of the world.

Further Reading

There exists a number of excellent contemporary textbook treatments of vertical integration; including, for the UK, Clarke (1985) and Wat-erson (1984), and for the US, Scherer (1980). Machlup and Taber (1960) is a useful early reference, and Kaserman (1978) offers a thorough, but now rather dated, survey. The impact of Williamson's writing will already be obvious and the references cited throughout the chapter need not be repeated here. Silver (1984) offers a lively, if sometimes loose, critique of models (other than his own) which purport to offer a generalized explanation of integration.

We should also point to two deliberate, but major, omissions in our own treatment. The first is Stigler's (1951) ambitious 'life-cycle hypothesis'. He argues that in the years immediately following its birth, an industry will typically comprise firms that are essentially integrated.

But as the industry grows, disintegration will emerge as it becomes more efficient to hive off some activities, such as the production of inputs, to specialist firms who can attain scale economies by supplying the industry as a whole. Later, with the contraction of the industry's market, re-integration emerges as the market becomes too small, once again, to support independent input suppliers. This thesis has been exposed to not altogether satisfactory empirical tests by Stigler himself, Tucker and Wilder (1977 and 1984) and Levy (1984).

Our second major omission, due to space limitations, is of the empirical literature on vertical integration. As it happens much of that literature is primitive and lacks the sophistication of the theoretical literature discussed in this chapter. To be fair, however, empirical research has always been severely limited by data problems. Those studies which have been concerned with the aggregate, industry level suffer from the fact that there is no totally satisfactory way of measuring the degree of vertical integration (see Hay and Morris, 1979, pp. 528–9). On the other hand, more micro, firm level, analysis requires the collection of data which is usually available only from the firms themselves, and which they may be unwilling to release for reasons of confidentiality. Nevertheless a number of interesting case studies are described in the reports of the British Monopolies and Mergers Commission.[22] Cowling *et al.* (1980, Chapter 10) includes an interesting case study of forward integration in the textile industry which is rare in its attempts to relate an empirical analysis back to the theoretical literature.

Notes

1   See the Monopolies Commission report on *Beer* (1969) for more detail on the British brewing industry.

2   It is as if the entrepreneur ranks all the possible opportunities for vertical integration in descending order of the market transaction costs involved, and then proceeds to internalize them within the firm until there comes a point where the cost of absorbing yet another activity exceeds any saving in transaction costs. The costs of internalization are rather loosely specified but amount, in effect, to a conventional neoclassical view that there is a limited entrepreneurial ability to coordinate a firm beyond a certain size: thus as the firm grows to include more and more stages, this increases the likelihood of entrepreneurial failure. This is a somewhat stylized picture since different activities will involve different costs of internalization (see Williamson 1975, pp. 118–30).

3   But see Flaherty (1981) for a rare attempt to 'operationalize' transaction costs. Also Monteverde and Teece (1982a, b) go some way to answering this criticism.

4   Thus the other input-supplying industries can be assumed to be perfectly competitive with horizontal industry supply curves. See Waterson (1984, pp. 86–9) for a discussion of the more complicated case of mutually related power.

5   This assumes no savings in marginal costs from integration; if there are, then integration will lead to a lower final price. Note also that if we reverse the positions, a downstream monopolist need not integrate with a perfectly competitive upstream industry as he too can earn monopoly profits in the first place.

6   Visually, it is clear that $p_B^* IHG$ in Figure 5.1 exceeds $p_B^{**} MLp_B^* + p_A^* JKc_A$ in Figure 5.2, but more rigorously, p_B^{**} cannot be the profit-maximizing price for a monopolist with costs $c_A + c_B$ since, at X^{**}, $MR > MC$ and it must pay to increase output – up to X^* of course.

7   Waterson (1984, pp. 99–106) provides a comprehensive survey of the literature on possible solutions to the bilateral monopoly problem.

8   Greenhut and Ohta (1976 and 1979) extend the analysis to integration involving oligopolists. Qualitatively their results confirm this conclusion.

9   Indeed this point is readily ceded and developed by Williamson (1983, pp. 527–8).

10   It is often the case that new products entail no major changes in production technology and require few if any new skills of the workforce.

11   Again, see Williamson (1979, pp. 253–4) for a discussion, in his terms, of the implications for organizational form of increasing the uncertainty surrounding transactions that involve specific assets.

12   Silver's analysis implicitly offers an interesting counterpoint to Stigler's (1951) model of fluctuations in organizational form over the product life cycle. While Stigler's model is fuelled by demand factors, Silver's relies on informational factors. The two are not necessarily inconsistent.

13   Porter and Spence (1977) discuss an alternative dimension of the integration-for-quality motive (but again driven by a scale economy dimension). They consider the case of an upstream producer who supplies a standardized input, with downstream producers choosing between buying that input and producing their own input to meet their specialized needs more precisely. In this case the trade-off is between quality and cost: the upstream supplier being able to produce at low cost by producing at larger scale and meeting the requirements of many downstream clients more or less approximately. The empirical applicability of this model has remained untested however.

14   The earlier model implied L-shaped isoquants which are probably inappropriate to most real-world contexts in anything other than the short run.

15   To see this, note that the isocost line for any given level of costs, Y, is defined by $Y = p_A A + p_c C$ where p_A and p_C are factor prices and A and C are factor quantities. The equation for the isocost line involves expressing C in terms of A as follows: $C = (Y/p_c) - (p_A/p_C)A$. Thus if Y^* denotes pre-integration downstream costs, the intercept of PP^* is (Y^*/p_C). Now consider the line MM^*: this shows the hypothetical level of costs associated with α if the A input was priced at cost, c_A, say Y^{**}; thus its intercept is $0M = (Y^{**}/p_C)$. It follows that $0P - 0M = PM = (Y^* - Y^{**})/p_C$ is that

part of pre-integration costs in B due to the A input being priced in excess of cost, i.e. the A monopolist's profit deflated by the constant p_C.

16   But Mallela and Nahata (1980) show that it can sometimes be profitable for the monopolist to *reduce* price in cases of low elasticities of substitution and demand.

17   Waterson (1984) provides a slightly more extensive discussion than we have time for here, and he also (1982) exends Warren-Boulton's methodology to the case of downstream oligopoly with qualitatively similar results.

18   This is not to deny that such a non-integrated entrant may be at a cost disadvantage *vis-à-vis* integrated incumbents if their integration was motivated by considerations of efficiency. The fact that other incumbents remain unintegrated must mean that unintegrated entry is possible, if not particularly profitable.

19   Perhaps the best (i.e. most balanced) discussion is to be found in Williamson (1979), who argues that, on balance, integration *may* raise entry barriers via increased capital requirements.

20   See Clarke (1985) for a discussion of this argument. The existence of free houses and off-licence sales by, amongst others, large supermarket chains ameliorates but does not remove this impediment to competition.

21   Brewing is dominated by a few large brewers in the UK, while there are thousands of pubs. If all pubs were independent, competition between incumbents should ensure that the restricted-licence barrier would not be translated into super-normal profits in all but the most isolated of districts.

22   See, for example, the reports on proposed mergers between: FMC and NFU (1975), Berisford and British Sugar Corporation (1981) and Pilkington and UKO (1977).

6 Conglomerate Firms

ROGER CLARKE

6.1 Introduction

Considerable attention has been given in recent years to conglomerate firms and their possible effects on the operation of the economy. As large diversified firms develop, apparently engaged in every aspect of production and distribution, inevitable questions arise as to why such firms exist and what possible effects they may have on economic welfare. Answers to these questions are, perhaps surprisingly, only tentative at this stage despite the considerable debate over conglomerates which has taken place in recent years. Nevertheless, some useful work on conglomerates has been done and we consider some of this work in this chapter.

Conglomerate firms can be distinguished from specialized firms in that they produce several goods and services. To some extent this definition is a matter of degree, however, in that some firms produce a number of products which are very closely related in demand and supply and would not be regarded as conglomerate, while other firms produce products which are less closely related (or not related at all). Thus, for example, a firm which simply produces different types of ready-to-eat breakfast cereal which are highly substitutable in demand (and possibly also supply) would not be regarded as a conglomerate firm, although it would be if it also diversified to produce orange juice or, more widely, to produce packaged foods.

For present purposes, we distinguish multi-product production of closely related goods and services from conglomerate operation on a broader front. In this latter category, firms may diversify laterally into products related to some extent in demand or supply or, alternatively, into entirely unrelated products. In the first case, *product extension* diversification is said to take place involving *marketing concentricity* when products are related in demand and *technological concentricity* with relationships in production.[1] Diversification into production of unrelated goods and services (such as newspapers and textiles) is then termed *pure conglomerate* diversification. In this chapter, we are concerned with why firms diversify either by product extension or in pure conglomerate form and what implications this may have for public policy.

Popular opinion suggests that pure conglomerates have been growing in importance in many Western economies in recent years, and that such firms have an undue influence (both economic and political) in the operation of those economies. In the US, where strong anti-trust policies on horizontal and vertical mergers have operated since the passing of the Celler–Kefauver Act of 1950, substantial conglomerate merger activity has taken place. Thus, for example, Scherer reports that pure conglomerate mergers accounted for only 3.2 per cent of large manufacturing and mining company assets acquired by merger in the US in 1948–53, rising to 15.9 per cent in 1956–63, 33.2 per cent in 1963–72, and 49.2 per cent in 1973–77 (Scherer, 1980, p. 124). Horizontal and vertical mergers (which were most likely to be subject to anti-trust action under the 1950 Act) showed a corresponding decrease in importance over the same period.[2]

A similar picture emerges from comparison of trends in concentration in the US in the post-war period. Scherer, for example, shows that unweighted average four-firm concentration ratios for a sample of 154 four-digit manufacturing industries increased only slightly in the period from 39.7 per cent in 1947 to 41.5 per cent in 1972 (Scherer, 1980, p. 70). In contrast, aggregate concentration in US manufacturing (as measured by the share of the largest 200 manufacturing corporations in US manufacturing assets) increased from 48.2 per cent in 1948 to 60.0 per cent in 1972 (Scherer, 1980, p. 126). This comparison shows that large firms increased their share of manufacturing capacity as a whole but not as a result of greater concentration in individual markets. An obvious explanation of this is that the largest firms in the economy grew by diversification rather than by increasing their individual market shares.[3]

A somewhat different picture emerges for the UK. In this case, controls on horizontal or large mergers were introduced only in 1965 (in the 1965 Monopolies and Mergers Act) and then with limited effect. Data available on mergers vetted under the legislation show that only 23 per cent of assets acquired by merger in 1965–83 were classified as conglomerate compared with 72 per cent classified as horizontal (Clarke, 1985, p. 264). There is some evidence that more conglomerate mergers took place after 1970 although horizontal mergers were by far the most important category even in the 1970s.[4]

More generally, trends in average market concentration have closely matched trends in aggregate concentration in UK manufacturing industry in the post-war period. Average three-firm employment concentration in three-digit UK industries increased from 29 per cent in 1951 to 41 per cent in 1968, while the share of the largest 100 firms in manufacturing net output increased from 22 per cent in 1951 (or 27 per cent in 1953) to 41 per cent in 1968 (Clarke, 1985, p. 25). Evidence in Clarke and Davies (1983) suggests that only about 10 per cent of the increase in aggregate concentration in the 1963–68 period (as measured by the Hirschman–Herfindahl index) was attributable to increases in diversification between three-digit (Minimum List Heading) industries, with the remaining 90 per cent associated with increases in market concentration. Aggregate concentration actually fell in 1971–77 matched by a corresponding fall in diversification between two-digit manufacturing (or broad manufacturing sector) industries.[5] In the UK, therefore, the evidence is that diversification and conglomerate growth have been much less prominent factors in relation to aggregate concentration than in the US.[6]

In the remainder of this chapter we consider what factors lead to conglomerate growth of firms and what effects such growth may have on the economy. We begin by considering transaction-cost economizing as an explanation of conglomerate firm growth in Section 6.2. Then other possible hypotheses relating to financial and managerial factors are considered in Section 6.3. Possible public policy issues relating to economic and political effects of conglomerates are considered in Section 6.4, and a summary and conclusions make up the chapter.

6.2 Transaction-Cost-Economizing Explanations of Conglomerate Growth

In Chapter 5 we saw that scope for economizing on market transaction costs arose in the context of vertical transactions of goods and services. Thus, under certain conditions, it might be more economical for a producer of an output X, say, to integrate backward into the supply of an important input, A, produced previously by an independent supplier. According to Williamson, this is more likely to be the case the more specialized are the assets used in production of A, the more recurrent are the transactions involved, and the greater is the uncertainty in the market. Given these conditions, transaction costs involved in arms-length contracts may be so substantial that vertical integration is required.

In the case of conglomerate firms no transactions of intermediate goods are involved and hence a somewhat different perspective is required. In this case, transaction-cost economizing arises, not in the internalization of intermediate product transactions, but in the internalization of production of *separate goods*. Such economizing will occur if the cost of conglomerate production of these goods is lower than with market provision.

Two broad explanations of why this might be so have been suggested in the literature. First, Williamson (1975, 1981) has argued that conglomerate firms (of the M-form type) have special advantages in allocating capital to high-value uses compared to the normal capital allocation process. Hence conglomerate firms have a general capital-allocation advantage relative to the outside capital market. Second, conglomerate firms may be better able to utilize the services of their specialized human and non-human resources by conglomerate growth than by their sale or lease on the market. In this case transaction-cost advantages in factor markets are involved. Both arguments are capable of considerable elaboration and we consider each in turn in what follows.

6.2.1 Williamson's Capital Markets Hypothesis

We begin by briefly considering Williamson's hypothesis. The basis of this argument is that conglomerate firms of the M-form type can establish internal capital markets which are particularly efficient at allocating capital to high-value uses. Top managers in such firms have access to better and more detailed information on investment opportunities within their firms and hence make superior investment decisions relative to the outside market. Also, they are able to exert more effective control over the uses to which their capital is put and hence are able to avoid control loss within the firm. On both counts, therefore, an M-form conglomerate can be more efficient as a 'miniature capital market' than the capital market at large, and this would provide a general explanation of the growth of multi-divisional, conglomerate firms.

This transaction-cost explanation centres on weaknesses of the capital market in obtaining information and controlling independent firm operations. An independent firm going to the market must persuade investors of the value of the opportunities that it offers; a task which in itself may involve no little cost. Its problem is complicated, however, in that it possesses hidden knowledge which is not generally available to the market. Hence, it has a problem of *signalling* its true potential to outside investors, while the latter have the problem of *screening* alternative investment opportunities which are presented.[7] An M-form conglomerate can have important advantages, in contrast, in obtaining better and more detailed information on the investment potential of one of its divisions, while at the same time anticipating less opportunistic behaviour of its divisional managers. These managers also know that a close watch will be kept on their performance following the expansion of their activities and this will make them less prone to exaggerate opportunities in the first place, as well as ensuring that they attempt to meet appropriate financial targets.

The arguments do not all go one way, however. In the first place, since, by definition, conglomerate firms must establish a *miniature* capital market, it may be that their attitudes towards risk differ from that of the capital market at large. As a general principle, conglomerates will be less able to diversify their risks compared to the market, so that one would expect them to forego risky investments which the market might be willing to accept. This argument, however, is countered by the possible superior information and incentive advantages of conglomerate operation. Second, managers in conglomerate firms may (for reasons which are discussed further in Section 6.3.2) be more risk-averse in their investments than shareholders, so that again risky investments are foregone. Third, managers may also pursue other policies (such as growth maximization; see again Section 6.3.2) against the interests of the stockholders. An example of this latter (which may well be relevant to US and UK experience of the past 20 years) is where managers in conglomerate firms favour (relatively safe) growth by acquisition to (potentially more risky) internal expansion and development of green-field sites. Each of these factors suggests that distortions in capital allocation can arise in conglomerate firms.

In addition, as noted by Williamson, the advantage that con-glomerates may have in allocating capital could be subject to dimin-ishing returns

'To be sure, this substitution of internal organization for the capital market is subject to trade-offs and diminishing returns. Breadth – that is, access to the widest range of alternatives – is traded off for depth – that is, more intimate knowledge of a narrower range of possible investment outlets – (Alchian and Demsetz, 1972, p. 793), where the general office may be presumed to have the advantage in the latter respect. The diminishing-returns feature suggests that the net benefits of increased diversity eventually become negative. Were further diversification thereafter to be attempted, effective control would pass back into the hands of the operating divisions with problematic performance consequences' (Williamson, 1981, p. 1559, n. 36).

As with many of Williamson's ideas, this trade-off is very much a conjecture in our current state of knowledge. Clearly, more work is needed (both theoretical and empirical) on this and other issues raised by Williamson, before firm conclusions can be drawn.

6.2.2   Resource-Utilization Arguments

A second argument is that conglomerate firms develop in response to opportunities for exploiting specialized resources. The basic point here is that firms consist of resources (e.g. knowhow, specialized capital equipment, etc.) which can be more efficiently exploited internally than via market transactions. This in turn arises because of market failure in the sale or lease of the services of such resources. In what follows we consider a number of examples of why such market failure may arise.

We begin, however, by briefly considering the recently developed idea of an economy of scope and its relation to the ideas of this section. This is then followed by a more general discussion of transaction-cost economies in relation to resource utilization.

Economies of scope.   An economy of scope refers to an economy in jointly producing two or more products compared to separate production (Panzar and Willig, 1975, 1981; see also Willig, 1979 and Baumol, Panzar and Willig, 1982). Put formally, an economy of scope exists if the minimized cost of producing output quantities q_1 and q_2 of goods 1 and 2 is lower in joint rather than separate production, i.e.

$$C(q_1, q_2) < C(q_1, 0) + C(0, q_2), \tag{6.1}$$

where $C(.)$ is the minimized cost of joint production. This definition, therefore, includes traditional joint products such as mutton and wool, or peak and off-peak electricity. More generally, however, it also includes any products for which the cost of joint production is lower than separate production. This might be the case, for example, when a firm possesses indivisible production capacity to produce a product 1 which can also be used to produce product 2, e.g. when a firm producing meat products owns a refrigeration plant which can be used to store other frozen products, such as ice cream. Another example might be where a firm acquires specialized knowledge in production of product 1 which has application to product 2, e.g. when a firm develops new technology, such as laser technology, in one use which has application elsewhere; or when a retail chain develops marketing expertise which enables it to diversify into new lines of retailing. In each of these cases, economies of joint production exist although, as we shall see in a moment, this, in itself, need not necessarily imply diversified operation.

A key feature of the examples cited above is that they each involve the use of a *sharable* or *quasi-public* input in production of two or more goods. That is, one (or several) inputs are used in production of goods 1 and 2 without complete congestion. As stressed by Panzar and Willig (1981, pp. 269–71), it is this quasi-public property of sharable inputs which gives rise to economies of scope. In the limit, an input (e.g. a technological development with several applications) may be purely public in that its use to produce good 1 in no way affects the quantity available to produce good 2. Thus, if k_i ($i = 1$, 2) are the services of such an input required to produce quantities q_1 and q_2 of goods 1 and 2, and β is the input price, the input cost would simply be

$$r = \beta.\max k_i.\tag{6.2}$$

At the other extreme, the input could be completely private in producing q_1 and q_2 with cost

$$r = \beta \sum_{i=1}^{2}.k_i.\tag{6.3}$$

Intermediate cases involve some sharing of the input between the two goods: hence the term quasi-public input. As long as production does involve an input which can be shared between several outputs (i.e. inputs are not all purely private) then an economy of scope will exist.

Clearly economies of scope are important in providing an incentive for joint production. This need not mean, however, that they are either necessary or sufficient for conglomerate operation (see, in particular, Teece, 1980). In the first place, as stressed by Teece, economies of scope do not necessarily imply a need for production within a single firm. The argument in fact is directly analogous to the argument that technological interdependence favours vertical coordination of production (e.g. in iron and steel production) but not necessarily vertical integration (see Chapter 5, Section 5.2.2). In this case an economy of scope (arising, say, from specialized knowledge or equipment) provides an incentive for the joint use of a sharable input but not necessarily for production of several outputs within a firm. Whether or not conglomerate operation occurs will depend on the market transaction costs in the sale or lease of sharable inputs relative to the costs of internal coordination.

Second, and perhaps less obviously, transaction-cost explanations of conglomerate firms based on shared inputs can, but need not, imply that economies of scope exist. The difference here is basically one of perspective between the neoclassical analysis of economies of scope as developed by Panzar, Willig and Baumol, and the institutionalist orientation of the transaction-cost approach. According to the latter, firms develop and evolve specialized resources which, at any point in time, may be capable of more generalized use, and this may give rise to conglomerate operation when market transaction costs are high. Economies of scope are, however, most readily viewed in a neoclassical perspective as providing cost savings in joint production (given input prices and technology) which are generally available to any multi-product firm. It follows that a firm may diversify to use its existing resources more fully (e.g. the spare capacity of its plant, its excess marketing expertise) even when no economies of scope exist (or indeed even if some diseconomies of scope exist). The transaction-cost approach thus places emphasis on the costs of transaction (and hence the available institutions in the market) rather than the costs of production and distribution.

In principle it would be possible to define economies of scope to include both production and transaction costs and hence include all resource-utilization arguments under the umbrella of economies of scope. Whilst this is a matter of definition, it should be noted that to take such a line runs the risk of obscuring the difference in perspective of the two approaches noted above. Given this, therefore, it is probably better to keep the two ideas separate, and this is the line taken in this chapter.

Transaction-cost economies.   According to traditional neoclassical theory, a firm employs inputs of capital and labour to produce a given product (or range of products) at least production cost. From this viewpoint, the firm will employ inputs just sufficient to produce its products in the requisite amount, using input markets to buy and sell input services as appropriate. In contrast to this, however, firms can be regarded as a bundle of resources rather than simply as intermediaries between inputs and outputs. Moreover, resources need not be wholly specialized to a particular range of activities and, at any point in time, may possess excess capacity. By using its resources to engage in new lines of activity a firm can both grow and become more profitable.

Various resources have been suggested as a basis for firm diversification, including indivisible physical capital, human capital, including technological know-how, and managerial expertise. In what follows we consider, in particular, the role of physical capital and human knowhow in fostering conglomerate growth.

These ideas have been discussed most fully by Teece (1980, 1982b) and we follow his work in what follows. Consider first the case of a physical asset which can be used in several directions. Thus a physical asset used to produce a product A (e.g. an automobile body stamping machine) may also have capacity to produce a product B (e.g. truck bodies) (Teece, 1980, pp.230–2). This asset could be owned by the automobile manufacturer, say, who contracts to produce trucks to order for a separate truck manufacturer. Alternatively, a separate firm might own the stamping facility and contract its services to separate automobile and truck manufacturers. Third, a multi-product producer could own the machine and produce both automobile and truck bodies. The key issue is which alternative is most likely to minimize the market transaction costs?

Following Williamson, Teece argues that market contracts are less likely the more specialized is the asset and the smaller the number of parties involved. Suppose the producer of A owns the machine and seeks to lease it to one or a limited number of producers of B. If substantial differences exist in the value of the machine when used to produce both products then scope for costly haggling over quasi-rents will exist. As previously discussed in Chapter 3, incentives will exist for each party to attempt to extract such rents and considerable transaction costs may result.

In such circumstances, intrafirm trading may economize on costly haggling in the market. By jointly producing both car and truck bodies, previous market transactions are brought within the control of the firm and subject to fiat. Problems in negotiating contracts in the market are thereby attenuated, leading to lower costs and hence higher profits. If this is the case with specialized physical assets in small numbers' conditions, then product extension conglomerate diversification will tend to take place.

A second important source of market failure identified by Teece is in relation to organizational knowhow. Teece stresses the tacit and fungible (capable of several uses) nature of organizational knowledge. Such knowledge is typically not written down in a set of blueprints but rather exists in tacit form, embodied in the routines of firm operation and the experience of groups within the firm. In Teece's view, such knowledge gives rise to a generalized capability to produce products and is a primary source of product extension conglomerate diversification.

In the case of organizational or managerial knowhow, firms can (and do) contract managerial services (e.g. in the form of a secondment) to other firms. Such a move may be appropriate on a one-off basis but is much less likely to be so if a continuing contract is required. In this case, transaction costs can be substantial in writing, executing and enforcing contracts. Haggling over terms of such contracts may be important *ex ante* both in relation to the prices and the performance criteria employed. Similarly, difficulties may arise in monitoring performance where outcomes rather than effort are more directly observable (see Chapter 2). Standard problems of small numbers' bargaining in the presence of uncertainty are likely to arise with consequent attenuation of the opportunities for market governance. Firms may therefore opt for intrafirm governance in such situations.

Similar points apply in the case of technical knowhow. In this case, there may be problems in recognizing opportunities for market contracts given the secretive nature of much technical information. In addition, problems arise on the buying side in valuing information, given that the seller cannot fully reveal its content prior to sale. Issues discussed above are raised when continuing and specialized contracts governing technology transfer are required. As noted by Teece,

'The seller is exposed to hazards such as the possibility that the buyer will employ the knowhow in subtle ways not covered by the contract, or the buyer might 'leap frog' the licensor's technology and become an unexpected competitive threat in third markets. The buyer is exposed to hazards such as the seller asserting that the technology has superior performance or cost-reducing characteristics than is actually the case; or the seller might render promised transfer assistance in a perfunctory fashion. While bonding or the execution of performance guarantees can minimize these hazards, they need not be eliminated since costly haggling might ensue when measurement of the performance characteristics of the technology is open to some ambiguity. Furthermore, when a lateral transfer is contemplated and the technology has not therefore been previously commercialized by either party in the new application, the execution of performance guarantees is likely to be especially hazardous to the seller because of the uncertainties involved.' (Teece, 1980, p. 229)

These problems are most acute when a continuous exchange of knowhow is required in the context of essentially new ('idiosyncratic') applications of ideas (Williamson, 1979). Such circumstances will, according to Teece, most often lead to the diversification option being selected.

Limited evidence on these various hypotheses is currently available. It is, however, known that conglomerate diversification is closely associated with research and development activity in different firms and industries. At the industry level, for example, Gorecki (1975) found, in a sample of 44 two-and-a-half-digit UK manufacturing industries in 1963, that research intensity (measured as the number of scientists and engineers per 100 persons employed in 1959–60) was positively and statistically significantly related to the average diversification of firms classified to a particular industry. This effect was mainly attributable to research activity in consumer goods industries.[8]

At the firm level, Teece (1980, pp. 241–6) similarly reports a positive and significant effect of technological intensity on diversification of large US oil firms into other energy activities in 1975. Specifically, he found, for a sample of 22 large firms, that

$$Y = 0.59 + 2.87X_1 + 20.03X_2 + 1.64X_3 \quad \bar{R}^2 = 0.38 \qquad (6.4)$$
$$\;\;\;\;\;\;(0.80)\;\;(2.47)\;\;\;\;\;(2.31)\;\;\;\;\;(2.15)$$

where Y is the number of other energy activities engaged in, X_1 is a measure of cash flow (relative to re-investment opportunities available to the firm), X_2 is cumulated applied research expenditures over 1965–75 (as a measure of the firm's stock of technological knowhow) relative to sales, and X_3 is a dummy variable with a value of one for an M-form firm (zero otherwise) (t ratios in parentheses). All variables have the expected signs and are statistically significant at the 5 per cent level. The result for technological intensity, in particular, is also consistent with descriptive evidence presented by Teece (1980, pp. 233–40) which links oil-firm diversification into alternate fuels with sharing technological knowhow across fuels.

6.3   Financial and Managerial Theories

Transaction-cost economizing is by no means the only explanation of conglomerate growth, and in this section we consider two other groups of hypotheses which have been suggested. We begin by considering financial reasons for conglomerate growth focusing primarily on risk-reduction issues. Such factors are in fact quite complicated and we consider only some basic issues here. Second, we consider managerial motives for conglomerate growth linked to the separation of ownership from control. Managers may diversify in order to promote firm growth or to effect risk-reduction benefits for themselves and each of these possibilities is briefly discussed.

6.3.1   Financial Theories[9]

The argument that diversification confers risk-reduction benefits is directly analogous to the usual risk-spreading arguments of 'not having all one's eggs in one basket'. Specifically, a conglomerate firm engaged in several lines of activity is less likely to have a large variance in performance (as measured, for example, by its group rate of return) compared to a specialized firm because poor performance in one or several lines is likely to be offset by better performance elsewhere. In the case of two lines of activity with similar characteristics, the more negative is the correlation in performance, the lower will be the corresponding variability in returns of the group, with, in the limit, complete stability of returns with a perfect negative correlation. In more typical cases, with a zero or positive correlation, some risk reduction will be experienced, the more so the less positive is the correlation. Conglomerate firms, therefore, can offer benefits in terms of less financial risk by appropriate operation of diverse activities.

These points can be illustrated by a simple example. Consider a firm which employs capital in amount K in each of two activities, and let the rate of return in activity i be $r_i = \pi_i/K$ where π_i is the profit in activity i. Assume also that r_i varies from year to year but has the same mean, μ, and variance, σ^2, for each activity. Then the rate of return for the firm as a whole is

$$r = (\pi_1 + \pi_2)/2K = 1/2(r_1 + r_2). \tag{6.5}$$

Moreover, it can be shown that the standard deviation for the group rate of return is

$$\sigma_r = \sigma\sqrt{[(1 + \rho)/2]}, \tag{6.6}$$

where ρ is the correlation coefficient between r_1 and r_2 (see Clarke, 1985, p. 222, n. 13). Hence, when r_1 and r_2 are independent ($\rho = 0$), $\sigma_r = \sigma/\sqrt{2}$, while for perfect positive correlation ($\rho = 1$), $\sigma_r = \sigma$ and with perfect negative correlation ($\rho = -1$), $\sigma_r = 0$. The standard deviation of the group rate of return falls monotonically as the correlation coefficient, ρ, falls from $+1$ to -1, i.e. as the rates of return of the two activities are less positively correlated.

The potential gains from risk reduction are most likely to arise in the early stages of diversification when a previously specialized firm diversifies into new activities. Several reasons for this can be given (see Prais, 1976, pp. 92–100). First, by the law of large numbers, amalgamation of independent and (for simplicity) equal-sized business units with similar characteristics, will lead to reductions in the variability of the group rate of return (measured by the standard-deviation group rate of return) in inverse proportion to the square root of the number of units. This means, amongst other things, that the greatest reductions in risk occur at the earliest stages of diversification.[10] Second, in practice positive rather than zero (or negative) correlations between rates of return in different lines of activity tend to exist because constituent parts of a firm face the same general economic climate and are subject to the same managerial influences. The existence of such positive correlations tends to reduce the scope for risk reduction by diversification, as well as implying that the effective minimum risk level is attained after adding fewer business units.[11]

These points can be illustrated by means of simple numerical examples. For example, even with no correlation between activities a conglomerate firm attains 80 per cent of its potential risk reduction by adding a total of 25 equal-sized and similar business units, and 50 per cent reduction by adding just four such units. With a positive correlation between activities, risk-reduction opportunities are reduced further. Thus, with a correlation of 0.5 between each unit, the corresponding figures are six business units and (just over) two business units.[12] Clearly, therefore, risk reduction is unlikely to be a strong motive for continued diversification (except in the odd case) for already highly diversified firms. It may, however, be a more important factor for firms of a less diversified nature.[13]

Even if potential exists for reduction of financial risks in conglomerate operation, this need not imply that shareholders benefit from such operation. Whilst several early studies (e.g. Adelman, 1961) argued that risk reduction associated with conglomerate activity directly benefits shareholders, more recent work has been more sceptical. In particular, Levy and Sarnat (1970) have argued that shareholders do not gain directly from reduced variability in rates of return in conglomerate firms. This is because they can, at least in principle, obtain equivalent protection by diversifying their holdings of specialized company shares. From this point of view, therefore, the conglomerate firm performs a similar function to that of a unit trust in reducing risks to investors. Given that investors are risk-averse, they can seek to diversify risks on the market by holding appropriate portfolios of shares in specialized companies and/or by investing in unit trusts. Only in so far as conglomerate firms offer risk-reduction opportunities not available on the market (which are, perhaps, difficult to conceive of) will they provide an additional direct benefit to shareholders.

It has also been recently recognized (see, in particular, Galai and Masulis, 1976) that shareholders can actually lose from risk reduction in a conglomerate firm. To see this, consider a pure conglomerate merger of two equal-sized firms in which no capital restructuring takes place. Whilst under certain simplified conditions (perfect capital markets, no synergistic advantages, etc.) this will imply that the value of the group is merely the sum of the values of the separate firms, it will also mean (when risk reduction has occurred) that bondholders have gained at the expense of equityholders. The reason for this is that the reduced variability in the rate of return means that the risk of bankruptcy has decreased, and this directly benefits the bondholders in the new group. Conversely, since the shareholders now have to cover the claims of bondholders in both units, the value of their equity correspondingly reduces. In effect, the formation of a conglomerate firm (with no alteration in financial structure) will weaken the value of the claims of the shareholders and raise those of the holders of debt. This effect alone would lead equityholders to resist the formation of conglomerate firms.

This argument, however, may be outweighed by other possible effects. In the first place, the firm can reorganize its financial structure by issuing more debt and correspondingly retiring equity (see Galai and Masulis, 1976, p. 69) to neutralize the above effect. If it does this then, *ceteris paribus*, equityholders will be indifferent to the change. Second, and more important from a practical viewpoint, the ability of firms to increase their debt capacity increases the after-tax value of the firm in that, by convention, interest payments on debt are deductible before payment of corporation tax. Hence, by reducing the risk of bankruptcy, the conglomerate firm can raise a greater proportion of capital as debt (i.e. increase its gearing) with consequent tax advantages to the shareholders. This benefit could provide significant incentives for the formation of conglomerate firms in situations where risk reduction is important.

The increase in debt capacity also confers other benefits. First, a reduced risk of default should lower bondholders' required rate of return for investing in a firm, thereby providing an opportunity for cheaper finance. Second, as argued in particular by Prais (1976, pp. 103–5), such finance may be particularly cheap in periods where investors fail to anticipate inflation fully and thereby lend at low (or even negative) real interest rates. According to Prais real interest rates on debenture finance in the UK were very low for much of the post-war period (being actually negative in the early 1970s, as well as in the early 1950s) and this provided a strong incentive for capital restructuring. Prais suggests that some part at least of the growth of conglomerate firms in post-war Britain may be attributable to the cheap debenture finance that has been available.

All of the above effects rely ultimately on the reduced variability in rates of return consequent on the formation of conglomerate firms. It is well known, however, that large firms have *per se* advantages in raising finance, independent of risk-reduction effects. These arise partly from the relatively fixed costs associated with raising capital (e.g. costs of issuing a prospectus, advertising, underwriting, and so on). More important, however, are the costs of capital itself, which appear to fall progressively as firm size increases. In his study Prais (1976, pp. 108–9) shows that quoted companies have a significant advantage over unquoted ones where the premium on quotation may approximately double the value of a company's shares. For quoted companies also, however, the market shows a preference for large companies over small companies even when such factors as variability of returns, and gearing, are taken into account. From a careful study of available evidence, Prais (1976, p. 111) suggests that this might be worth about one to two percentage points in the cost of capital for a large firm compared with a smaller firm (where the latter is defined as being one-tenth of the size of the large firm with an earnings yield of 10 per cent). Prais argues that part of this preference for large firms arises from the desire of financial intermediaries to invest in larger units and from the growth in importance of such intermediaries in the capital market in the UK and elsewhere.

The relationship of capital costs and firm size can give a general incentive for firms to grow independently of any conglomeration effect. Large firms, however, tend to be more diversified than small firms (since scope for expansion in individual markets is obviously limited) so that this effect can lead to conglomerate firm growth. Whilst it could be argued that the bias towards large firms found in the provision of capital merely reflects the operation of market forces (including transaction costs) in providing capital, it can also be argued that imperfections in the capital market give rise to important distortions tending to bias the market towards large (and conglomerate) firms (Prais, 1976, p. 113).

6.3.2 Managerial Motives

Another group of explanations of conglomerate diversification centre on managerial motives. In the first place, several authors (notably Marris, 1964 and Mueller, 1969) have argued that diversification is associated with growth maximization objectives of management. In the Mueller (1969) version (see also Mueller 1972, 1981 and Marris and Mueller, 1980), for example, it is argued that such effects are likely to be associated with the life cycle of the firm. Relatively young firms with ample investment opportunities will typically employ capital raised in the capital market to fund marginal investment projects, and, in this case, objectives of stockholder wealth and growth maximization will be largely coincident. In the case of mature firms, however, where investment opportunities are fewer, managers will seek to retain earnings to support growth objectives contrary to the interests of stockholders. Mueller argues that managers pursuing growth-maximizing strategies will adopt a lower cost of capital than the market rate and that this will lead them to make investments, including conglomerate acquisitions, which are not in the stockholders' interests.

Clearly, if such policies are pursued then we would expect firms to engage in mergers which, at the margin at least, are not profitable to their owners. A fair amount of evidence that has been produced is in fact consistent with this hypothesis (see Mueller, 1981). Such evidence applies even when horizontal mergers are considered. In the UK, for example, Singh (1971) found that at least one-half of a sample of 77 firms which engaged in horizontal mergers in 1955–60 experienced a fall in profitability in each of several years following the merger. Similar results were obtained by Meeks (1977) in a more extensive survey of 233 large firms which merged in 1964–72. More recently, a study of mergers in six European countries and the US (Mueller, 1980) similarly found little evidence of improved profitability through mergers. While in this case there was significant evidence of improved profitability in the UK,[14] increases and decreases in profitability were evenly matched across all European countries. Results for the US in this study and elsewhere also show a neutral or mixed effect of mergers on profitability (see Mueller, 1981 for details).

Managers may pursue other objectives than merely growth. Recent literature (Amihud and Lev, 1981; Marcus, 1982), in particular, has focused on managerial attitudes to risk which may give rise to specific incentives for conglomerate as opposed to horizontal or vertical firm growth. This literature stresses the asymmetrical position of managers compared to owners as far as risk reduction is concerned. As noted in Section 6.3.1, owners of firms (i.e. shareholders) are able to fully diversify their risks by choosing an appropriate portfolio of shares. Managers in a company, in contrast, cannot typically diversify their risks in this way. Managers work for one company at a time and hence the risk associated with their income will be more closely related to the performance of that firm. This will be partly because managerial compensation is directly linked to firm performance (e.g. in stock options, bonuses, etc.) in a non-diversifiable way. In addition, however, managers also face employment risk if the firm significantly underperforms or goes bankrupt, with attendant adjustment costs in finding new employment. Managers, therefore, have an incentive to reduce the variability in performance of the firm and hence adopt a diversification strategy.

The incentive for managers to avoid risks has been explored (in a non-diversification context) by Marcus (1982). He assumes that some part of managerial compensation takes the form of non-tradeable equity in the firm. Whilst other owners of the firm are able to diversify their portfolios in accordance with their risk preferences, managers face a binding constraint in relation to their holdings of their own firm's shares. Such shareholdings, however, are in the interests of the owners in that they encourage effort and reduce agency costs. Marcus shows that in this framework, with effort not directly observable, equilibrium will involve managers under-investing in risky projects or over-spending on risk-reducing activities in order to reduce the risks associated with their shareholding constraint. Such activities will be suboptimal from the point of view of independent owners, although given the agency relation involved they will be accepted because of the extra incentives and hence profits that they generate. Hence, managerial risk reduction will be an optimal outcome of the agency problem associated with encouraging managerial effort.

Some evidence consistent with the risk-reduction hypothesis is presented by Amihud and Lev (1981). They consider two tests of the hypothesis. First, they look at the association between large corporate acquisitions (assets acquired in excess of $10 million) and management control for 309 large US firms in 1961–70. This test shows that management-controlled firms (those where no single party held 10 per cent or more of the company's stock) accounted for significantly more conglomerate acquisitions than owner-controlled firms.[15] No similar pattern was observed for horizontal and vertical mergers, thereby offering support for the diversification hypothesis. Second, they considered the correlation between the firm net income/equity ratio and the corresponding economy ratio for their firms over the period 1957–72. In this case, higher correlations between these variables (as measured by the r^2 statistic) indicate a closer correspondence between firm and general industry performance which one would expect with more diversified firms. Again, they found that greater diversification (measured by these R^2 statistics) was significantly higher in management-controlled firms.

These results are consistent with the view that managers diversify their firm's activities for risk-reducing reasons.[16] They do not unambiguously confirm this hypothesis, however, because management control may itself be endogenous such that greater firm diversification itself is likely to imply weaker owner control. Also, the results could be consistent with simple managerial growth maximization, where conglomerate acquisition provides the greatest opportunities for firm growth. The tough anti-merger policy which has effectively barred most, if not all, horizontal and vertical mergers in the US since the early 1950s may have been important in this respect. Conglomerate firms appear to be linked with managerial control, but further work needs to be done to disentangle the various possible relationships involved.

6.4   Conglomerates and Public Policy

Conglomerate firms raise a number of economic and wider political issues of interest from a public policy point of view. Some authors argue that multi-market operation supports anti-competitive behaviour and possible resource misallocation. Others argue that conglomerate firms offer efficiency advantages, or, at worst, are neutral in their effects on economic behaviour. Writers are also divided on the wider political effects of conglomerate operation. Some of the various arguments are considered in this section.

6.4.1   Economic Issues

For simplicity we consider only four hypotheses concerning the economic effects of conglomerate firms in this section. We begin with pro-competitive effects of diversified new entry, and then consider possible anti-competitive effects arising from mutual forbearance, reciprocal dealing and predatory pricing.

Diversified new entry.   In addition to possible cost savings discussed in Section 6.2, conglomerate firms can provide important economic benefits in relation to diversified new entry. If a market is monopolized or otherwise yields excess monopoly profits then entry by conglomerate firms (provided that it is entry by new building and provided that it does not itself increase monopolization in the industry) should lead to more competition and lower prices. This is, of course, not a universal rule since it depends on the oligopoly game that is played after entry, but, nevertheless, it suggests the possibility of a welfare improvement associated with diversification.

The importance of this argument depends on the advantages of diversified entry relative to simple new entry by firms. Diversified entrants typically have easier (and less costly) access to capital required for new entry (either from the capital market or from internal sources) compared to *de novo* entrants. Hence, they are able to move more easily into markets offering excess profit opportunities and thus monopoly profits are more quickly competed away. In addition, since a diversified entrant has more resources available to support new entry, it is likely to be better able to withstand an initial period of loss-making after entry. This, in turn, means that established firms are more likely to accommodate a diversified entrant than engage in fierce competition once entry takes place. From a strategic point of view, therefore, diversified entry is more likely to meet with an accommodating response, and this in turn may mean that more such entry is encouraged. In addition, firms which seek to limit new entry must set lower prices and profits to deter diversified entry (Bain, 1956). Either way, therefore, monopoly power of established firms should be reduced.

Diversified firms may also be able to take advantage of cost savings in an initial production phase to facilitate new entry. In many industries, costs fall with accumulated output and experience, i.e. 'learning by doing' takes place. Such costs may be important to a new firm entrant who must consider the additional costs of gaining experience and so on in producing a new product. A diversified firm, however, may have access to experience and skills (production, marketing, etc.) in other markets so that it can compete on similar terms with established firms.[17] It should be noted that in this case economies of scope need not exist vis-à-vis specialist producers in the new industry. Nevertheless, such economies are available relative to a specialist entrant in the short run. This latter effect forms the basis of an important advantage for diversified firms.

Each of these arguments suggests that conglomerate firms serve an important social function in increasing competitiveness in an economy. Somewhat surprisingly, however, very little empirical work appears to have been done to assess their quantitative importance. Much more attention has been given to possible anti-competitive effects of conglomerate firms to which we now turn.

Mutual forbearance.   First, it is often argued that the growth of conglomerate firms can give rise to 'mutual forbearance' or 'spheres of influence' in the economy (see, for example, Scherer, 1980, pp. 340–2). This hypothesis was originally put forward by Edwards (1955) who argued that diversified firms tend to develop spheres of influence in product markets so that (by mutual understanding) competition is reduced. If conglomerate firms face each other in a number of markets, they will recognize that attempts to force vigorous competition in one market could lead to retaliation in others. Each firm, therefore, will recognize the primacy of interest of some firms in particular markets and allow a reduced degree of competition in all the relevant markets.

In a sector (or, indeed, an economy as a whole) dominated by conglomerate firms, therefore, one would expect reduced competition and higher prices and profits due to mutual forbearance.[18]

The validity of this hypothesis depends on entry conditions in the relevant markets and would not apply if entry conditions for independent firms were easy. In addition, it requires conglomerate firms to face each other in various markets which is most likely to happen within industrial sectors. Given these conditions, however, it seems likely that firms will develop spheres of influence to raise their overall profitability. Whilst the evidence is fragmentary, Scherer (1980, pp. 341–2) cites examples including the case of the international chemicals industry in the inter-war period where explicit evidence of mutual forbearance of the major conglomerate firms (Farben in Germany, ICI in England and du Pont in the US) has been found (see Kahn, 1961). Further examples relate to international merchant-marine cartels and banking (Scherer, 1980, p. 342).

Some limited evidence is also available from econometric studies which suggests that prices and profits are positively associated with diversification. Rhoades (1973), for example, considered determinants of price–cost margins in 241 four-digit US manufacturing industries in 1963. Using OLS regression he found that

$$Y = 15.64 + 0.11X_1 - 0.08X_2 + 0.06X_3 + 0.11X_4 + 7.08D - 0.08X_5,$$
$$\quad\quad (3.32) \quad (3.35) \quad (3.02) \quad (4.86) \quad (6.12) \quad (2.59)$$

$$\bar{R}^2 = 0.32; \tag{6.7}$$

where Y is the industry price–cost margin, X_1 is the four-firm concentration ratio, X_2 is the ratio of primary to total employment of firms classified to an industry, and other variables reflect market growth, the capital/output ratio, a producer–consumer goods dummy variable (consumer goods $= 1$) and an index of the geographic concentration of markets, respectively (t ratios in parentheses). The negative coefficient on X_2 is statistically significant at the 1 per cent level indicating that greater diversification is associated with higher price–cost margins. This result is, therefore, consistent with the mutual forbearance hypothesis, although it does not rule out other possible explanations (e.g. economies of scope, other market power effects) of the price–cost margin/diversification relationship.[19]

Clearly, scope exists for more carefully specified statistical work on the mutual-forbearance hypothesis as well as further case-study work on particular sectors of the economy. It seems likely that mutual forbearance could be an important factor in the operation of some sectors in the economy and so be of some public policy concern.

Reciprocal dealing. A second argument is that conglomerate firms engage in reciprocal dealing arrangements which reduce competition and generally lead to resource misallocation. A classic case of this would be where a conglomerate firm purchases a significant part of the output, X, of an industry whilst at the same time supplying an important input, Y, to that industry. Then the firm may insist that the industry concerned purchase its product Y as a condition for purchase of their product, X. Such a requirement at the very least would distort the distribution of sales of product Y towards the conglomerate firm, and may also imply direct misallocation of resources.

In principle, reciprocal dealing could be enforced by a single product firm. For example, a supplier of steel (X) may insist that suppliers of its replacement steel-producing equipment (Y) purchase their steel from it. Conglomerate firms, however, have particular scope for reciprocal dealing agreements in that their multi-product operation increases both the number of potential reciprocal relationships involved and the power of the firm to insist on reciprocal arrangements. Thus, for example, suppliers of office stationery (X) may be encouraged to purchase a particular company's production machinery (Y). If that company is in turn part of a large conglomerate firm using its office stationery in various subsidiaries (including possibly a retail stationery chain) then the power of the firm to insist on a reciprocal deal is enhanced. A conglomerate firm has more leverage in insisting that a supplier takes one of its own products than might a specialist firm producing a single product.

Available evidence in the US suggests that reciprocity is a widespread business practice (Scherer, 1980, p. 342). At the same time, however, there is considerable disagreement as to its likely economic policy importance. On the one hand, some economists argue that reciprocal dealing is only likely to be successful when products offered are of similar price and quality to independent alternatives, and that its only effect therefore will be to switch sales towards conglomerate firms rather than to misallocate resources. On the other hand, it is suggested that reciprocal dealing can lead to significant distortions in economic resource allocation, imposing deadweight welfare losses on society at large. *Inter alia*, such distortions will lead to greater concentration of economic production both within markets and in the economy as a whole. No systematic evidence appears, however, to be currently available to consider how important such effects might be.

Predatory pricing.   Finally, we may briefly mention predatory pricing, or more generally predatory tactics, in relation to conglomerate firms. Predatory pricing arises when a dominant firm or firms cut price in a market in order to eliminate or discipline smaller rivals and thereby to raise prices and profits in the long run. Non-price predatory tactics may also be used such as very aggressive advertising campaigns or, more directly, attempts to cut off input supplies or sales outlets to rivals, threats or even sabotage. Among other things, predatory action requires that predator firms are financially able to withstand short-term losses in order to reap longer-term rewards. This, in turn, is particularly likely to be the case if predator firms are diversified and hence able to cross-subsidize temporary losses in a particular market with profits earned elsewhere. In addition, conglomerate firms can also benefit in that predatory action in one market may discourage competition of small firms or potential entrants in another of the firm's markets.

Predatory pricing will, in the long run, give rise to high prices and profits. Its association with conglomerate operation is, therefore, consistent with evidence for a positive price–cost margin/diversification link cited above. Some case-study evidence for its existence is also available (see Scherer, 1980, pp. 335–42; Utton, 1979, Chapter 5).

6.4.2   Political Issues

In addition to possible economic effects of conglomerate firms, concern has also been expressed over their possible wider political effects. Indeed, in the popular view, this concern is possibly of most importance. To some extent concern is with large firms (big business) *per se* and is not necessarily linked to the diversification of a firm's activities. Some diversification arguments also exist, however, and we consider these briefly here.

The main arguments concerning big business relate to the concentration of decision-making within a single hierarchical unit and the possibilities for exercising power associated with large financial resources. Large conglomerate firms, as we have seen, may be able to wield economic power within individual markets. More broadly, however, they may also wield power in the legal and political spheres. They may, for example, be better able to defend patent and other rights in the courts because of the large financial resources available to them. Also, they may be better able to lobby politicians and ministers on policy issues pertinent to their economic interests. Such firms, it is argued, will have incentives to undertake lobbying because of the large economic rewards at stake. Moreover, in so far as economies of scale operate in lobbying activities (setting up a research unit, disseminating information, coordinating campaigns, etc.), they may be economically feasible only for larger groups. Whilst the example of the farmers shows that effective lobbying can be attained by groups of small businesses, organizational problems may in some circumstances make this a less cost-effective option.

The particular advantages of conglomerate operation in the political sphere may be associated with economies of scope in lobbying activities. That is, costs of lobbying (or indeed defending patents, etc.) in a number of areas may be lower for a conglomerate firm than for equivalent specialized firms. The lobbying organization employed by the firm may be shared over a number of activities. The goodwill generated with officials and politicians in one area may be made use of in other areas. Advantages in bargaining may be obtainable when a number of points of contact (e.g. in relation to possible grants and employment creation) are being discussed. In each of these cases it is conceivable that specialized firms could cooperate to produce the desired effect. As in the production sphere, however, the transaction costs associated with such cooperation will often favour hierarchical control.

Political influence can be a difficult thing to gauge since it may take a variety of forms, which are often difficult to measure. Studies that have been done have looked at such things as tax concessions, import duties and political contributions in relation to various attributes of the firm. One study by Marx (1980) has particularly focused on conglomerate operation. Using a matched sample of 75 conglomerate and non-conglomerate firms of similar size, he found no relationship between conglomerate operation and income taxes paid or tax incentives received, nor in relation to voting patterns in the US Congress. He did, however, find a positive relationship between conglomeration and campaign contributions, as one might expect given the greater possible value of political goodwill to a conglomerate firm.

6.5 Summary and Conclusions

In this chapter we have considered the reasons for and the possible effects of conglomerate firm growth. In Section 6.1, trends in conglomerate diversification in the US and UK in the post-war era were considered, and evidence for greater conglomerate growth in the US was presented. This trend may be linked to tighter controls on horizontal and vertical mergers in the US since the early 1950s. Section 6.2 considered transaction-cost economizing as a reason for conglomerate growth, whilst Section 6.3 considered other financial and managerial hypotheses that have been suggested. Finally, in Section 6.4, competitive effects of conglomerates were considered together with possible broader political effects of conglomerate firms.

The arguments presented clearly show no consensus on the causes and effects of conglomerate firm growth. Whilst, traditionally, conglomerate firms have been viewed with suspicion (what Williamson has referred to as the 'inhospitality' tradition), more recent work has suggested that conglomerate firms can have socially beneficial effects. In addition to the advantages of diversified entry, work stemming from Williamson's (1975) contribution stresses their possible transaction-cost-economizing advantages. Such firms can make efficient use of under-utilized resources in the presence of market transaction costs, and may (perhaps more contentiously) have capital allocation advantages when organized along M-form lines. Possible non-beneficial effects (due to mutual forbearance, reciprocal dealing, etc.), however, must also be borne in mind. Clearly there can be both social benefits and costs associated with conglomerate firm operation and further research (both theoretical and empirical) is needed to disentangle the various factors at work.

Further Reading

A useful discussion of transaction-cost economizing and asset utilization as a basis for conglomerate diversification is given in the two papers by Teece (1980, 1982b). Williamson's own discussion is given in Williamson (1975, Chapter 9, and 1981). See also Sutton (1980, Chapter 4).

Financial theories of diversification can be complex. A useful introductory treatment is given in Prais (1976, pp. 92–123). See also Monroe (1981) for a fairly recent survey. Managerial theories are discussed in Marris and Mueller (1980) and Mueller (1981). See also the excellent empirical paper by Amihud and Lev (1981).

Public policy and other material is discussed in Scherer (1980, Chapter 12). See also the recent symposium edited by Blair and Lanzillotti (1981) where many of the issues raised in this chapter are discussed in greater detail.

Notes

1   These definitions are based on classifications of conglomerate mergers employed by the Federal Trade Commission (FTC) in the US. See the FTC Annual Statistical Report on Mergers and Acquisitions. The FTC

also distinguish *market extension* mergers into new geographic markets which are not considered explicitly in this chapter.

2   Specifically, horizontal (vertical) mergers accounted for the following proportions of manufacturing and mining assets acquired: 36.8 (12.8) per cent in 1948–53, 19.2 (22.2) per cent in 1956–63, 12.4 (7.8) per cent in 1963–72 and 15.1 (5.8) per cent in 1972–77.

3   This comparison is essentially crude being based on aggregate and market concentration ratios. Formal relationships between aggregate concentration, market concentration and diversification can be derived for other concentration indices: see Clarke and Davies (1983, 1984). In principle, changes in industry size rather than conglomerate growth could explain the disparity in US trends in aggregate and market concentration, although this is unlikely.

4   These figures are biassed towards horizontal mergers in that a large market share for the merged company (33 per cent of the market in 1965 reduced to 25 per cent in 1973) was one criterion used for merger vetting. The largest mergers (originally with £5 million assets acquired or more) were also vetted. Bearing this in mind it seems clear that horizontal mergers were the major type of mergers in the UK in the period.

5   Data limitations prevent more detailed analysis of the 1971–77 period. A slight fall in diversification between two-digit industries (or sectors) was also recorded for 1963–68. For further details see Clarke and Davies (1983).

6   Some recent evidence (White, 1981a) has suggested that aggregate concentration in US manufacturing (and more generally) has not increased in the 1960s and 1970s and may even have decreased, notwithstanding the substantial US merger activity of the late 1960s. See also the comments of Feinberg (1981) and the reply by White (1981b). For the UK, recent work by Goudie and Meeks (1982) suggests a greater role for conglomerate mergers than we have suggested here.

7   As noted in Chapter 2, such hidden knowledge problems are facets of the general problem of adverse selection.

8   Such positive correlations have been reported in a number of studies: see, for example, Gort (1962), Amey (1964), Grant (1977) and Wolf (1977).

9   This section draws, in particular, on the work of Prais (1976). See also Clarke (1985, pp. 209–12) and Monroe (1981).

10   Thus with n lines of activity of the same size, each with a rate of return r_i with mean μ, and variance, σ^2, the group rate of return $r = 1/n . \sum_{i=1}^{n} r_i$ will have mean μ and standard deviation $\sigma_r = \sigma/\sqrt{n}$ if the rates of return are independent (see, for example, Wonnacott and Wonnacott, 1972, p. 121). This implies that $\partial \sigma_r/\partial_n = -0.5 \, \sigma . n^{-3/2} < 0$ but $\partial^2 \sigma_r/\partial_n^2 = 0.75\sigma . n^{-5/2} > 0$.

11   In this case, given equal-sized units with similar characteristics as in the previous footnote, the standard-deviation group rate of return is $\sigma_r = \sigma\sqrt{[(1 + (n - 1)\rho)/n]}$ where ρ is the correlation between any pair of units

(Prais, 1976, p. 95). This expression has a lower limit of $\sigma\sqrt{\rho}$ (as n tends to infinity), and a firm reaches within (say) 10 per cent of this limit as $n^* = (1 - \rho)/(\cdot 21\rho)$. Hence $\partial n^*/\partial\rho = -1/(\cdot 21\rho^2) < 0$.

12   With reference to the previous note, the lower limit on risk reduction is $\sigma_r = 0$ with $\rho = 0$ and $\sigma_r = 0.71\sigma$ with $\rho = 0.5$. The figures cited relate to 80 per cent and 50 per cent reductions over the relevant range.

13   Greater incentives for diversification can arise if negative correlations between units can be obtained. As explained in Prais (1976, n. 20, p. 261), however, scope for such negative correlations is limited by the essential logic of correlation analysis. In the equal correlation case of Note 11 for example, it is readily seen that non-negative σ_r requires $\rho \geq -1/(n - 1)$ which rises to zero as n goes to infinity.

14   The study of the UK, by Cosh, Hughes and Singh, related to takeovers which took place in 1967–69. It is not clear at the present time why this study obtained different results from most other UK studies (see also Firth, 1979 and Cowling et al., 1980).

15   They also found that weak owner-controlled firms (where a single party owned between 10 and 30 per cent of the stock) engaged in more conglomerate acquisitions than owner-controlled firms although to a lesser extent.

16   Although we may note that for some conglomerate firms presumably in Amihud and Lev's sample scope for risk reduction by merger may have been small given their already diversified state. In such cases managerial risk reduction would have been a past but not a continuing reason for conglomerate growth.

17   Examples of this might be where a manufacturer of motor cars diversifies into bus and truck production, or where a producer of local newspapers diversifies into national newspapers and magazines (see, for example, the recent case of Eddie Shah's new entry into national newspapers in the UK).

18   Contrast the argument in Chapter 4, Section 4.5.2, wherein the threat of retaliatory entry by one firm into another's market may lead to less entry all round. In that case, mutual forbearance arises at the pre-entry stage rather than in relation to actual competition in the market.

19   A similar positive relationship is also found in Miller (1969). In a follow-up study, Rhoades (1974) found a negative effect of diversification on price–cost margins in 117 two-and-a-half-digit US industries in 1967. In this case, diversification related to multi-product activity on a broader scale than in his earlier study, and it may be that this factor explains the divergence in results. The earlier study which captures more narrow spectrum diversification would ceteris paribus be expected to more readily capture mutual forbearance effects.

7 Multinational Firms

MARK CASSON

7.1 Introduction

The economic theory of the multinational enterprise (MNE) lies at the interface of three separate specialisms: the theory of the firm, international trade theory, and international finance. Unfortunately, it is difficult to integrate these three branches of theory. As they are conventionally formulated, some of the assumptions made by each are inconsistent with those made by the others. Writers on the MNE have tackled this problem by re-formulating the constituent theories – notably the theory of the firm. The result is a theory which deals comprehensively with both the spatial and organizational aspects of the firm. The modern theory of the MNE is, in fact, a general theory of the enterprise in space and, as such, embraces theories of the multi-regional and the multi-plant firm. The theory of the uninational single-plant firm under perfect competition – a theory which used to be known quite simply as 'the theory of the firm' – turns out to be a quite trivial special case.

The study of the MNE is also valuable because it emphasizes a couple of points which have been rather neglected in the past. First, it demonstrates that the internal workings of large firms are a subject of intrinsic interest to the economist. When the value added by one of the world's largest multinationals can exceed the GNP of a small country, the idiosyncrasies of decision-making within the enterprise are clearly important for the global allocation of resources. It can be misleading, therefore, to talk of a 'representative firm' when analysing an MNE, and to attempt to explain its behaviour as though it were a 'black box'.

The second point concerns the importance of stylized facts as a stimulus to theoretical development. Empirical study of MNEs has yielded an intriguing set of stylized facts, some of which are summarized in the list below, and the modern theory of the MNE successfully explains them.

Some Stylized Facts about MNEs

(1) *Historical pattern of growth.* MNE control of world manufacturing production grew very rapidly during the 1950s and 1960s, but has levelled off since then. In the 1920s and 1930s international cartels controlled some of the industries (e.g. chemicals) which MNEs now dominate. To some extent, therefore, there has been a substitution of one form of international control of production for another. Substitution along similar lines is evident in the marketing field, where many companies have replaced independent overseas sales agents with wholly owned foreign sales subsidiaries.

(2) *Country of origin and the structure of international production.* Three main types of MNE can be distinguished: (a) the US-based MNE which grew rapidly in the 1950s and early 1960s, and undertakes import-substituting investments in other developed countries (notably in Europe); (b) European-based MNEs which undertook backward integration into agriculture and minerals in the colonial territories in the 1920s and 1930s; and (c) Japanese MNEs which have invested in offshore 'export-platform' investments in the low-wage, newly industrializing countries of SE Asia in the 1970s. There are plenty of hybrids, though: US MNEs which have invested in agriculture and minerals in Latin America, European MNEs that have cross-invested in Europe and in the US, and Japanese MNEs which have recently begun to undertake import-substituting investments in Europe and the US.

(3) *Industry characteristics.* US MNEs predominate in industries with high R&D/sales ratios and high advertising expenditure/sales ratios (as indicated by data relating to the US economy); also in industries with high ratios of salaried/weekly paid staff, and of administrative staff/production workers, and with high five-firm concentration ratios in the host country.

(4)   *Firm characteristics.*   Within an industry, MNEs appear to have the characteristics typical of the industry – as noted above – *only more so*. They undertake more R&D, have a relatively high proportion of administrative staff, and so on. They also offer higher wages, use different systems of wage negotiation – preferring to deal with fewer unions – and tend to export a higher proportion of their output than their indigenous competitors. Case-study evidence suggests that many MNEs enjoy privileged access to either technology, reputable brand names, or managerial techniques (usually – though not invariably – techniques that are specific to the industry). Enterprises that produce in a very large number of countries tend to concentrate on a narrow range of products, whilst those that produce in very few countries tend to produce a wider range of products.

(5)   *Contractual alternatives to the MNE.*   Licensing, franchising, subcontracting and joint ventures (as well as cartels) are all alternatives to the MNE so far as the international control of production is concerned. Licensing appears to be most common in industries such as float-glass, where process technology is easy to patent, and in publishing, where copyright protection is relatively secure. Franchising is common in food and in certain service industries, such as hotels. Subcontracting is widespread in many industries, whilst joint ventures are common in heavy chemicals and in component manufacture for mass-assembly, where there are significant economies of scale. These alternatives to the MNE have been used more frequently during the last 10 years than they were in the early post-war period.

(6)   *Vertical integration between primary and manufacturing industries.*   Backward integration into minerals is much more common in some industries than others. It is common, for example, in aluminium and copper, but not in tin. Within the energy sector, it is common in oil but not in coal. Likewise, backward integration into agriculture is common in bananas, but not in cocoa, grain or cotton.

Sources: Buckley (1985), Buckley and Enderwick (1984), Casson and associates (1985), Dunning (1981, 1983), Dunning and McQueen (1982), Hennart (1982), Pearce (1983), Stuckey (1983), Wilkins (1970, 1974), Wolf (1977).

The need to explain facts has guided the development of the theory throughout, and this has conferred on the theory its major strength relative to other branches of economics, namely its immediate practical relevance.

The economic theory of the MNE can be viewed as an application of certain broad theoretical insights to the specific problems of coordinating economic activity over space. In each case, however, the theory of the MNE gives a special 'twist' to the theory in the course of the application.

The concept of 'principals' and 'agents', for example, is widely used to examine relations between the owners and managers of a firm (Jensen and Meckling, 1976). The same concept is used in the theory of the MNE to analyse relations between the overall management of a production process and the management of an individual operation (see Chapter 2). It is argued, for example, that under certain conditions agency problems are less acute when each of the individual operations involved in the process belongs to the same ownership unit. Common ownership gives the high-level manager the right of access to information utilized by the lower-level managers and so reduces their scope for strategic or deceitful use of the information at their disposal. The advantage of reducing information asymmetry through common ownership explains why high-level managers of a firm may prefer to control an overseas production activity directly rather than subcontract the activity to an indigenous firm.

Strategic behaviour, in general, has a key role in the economic theory of the MNE. But while writers on the 'new industrial economics' emphasize the strategic issues created by scale economies (Spence, 1977; Eaton and Lipsey, 1978), the issue that dominates the economic theory of the MNE is the exploitation of proprietary knowledge. One reason why scale economies are not so important in the study of MNEs is quite simply that scale economies encourage the concentration of global production on just a few locations, and therefore discourage multinational operations. Since, on the other hand, knowledge is an internationally transferable asset, possession of proprietary knowledge positively encourages multinational operations.

Transaction-cost theory also has a prominent role in the economic theory of the MNE. Writers on the MNE have, however, evolved their own traditions in applying transaction costs to the theory of the firm. One reason for this is their preoccupation with transaction costs in the market for knowledge. Another reason is a purely historical one – the first application of the Coasian concept of internalization to the MNE by McManus (1972) antedates Williamson's formulation of 'markets and hierarchies' theory (Williamson, 1975) and its application to the MNE by Teece (1982a). Literature on the MNE is therefore refreshingly free from the jargon which is so conspicuous a feature of conventional 'markets and hierarchies' theory. Moreover, during the past decade, writers on the MNE have had far greater success in deriving testable propositions from transaction-cost theory than have writers outside this field, as the following pages show.

7.2   The Evolution of the Theory

The pioneering work in the modern theory of the MNE is Hymer's doctoral dissertation, written under Kindleberger's supervision at MIT and submitted in 1960 (Hymer, 1960). This work, however, remained unpublished until 1976, and much of what was known of it came from the summary of Hymer's argument in Kindleberger (1969). Unfortunately, Kindleberger's book, being based upon public lectures, revealed only some of Hymer's analytical insights. By the time of its publication Hymer had become a publicly committed Marxist and had modified his views of the MNE quite considerably as a result. Hymer's theory was not, therefore, properly disseminated until the late 1970s, by which time a considerable amount of independent work had been done along similar lines.

Hymer's contribution to the theory of the MNE has recently become a matter of some controversy (see Dunning and Rugman, 1985; Kindleberger, 1984; Teece, 1985) and the following remarks are intended, in part, to clarify some of the issues in this controversy.

At the time of writing his thesis, Hymer's stance reflected the general concern of anti-trust economists in Canada and Western Europe over the growing impact of US foreign investment on their national economies (Rowthorn, 1979). But in order to analyse their national impact, it was necessary to understand what the MNEs were doing abroad in the first place. Hymer's basic premise was that the first-time foreign investor incurs costs of acclimatizing to the business environment abroad. How then, was it possible for US firms to produce abroad so successfully in competition with indigenous firms? Hymer argued that US foreign investors possessed various advantages over their US rivals. Drawing explicitly on Bain (1956), Hymer showed that many of these advantages were of a monopolistic or monopsonistic type. He supported his argument by empirical evidence drawn from various sources, particularly Dunning's study of US investment in Britain, which showed that US firms possessed superior technology and management skills (Dunning, 1958).

Another question considered by Hymer was why US managers did not attempt to have the 'best of both worlds' – transferring their technology, whilst avoiding the costs of doing business abroad – by licensing their technology to indigenous firms. Hymer's answer was essentially that the market for knowledge is not perfectly competitive. Hymer did not, however, clearly distinguish between two types of market imperfection. The first type is associated with market structure – in the sense of the concentration of buyer and selling power, and the related phenomenon of strategic interdependence between oligopolistic firms. The second is associated with transaction costs incurred in connection with defining property rights and negotiating, monitoring and enforcing contracts.

The two types of imperfection are logically quite distinct. They are related, though, because market structure can influence transaction costs, and conversely the level of transaction costs can affect market structure. When the market structure is one of bilateral monopoly, for example, the costs of negotiating a price are liable to be very high. Conversely, when transaction costs are high because information on price and quality is difficult to obtain, the volume of trade will be low and monopoly is liable to prevail.

Hymer's failure to distinguish clearly between market structure and transaction costs meant that when analysing licensing he tended to argue directly from market structure, rather than from market structure to transaction costs, and from transaction costs to licensing. Although he mentions uncertainty and some other factors which affect transaction costs, he failed to relate his discussion explicitly to the work of Coase (1937). This crucial step was taken, largely independently, by a number of writers including McManus (1972), Buckley and Casson (1976), Brown (1976), Swedenborg (1979) and Hennart (1982). These writers look to institutional economics and the theory of property rights for an answer to the question 'Why are plants in different countries brought under common ownership and control?'. The answer is 'Because the transaction costs incurred in intermediate products markets can be reduced by internalizing these markets within the firm'.

Once the licensing decision was perceived as a special case of this more general issue, a number of other matters began to fall into place. The investments of European firms in colonial mining ventures could also be explained by internalization. The raw materials and semi-processed products traded within the European-owned mining firms were one type of intermediate product, while the knowhow traded between the research division and the manufacturing division of the US high-technology firm was just another type of intermediate product. The fact that in the second case the intermediate product – knowledge – has some of the characteristics of a 'public' good (Johnson, 1970) explains why the high-technology firm is not only 'vertically integrated' between research and manufacturing, but 'horizontally integrated' within manufacturing too.

The transaction-cost approach can be used to tackle another issue raised by Hymer, namely the importance of collusion in explaining horizontal integration by MNEs. Hymer emphasized that global profits in an industry can be enhanced by collusion between producers in different localities, and he perceived that the MNE was a vehicle through which such collusion can be organized. But collusion can be effected through alternative arrangements – notably a cartel – and without a theory of transaction costs Hymer could not explain why, in certain industries and at certain times, an MNE prevails and, in other industries and at other times, an international cartel. The role of collusion in international operations is examined in Section 7.3.

A theory of collusion is, in fact, implicit in modern analysis of the licensing decision. Because of the 'public good' character of knowledge, the proceeds of the competitive exploitation of knowledge are normally insufficient to defray the costs of research. If the research is privately financed, therefore, monopoly rents must be earned, and this in turn implies that when several plants exploit the same knowledge, they must normally collude. The role of collusion in the commercial exploitation of knowledge is considered in Section 7.4.

Recently, a number of general theories of the MNE have appeared which claim to provide the theoretical synthesis that Hymer could not: Dunning's 'eclectic theory' (Dunning, 1977, 1981, 1985a), Rugman's generalized internalization theory (Rugman, 1981) and Teece's 'multinational' version of Williamson's 'markets and hierarchies' theory (Teece, 1982a; Williamson, 1975, 1979). In fact, none of the theories is general, for reasons explained below. Moreover, there appear to be few substantial differences between the theories. Most of the differentiation seems to lie in the terminology in which they are expressed. With certain qualifications it is possible, when terms are suitably defined, to translate one theory into another and then back again (for other criticisms of these theories, see Casson 1984a).

The relationship between Hymer's theory and the 'general' theories is illustrated schematically in Figure 7.1. Hymer emphasizes market structure at the expense of transaction costs, but applies his market-structure analysis to both intermediate and final product markets. This provides a unified and quite distinctive approach. The general theories emphasize transaction costs in intermediate product markets, but fall back on market-structure consideration where final product markets are concerned. They partially remedy Hymer's omission of transaction costs, but at the expense of losing the unity of approach.

The figure illustrates quite clearly a common weakness of both the Hymer and 'general' theories – namely, the lack of attention to transaction costs in final product markets. It is the drive to minimize these costs that explains the marketing function of the firm. The firm incurs marketing costs in order to reduce buyers' search and information costs, so that *overall* transaction costs are reduced.

Marketing has important implications for the firm's operations. Mar-

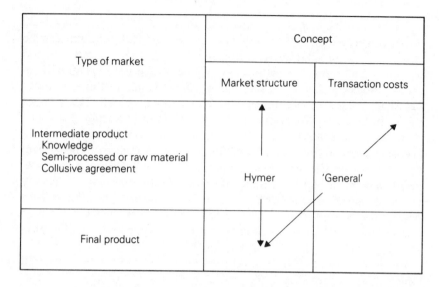

Figure 7.1   The logical structure of the theory of the MNE. *Note*: A truly general theory would be represented by a four-pointed star at the centre, indicating that it would take full account of interdependencies between market structure and transaction costs in both intermediate and final product markets.

keting considerations can stimulate forward integration into the physical distribution of the product, and also backward integration into the supply of components and raw materials. The firm normally faces a trade-off, in which higher transaction costs in intermediate product markets generate lower transaction costs in final product markets, and *vice versa*. Marketing is particularly crucial for the MNE because of the geographical diversity of its market area. Some of the strategic implications of marketing are considered in Section 7.5.

The emphasis on knowledge – and on the internalization of the market for knowledge in particular – means that the theory of the MNE is well adapted to handling dynamic issues concerned with innovation and the growth of the firm. Unfortunately, the full potential of the theory has yet to be realized in this respect. Section 7.6 shows how internalization theory can be used to develop a simple model of the growth of the firm. According to the model, the firm can choose between alternative strategies for promoting market growth, and the strategy mix it chooses will reflect the aptitudes of its researchers. Some firms will opt for strategies that rapidly turn them into multinationals, whilst others will not.

The conclusions are summarized in Section 7.7. The contribution of the theory of the MNE to the theory of the firm, it is claimed, lies not in the ready availability of a general theory, but in a number of separate specific contributions. A truly general theory would emphasize more strongly both the mutual interdependence of market structure and transaction costs, and the close connections between intermediate and final product markets. It would analyse in more detail a wider range of issues, and in particular would give more attention to the dynamics of the growth of the firm. While a satisfactory general theory is still some way off, however, the contributions summarized below all help to advance the theory towards this goal.

7.3   Horizontal Integration as Interplant Collusion

The standard model of the horizontally integrated MNE is due to Horst (1971, 1974). A more sophisticated version of the model is presented by Batra and Ramachandran (1980), but only a highly simplified version is used here. The model is used to illustrate Hymer's insight that an MNE may be formed in order to profit from collusion. The basic approach is similar to that of Fellner's joint-profit-maximizing theory of collusive oligopoly (Fellner, 1949) which was probably known to Hymer; the details are different, though, because of the spatial disaggregation of the product market which arises in the case of the MNE.

Consider an industry producing a homogeneous product in which there is initially a single-plant monopoly in each of two countries. There are no barriers to trade. Initially each monopolist charges a uniform price which he sets independently of the other firm's price, and sells only to customers in his home country. Figure 7.2 shows the demand curves D_1, D_2 in each country, the corresponding marginal-revenue curves MR_1, MR_2, and the marginal-cost curves for each plant MC_1, MC_2. Independent profit maximization by the monopolists generates equilibrium prices P_1, P_2 and equilibrium outputs Q_1, Q_2.

This equilibrium is unstable, however, unless the costs of international transport are prohibitively high. Since the price is higher in country 2 than in country 1, $P_2 > P_1$, there is an incentive for independent arbitragers to buy in country 1 for export to country 2. Secondly, there is an incentive for each monopolist to invade the other's market. This is because the price in country 2 exceeds the marginal cost in country 1, $P_2 > C_1$, and conversely the price in country 1 exceeds the marginal cost in country 2, $P_1 > C_2$. Finally, even if both

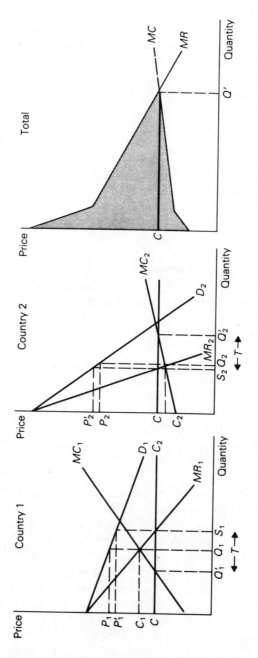

Figure 7.2 Horizontal integration

independent arbitrage and mutual invasion could somehow be avoided, it would be efficient for the monopolists to switch some production from country 1 to country 2. This is because the marginal cost of production in country 1 exceeds the marginal cost of production in country 2, $C_1 > C_2$.

The joint profits of the monopolists are maximized when they agree (1) to sell, if possible, only to final consumers in each market, and so protect one another's markets by denying supplies to independent arbitragers; (2) not to invade each other's markets; and (3) to concentrate production on the lowest cost plant, and export the surplus for sale by the other monopolist.

Formally, the joint profits of the monopolists are maximized when the prices can be set independently in each market according to the local elasticity of demand, when the marginal costs of production are equalized across countries, and when the marginal revenue in each country is equal to the common level of marginal cost. (A fourth possibility, that the monopolists could discriminate between consumers within each market, is ignored.) These conditions assume zero transport costs; if transport costs are incurred then the conditions are modified slightly.

The determination of the joint-profit-maximizing equilibrium is illustrated in the right-hand quadrant of the figure. The curve MR is the horizontal summation of the curves MR_1 and MR_2, and MC is the horizontal summation of MC_1 and MC_2. The international equilibrium level of marginal cost is C, and total international output is Q'. Q'_1 is produced in country 1, and S_1 is sold, with $T = S_1 - Q'_1$ being imported from country 2. Correspondingly, Q'_2 is produced in country 2, and S_2 is sold, with $T = Q'_2 - S_2$ being exported to country 1. The prices in the two countries are P'_1 and P'_2 respectively. The joint profit is measured by the shaded area in the right-hand quadrant.

There are three main institutional mechanisms by which this joint-profit-maximizing equilibrium could be achieved. The first is for the two monopolists to negotiate an agreement prohibiting sales to arbitragers and outlawing market invasion, and then to bargain jointly over the level of arm's length trade between them. The second is for them to organize a cartel. The third is for them to merge to form an MNE.

The relative advantages of these arrangements have been examined by Casson (1985), drawing on earlier work by Robinson (1941) and Williamson (1975, Chapter 12). The cartel is more effective than an arm's length agreement in the long term because it allows a sales syndicate to be set up to organize trade between the companies. By offering to buy unlimited quantities from the companies at the parametric price C, the syndicate can ensure that both plants will incur similar levels of marginal cost. By marking up the price C by a factor related to the elasticity of demand in each market, the syndicate can fix prices which equate marginal revenue in each country to marginal cost. The profits of the syndicate are then distributed between the two firms. In this way the monopolists can collude whilst retaining control of their own outputs. Production is rationalized without the producers having to divulge their costs to each other. If market conditions change then the syndicate simply announces a new parametric buying price, and the producers adjust their output accordingly. Once the syndicate has been established, therefore, there is no need to renegotiate 'from scratch' arm's length contractual arrangements between the firms. The sales syndicate is, in fact, only one of several systems that cartels can use, and the system that is preferred will reflect technical and market conditions in the industry concerned.

The main weakness of a cartel is that there is normally an incentive for members to cheat – particularly by secretly invading one another's markets. A common form of cheating is to offer special discounts to large customers who can be supplied direct from the factory rather than through normal sales outlets. Complete financial consolidation of the monopolies not only improves the ability to monitor price cutting but practically eliminates at source the incentive to cheat. When plants are located in different countries, financial consolidation leads to the creation of an MNE. The main obstacle to financial consolidation is the attitude of governments, who are often opposed to foreign control of industries of strategic importance. Strategic industries such as shipping and aviation, and the mining of key raw materials, therefore tend to be dominated by international cartels rather than by MNEs. More generally, whenever the international political climate worsens, and the owners of MNEs begin to fear expropriation of their foreign assets, there is an incentive to split up MNEs and form a cartel instead. Conversely, when the political climate improves – as it did in post-war Europe – there will be a tendency to abandon cartels and establish MNEs in their place.

Other considerations include the heterogeneity of the product, and in particular the pace of new product innovation. It is far more difficult to control non-price competition than to control price competition, and this means that a cartel is liable to disintegrate under the pressure of administrative work when products are varied and changing. Progressive conditions favour the MNE over the cartel.

It is also difficult for a cartel to rationalize production in an industry that affords substantial economies of scale, since this may involve closing down members' plants and preventing the plants from being sold off cheaply to potential entrants. The MNE is therefore more effective than a cartel in industries characterized by economies of scale. Several other, more minor, considerations are considered in Casson (1985).

7.4 The Role of Collusion in the Exploitation of Proprietary Knowledge

In the discussion of horizontal integration it was implicitly assumed that in each country there was some barrier to entry which afforded each domestic producer a degree of long-run monopoly power. In the theory of the MNE, analytical developments have focused upon one particular type of barrier to entry, namely possession by the firm of exclusive knowledge.

In the theory of the MNE, the concept of knowledge is a very broad one. To begin with, it includes at least three distinct types of knowhow: (1) technical knowhow, i.e. technological expertise in producing goods and services; (2) marketing knowhow, i.e. expertise in selling things, and in purchasing them too; and (3) managerial knowhow, i.e. expertise in administration, delegation, and all aspects of decision-making not included in (1) or (2).

Knowledge has a value and so there is, in principle, a market for it. In practice, the market for knowledge is a quite peculiar one. It has a number of features which, though they are not unique when considered separately, are not found all together in any other case:

1　there is considerable uncertainty about the quality of the product;
2　the product is indivisible, but the capacity of any one unit to generate services is theoretically infinite; this means that the supply of just one unit is normally sufficient to satiate the buyer's needs;
3　the supply of the product is irreversible; this means that it is not normally feasible to supply it 'on approval';
4　property rights to the product may be ill-defined and, where they exist, are costly to enforce;
5　the product may have multiple uses; and
6　the first unit is normally expensive to produce, but thereafter any one unit can normally reproduce itself fairly easily; this means that the marginal cost of supply is very low compared to the average cost; it also means that each customer becomes a potential competitor of the seller from whom he bought the product.

What is sold in the knowledge market is not a certainty, but a claim which may be either true or false. In the absence of a decisive test for truth, opinions may differ about the veracity of the claim. This is a special case of a more general problem of quality uncertainty which affects nearly all markets. In the case of knowledge, the paramount quality of the product is its truth, although *provided that it is true*, other qualities are important as well, such as its relevance to commercial operations.

A common response to quality uncertainty is for the supplier to offer a small sample of the product to the buyer. In the case of knowledge, the only sample that can usually be offered is the knowledge itself, and once the buyer has acquainted himself with it he has no need to make a purchase. It is pointless for the seller to insist that the sample be 'returned' to him because the buyer can memorize the details. Indeed, once the buyer has memorized the details he is in a position to set up in competition with the seller to supply the knowledge to third parties.

The problem of marketing knowledge described above is known as the 'buyer uncertainty' problem (Buckley and Casson, 1976; Casson, 1979). Some writers on the MNE, notably Vaitsos (1974) have, however, used the term in an unfortunate way. They suggest that buyer uncertainty leads buyers to pay too much for their knowledge, whereas the theory actually suggests that the reverse will be the case. Typically, it is alleged that 'buyer uncertainty' leads government officials and private licensees in developing countries to pay too much for advanced technology obtained from Western enterprises. The argument rests upon the implicit assumption that the buyers are stupid enough to believe uncritically all of the claims made for the new technology, and that they fail to 'shop around' amongst alternative suppliers of technology before concluding a deal. In fact, the buyer-uncertainty argument suggests that the seller of knowledge will normally have to compensate the buyer for suspicions about its quality which the seller, for strategic reasons, cannot allay. The buyer may, of course, occasionally make a mistaken purchase. But because of the greater risks he perceives he will, on average, demand a higher return on imported technology, and this means that the price offered to the seller will be low. The low price explains, in turn, why corporations are reluctant to license and prefer, where possible, to undertake foreign investment instead.

The problem of buyer uncertainty is also an element in what Magee (1977) calls the 'appropriability problem' and Rugman (1981) calls the 'dissipation problem'. These terms are not, however, very specific, and might well apply to another problem which is logically quite distinct from buyer uncertainty, though often occurs along with it. This is the problem of efficiently decentralizing the exploitation of proprietary knowledge amongst a group of licensees.

Consider a firm which is licensing technical knowhow to other producers in the same industry. It has invested heavily in developing the technology and, in the long run, cannot remain in the innovation business unless the rents accruing from the exploitation of technology cover the costs of its development. But because the marginal cost of utilizing technology is very low, unrestricted competition in the exploitation of the technology will eliminate practically all producer rents. A firm that has developed a new technology can therefore only recover its costs through the exercise of monopoly power.

Suppose that the firm nominates one licensee in each country. If the product cannot be traded, because of prohibitively high transport costs or tariffs, say, then each licensee has a national monopoly and in order to extract a monopoly rent the licensor can simply charge each licensee a lump sum annual fee equal to his expected super-normal profit. If the product can be traded then the licensor has a problem. He must prevent the licensees from invading one another's markets by bidding down prices, for in this way they will dissipate rents that could be appropriated by the licensor. The licensor can choose between two main strategies. One is to provide each licensee with an exclusive sales area, and to prohibit each licensee from selling outside this area. This restores the national monopoly situation described above. It is a simple concept in principle, but the export restrictions may be difficult to enforce in practice – particularly as such restrictions are illegal in many countries.

The second strategy is to structure the schedule of licence fees so that it discourages price cutting by raising the marginal costs of licensees. This is normally an inadequate substitute for export prohibition, but there is one case in which it is fully effective (Casson, 1979, Chapter 2). This is where there are no barriers to trade in the product, so that all the licensees are competing in a single integrated market. In this case, the licensor can appropriate the entire monopoly rent in the industry by levying a royalty on each unit produced that is equal to the mark-up of the industry-wide monopoly price on the licensee's minimum average cost of production. By basing the royalty on the minimum average cost of the most efficient licensee the licensor can ensure that only the lowest cost producers in the industry remain in business.

The situation is illustrated in Figure 7.3. In the left-hand quadrant the curves MC and AC represent the cost structure of a least-cost licensee, and they determine the minimum average cost MAC and its associated level of output Q. Equilibrium in the industry as a whole is illustrated in the right-hand quadrant. It is assumed that adjustments to industry output are effected by the entry and exit of least-cost licensees, and not by the adjustment of the licensees' outputs. Thus, if the indivisibility of firms is ignored, the industry marginal-cost curve IMC is horizontal at a level MAC. The industry marginal-revenue curve

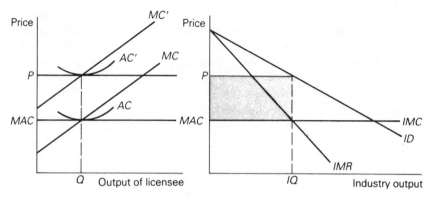

Figure 7.3   Licensing in a competitive industry

IMR is derived from the industry demand curve *ID* in the usual way. The intersection of *IMR* and *IMC* indicates that industry-wide profit is maximized with a price *P* and industry output *IQ*. This determines the equilibrium royalty rate *P* − *MAC*. The costs of the licensee, inclusive of royalty, are indicated by the curves *MC'* and *AC'*. It can be seen that a profit-maximizing licensee can just break even by continuing to produce an output *Q*. The full monopoly rent, measured by the area of the shaded rectangle in the right-hand quadrant, is appropriated by the licensor.

When transport costs are high but not prohibitive, and export restrictions are difficult to enforce, it is hard for a licensor to devise a structure of royalty fees which provides suitable incentives for licensees. To maximize monopoly rents in this situation it is normally necessary for the owner of the knowhow to retain overall control of marketing. Instead of licensing production, it is better to subcontract it. The subcontractor, in this case, is an independent producer who, like a licensee, uses the client's technology to produce his output. But under subcontracting the output is sold back to the client and not directly to final consumers. The client can avoid the subcontractor appropriating some of the monopoly rents by offering the subcontractor a package deal in which the price is tailored to the average cost of producing a stipulated quantity of output. If the client does not know the structure of the subcontractor's costs then a similar result can be obtained by eliciting competitive tenders for various quantities of output.

The discussion suggests that the MNE is particularly effective as a vehicle for the commercial exploitation of knowledge when the knowledge is difficult to patent, and when the global market is difficult to segment because transport costs are low, export restrictions are illegal, etc. Conversely, licensing is a viable alternative to the MNE when patent protection is effective and market segmentation is easy.

7.5 Marketing Strategy and Vertical Integration

It was emphasized in Section 7.2 that transaction costs in the final product market have received little attention either from Hymer himself or from the expositors of 'general theories' of the MNE. The emphasis of the theory has been very much upon intermediate product markets – and quite rightly so. But intermediate and final product markets are very closely linked, and the exclusive emphasis on intermediate products has led to imbalance in the theory. This section attempts to restore the balance by focusing upon a very important link between intermediate and final product markets. This link is forged by marketing requirements in the final product market, which have important implications for the organization of intermediate product trade.

The function of marketing is, quite generally, to reduce transaction costs. More precisely, in the absence of marketing activity, lack of information is a formidable obstacle to any kind of trade. Buyers and sellers incur transaction costs in attempting to overcome such obstacles. When buyers require a customized product they normally incur most of the transaction costs themselves, for the onus falls upon them to specify their requirements, to seek out potential suppliers and, where appropriate, put production out to tender. When buyers and sellers are trading second-hand assets – houses, financial assets, used motor vehicles, etc. – the buyers must select their specific requirements from a very heterogeneous supply. The transaction costs are normally incurred by specialized brokers and stockholding middlemen, who provide a service which matches up the idiosyncrasies on both sides of the market. When products are mass-produced, however, the sellers nromally incur most of the transaction costs. The design and development of the product are both speculative activities undertaken before sales commence, and the seller must build up the market in advance by communicating with customers, both through mass media and through decentralized retail outlets.

The ultimate incidence of transaction costs is, of course, governed by conditions of supply and demand. Those who initially incur the costs can usually pass some (or indeed all) of them onto others. Efficiency considerations suggest that, loosely speaking, those who incur the costs should invest in marketing up to a margin where their costs are equal to the savings of transaction costs their efforts afford to others. They recoup their costs by adjusting the prices at which they buy and sell, within the limits set by competitive forces.

Lack of attention to transaction costs in final product markets is reflected in the fact that general theories of the MNE have little to say about marketing. They recognize that marketing skill is one of the competitive advantages that a firm may enjoy over its rivals, particularly if it possesses a reputable brand name (Caves, 1971). More generally, marketing often confers an advantage on *all* established firms in an industry over *all* potential entrants, because consumers are reluctant to purchase untried products. But for analytical purposes this marketing skill is usually treated as if it were exactly analogous to a technological advantage, and as if the major strategic issue facing management were how this marketing advantage could be sold.

There are, however, a few isolated contributions which analyse in some detail the marketing activities of MNEs. The transaction-cost approach to marketing outlined above is based upon Casson (1982a, Chapter 9) and is applied to the MNE in Casson (1982b, 1985). A synthesis of the transaction-cost approach and conventional marketing theory has been developed by Brown (1984) in a very interesting paper which also considers applications to the MNE. Nicholas (1983; see also Nicholas, 1982) has studied the marketing strategies of the MNE from a historical standpoint, drawing widely on business history case studies, and charting the movement of forward integration in which the overseas sales agency is replaced by the wholly owned foreign sales subsidiary.

To analyse the impact of marketing on integration it is important to appreciate that so far as the typical buyer is concerned, 'the product *is* what the product *does*' or in other words, it is the function that the product performs that is crucial. The standard of performance achieved by the product reflects, in part, the qualities of the design, materials and workmanship embodied in it. Normally these qualities vary from producer to producer, and even for a given producer, from one unit of output to the next. Since the product is defined by performance and not appearance, the quality of the product cannot usually be assessed by inspection. And since the producer is in a better position to monitor production than the consumer, wherever quality is variable there is a potential asymmetry of information. Thus it is usual for the producer to advertise claims about the performance of the product. This is particularly important for novel and sophisticated products sold to first-time buyers; it is less important for simple and mature products sold to repeat buyers.

It was noted in Section 7.4 that a seller's claims are often viewed sceptically, so that a good deal of marketing skill resides in persuasion. The persuasiveness of a claim can often be increased by providing the buyer with a guarantee, over and above the seller's statutory obligations. But if a guarantee is offered, it becomes important not to pitch the claims too high, otherwise there will be loss of goodwill, and possibly a large number of claims. Thus the choice of a claim structure is a finely balanced one, and having settled upon it, the producer must ensure that his salesmen neither under-sell nor over-sell the product.

A second important aspect of marketing is that what the consumer purchases is a package. To begin with, the product is usually packaged with a certain amount of retail service. The service may include help with the evaluation of the product, discretion over the time and place of delivery, and various options for customizing the product. The level of service is governed by, amongst other things, the retailer's investment in display facilities and product inventory.

The link between marketing and the MNE is forged most strongly by the fact that product reputation is often packaged, with one person – normally the final manufacturer – assuming responsibility for the overall coordination of marketing effort. His responsibility may extend from the quality of the components embodied in the product to the quality of service supplied at the retail level. The same person often assumes overall product liability as well. This means, for example, that the assembler of a multi-component good underwrites for the consumer the quality of all the components. The person who assumes overall responsibility for product quality and standards of service may be identified with the 'channel leader' found in the marketing literature. It is the channel leader who takes the strategic decisions about forward and backward integration. The key issue is the same in both cases – how best to achieve high standards in quality control. The optimal degree of integration is governed by a trade-off. The wider is the field of integration, the easier it is to maintain quality by regular supervision, but the greater is the diversity of the activities that must be managed, and hence the greater are the demands imposed upon the management team.

In the case of forward integration, the average size of the retail unit is normally much smaller than that of the final stage of manufacture, and so diversity manifests itself in the number and geographical spread of the retail operations that must be managed. In the case of backward integration, there are usually many different components that make up a single finished product, and so diversity manifests itself in the variety of production activities that must be managed. The problem of diversity becomes more acute at the retail end if the retailer has to stock a range of other products too. Diversity becomes more acute at the component end if there are major economies of scale in component production, or if numerous by-products are generated in component production, because the management then becomes involved with either utilizing the surplus output and the by-products from component production, or marketing them to other firms.

The more acute the problem of diversity, the greater is the incentive for the firm to use subcontractors. But in selecting subcontractors, the firm faces exactly the same problems of quality uncertainty as does the consumer in selecting the final product. However, while the consumer may be only a small-scale occasional purchaser, the manufacturer makes large-scale regular purchases from his subcontractors, and so can afford to invest in a monitoring system.

In some cases the component may be so much simpler than the finished product that it can be tested by inspection. In most cases, however, the assurance of quality comes from inspecting workmanship on the spot. If neither the manufacturer nor the subcontractor has trade secrets to protect, then putting the manufacturer's representative into the subcontractor's plant is a simple solution. If the manufacturer has a trade secret to protect, however, then he needs a sanction over the subcontractor to prevent theft of the secret; he may, for example, arrange to pay the subcontractor in arrears, so that in the event of a disagreement payment can be withheld for goods already supplied.

If the subcontractor has a trade secret of his own to protect then on-the-spot monitoring by the manufacturer may prove unacceptable. In this case the manufacturer may have to use indirect information signalled to him by the observable aspects of the subcontractor's behaviour (cf. Spence, 1974). In the construction industry, for example, a major influence on the care and attention exercised by the subcontractor's workforce is the payment system. Piecework payment encourages workers to increase their output by sacrificing quality, whereas time-rate payment does not. When the manufacturer has a choice of subcontractors, therefore, he can use the payment system as an indicator of the subcontractors' attitude to quality, and employ only subcontractors who use the time-rate system.

The prevalence of trade secrets within an industry tends to reflect the stage of the product life cycle. Early in the product's life, trade secrets are common, and so subcontracting is hazardous. As the product matures, however, knowledge diffuses, monitoring becomes easier to arrange, and subcontracting becomes more common.

Another influence on quality is the subcontractor's choice of materials. It is difficult to observe this, or to obtain suitable signals about it. The manufacturer can, however, control this through a restrictive agreement which ties the subcontractor to materials supplied through the manufacturer. Although such agreements are not popular with subcontractors, they are fairly common in practice.

It was noted in Section 7.2 that market structure is a major influence on transaction costs in intermediate product markets, and this is reflected in the fact that subcontracting is much easier to arrange when there are many competing subcontractors than when there are just one or two. Not only is the manufacturer likely to obtain more favourable terms (by a simple market-structure argument), but the negotiation costs associated with bilateral monopoly and other small numbers' situations will be avoided (transaction-cost argument).

Market structure, too, varies over the life cycle of the product. Moreover, market structures in the intermediate and final product markets tend to be linked over the cycle (in manufacturing industries, at least). Early in the life cycle, there are few suppliers of the final product – and therefore few buyers of the product-specific components embodied in it – and few potential suppliers of these components too. Monopoly in the final product market is therefore associated with bilateral monopoly in the intermediate product markets. Because of the high transaction costs the monopolist undertakes little subcontracting. As the product matures, there become more suppliers of the final product, more buyers of the product-specific components, and more potential suppliers of them. Competitive conditions prevail in both final and intermediate product markets, and the competitors in the final product markets rely more heavily upon subcontracting than did the monopolist that preceded them.

This life-cycle trend toward more competitive market structures reinforces the trend noted earlier for trade secrets to be eliminated as the product matures. Taken together, these considerations suggest that subcontracting will grow substantially over the lifetime of a product. It should be emphasized, however, that the form taken by the life cycle may well vary significantly from one industry to another because of technology and other factors specific to the industry.

A number of other considerations affect the subcontracting decision (see Casson, 1984b), and there are two of them that are specific to MNEs. One is that opportunities for transfer pricing are lost when foreign subcontracting replaces ownership of a foreign subsidiary, and the other is that exposure to expropriation risk is reduced at the same time. Apart from these two specific considerations, however, it can be argued that transaction costs generally are much higher where international operations are concerned. Where quality control is at a premium, it is often difficult to rely upon foreign subcontractors, particularly in developing countries. The foreign enterprise lacks the expertise to identify the appropriate subcontractors and to liaise effectively with them. Dissatisfaction by MNEs with local subcontractors occurs even in developed countries such as Britain where, over a span

of 30 years, first US and then Japanese MNEs have expressed res-
ervations about the quality of subcontractors' work (Dunning, 1985b).
Because of their emphasis on the marketing of new products, it appears
that MNEs are often reluctant to subcontract work to the same extent
as their indigenous competitors. The extent to which MNEs use local
subcontractors in host economies has now become a major issue in
political debate over MNEs.

The need for effective strategic management by channel leaders has
been widely recognized in recent years. The Japanese are commonly
credited with having pioneered new methods of managing multi-stage
production and distribution channels, based on low inventories of intermediate products, automated quality control and informal long-term
understandings with their subcontractors. It can be argued, however,
that in some respects the Japanese have merely adapted best practice
techniques from successful Western enterprises, and harnessed them to
cultural forces which make for high productivity in their workforce.
While there may be controversy over the nature and extent of the
Japanese contribution to channel management, however, there is no
doubt that a full understanding of the phenomenon requires economists
to take greater account than before of the strategic links between
intermediate and final product markets.

7.6   The Growth of the Firm

The theory of transaction costs provides a useful basis for a theory of
the growth of the firm. Consider the three functions of production,
marketing and R&D. Each is linked to the others by flows of information, as indicated in Figure 7.4. The very high transaction costs
associated with knowledge suggests that these activities will all be
carried on within the same enterprise. The internalization of knowledge
has important implications for growth. The firm's production division,
for example, becomes committed to exploiting all the knowledge generated by its R&D division. If a steady level of expenditure on R&D
generates a continuous flow of new knowledge then the consequent
improvements to technology, product quality, etc., will steadily increase
the firm's potential market (assuming a stable environment). This
generates an 'acceleration' mechanism by which the *level* of R&D
activity governs the *rate of growth* of production.

The original objective of Buckley and Casson (1976) was, in fact, to
use the concept of internalization to develop a model of the growth of
the MNE. This objective has largely been abandoned by later writers
on the MNE, who have taken the technological capability and the

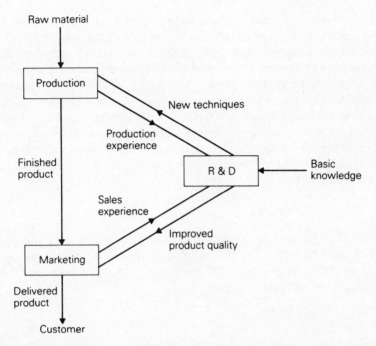

Figure 7.4   Integration of production, marketing and R&D. *Source*: Adapted from Buckley and Casson (1976), figure 2.1; see also Hymer (1979), figure 1.

marketing and management skills of the firm as given (see Buckley, 1983). An extension of the Buckley and Casson model is presented below.

It is assumed that the firm grows either by entering new markets or by increasing its penetration of existing ones. At any time $t > 0$, the firm produces a range of $N(t)$ different products, each of which is sold in $M(t)$ national markets. Each market is serviced by local production, so that $M(t)$ is also an index of the multinationality of the firm's operations. Each product has to be adapted, to some extent, to local conditions (though the adaptation may be quite superficial, and concerned only with packaging and branding to suit national tastes). The average quality of the firm's products, as perceived by consumers in a representative country, is measured somehow by an index $Q(t)$. It is assumed that $Q(t)$ is reflected in the extent of the typical product's penetration of a national market.

The technology of production is constant over time, as are factor prices. Production and marketing take place under constant returns to scale, so that the marginal cost of output is a constant, c, which is independent of time.

In each national market, the demand for each product is a function solely of its own price, all other relevant factors being assumed to be constant. It is assumed that the size of the market and the price-dependence of demand is the same for all products and in all countries, and that the firm sets the same price, p, for all products everywhere. In the light of the other assumptions made about cost of production and demand, the optimizing strategy for the firm is in fact to maintain a constant price. It simplifies the presentation of the model, however, if this property of the solution is included amongst the assumptions. Worldwide demand for the firm's output, $X(t)$, may thus be expressed in the form

$$X(t) = A(t).D(p) \tag{7.1}$$

where $D(p)$ satisfies the usual conditions of differentiability and negative slope. The factor $A(t)$ measures the scale of demand, as governed by the number of products, the number of national markets, and the quality of the product

$$A(t) = M(t).N(t).Q(t) \tag{7.2}$$

R&D activity can be channelled in three main directions. First, it can be used to develop new products. A constant level of R&D activity directed in this way generates a constant logarithmic rate of change in the number of products, n. Secondly, it can be used to adapt existing products to the requirements of new national markets. A steady application of R&D in this direction generates a constant logarithmic rate of change in the number of national markets that are served, m. Finally, it can be directed to an overall improvement in the quality of products in the range. This increases the firm's penetration of each of the markets in which it operates; a steady application of R&D in this direction generates a constant logarithmic rate of change in the quality index, q. It follows that a constant level of R&D is associated with exponential growth in M, N, and Q:

$$M(t) = M_0 e^{mt}, \tag{7.3a}$$

$$N(t) = N_0 e^{nt}, \tag{7.3b}$$

$$Q(t) = Q_0 e^{qt}, \tag{7.3c}$$

whence the firm's global output also grows exponentially:

$$X(t) = A_0 D(p) e^{zt}, \tag{7.4}$$

where

$$A_0 = M_0 N_0 Q_0 \tag{7.5}$$

and

$$z = m + n + q \tag{7.6}$$

As already noted, production and marketing costs, $C_1(t)$, vary directly with global production

$$C_1(t) = cX(t) \tag{7.7}$$

The cost of R&D, C_2, is maintained constant over time, and so too are the rates of progress m, n, q. R&D takes place under decreasing returns to scale, and exhibits diminishing marginal rates of substitution as one line of research is pursued at the expense of the others. The costs of research are governed by a parameter, v, which is specific to the firm, and describes the particular aptitude of the research team for one kind of research rather than another. The cost function for R&D, therefore, is of the form

$$C_2 = C_2 (m,n,q,u) \tag{7.8}$$

The owners of the firm, it is assumed, can borrow and lend in a perfect capital market at a parametric rate of interest, r. This assumption is, of course, difficult to defend given the emphasis of this chapter on transaction costs. It may be taken, however, as a reasonable assumption for a company where management has an outstanding reputation in the capital market. The managers maximize the value of the firm, as measured by the present value, V, of the profit stream $\pi(t)$, where

$$V = \int_0^\infty e^{-rt} \pi(t) \, dt \tag{7.9}$$

and

$$\pi(t) = p X(t) - C_1(t) - C_2. \tag{7.10}$$

To solve for the optimizing behaviour of the firm, it is convenient to form the Lagrangian which can be expressed, using (7.1)–(7.10) in the form

$$L = A_0 (p - c) D(p)/(r - z) - C_2(m,n,q,v)/r + \lambda (m + n + q - z) \tag{7.11}$$

The first-order condition with respect to p gives the familiar formula for the equilibrium monopoly price:

$$p^* = (\eta/(\eta - 1))\ c \qquad (7.12)$$

where $\eta = -dD/dp/(p/D)$ is the own price elasticity of demand.

The first-order conditions with respect of m, n, q and λ determine the rates with which research progresses in each direction, and the marginal cost of research, as functions of the desired rate of overall market growth and the parameter of research aptitudes. The marginal conditions reduce to

$$\partial C_2/\partial m = \partial C_2/\partial n = \partial C_2/\partial q = \lambda, \qquad (7.13)$$

and the solutions are

$$m = m\ (z,v) \qquad (7.14a)$$

$$n = n\ (z,v) \qquad (7.14b)$$

$$q = q\ (z,v) \qquad (7.14c)$$

$$\lambda = \lambda\ (z,v) \qquad (7.14d)$$

The determination of the direction of research strategy conditional upon the rate of overall market growth is illustrated in Figure 7.5. The iso-cost surface ABC represents the various technically efficient options for channelling R&D in different directions. It is concave to the origin, indicating that there are diminishing marginal rates of technical substitution between different directions of research. The iso-z planes XYZ represents the different combinations of research progress which generate the target rate of overall market growth. The point of tangency, E, between ABC and XYZ indicates the optimizing research strategy, conditional upon z. The strategy m', n', q', represented by E, achieves the target rate of overall market growth at minimum cost. This optimizing strategy may vary from firm to firm, according to the research aptitudes, as reflected in the shape and positioning of the iso-cost surface. A special case of this trade-off between directions of research has been noted by Wolf (1977), who has emphasized that the development of new products (i.e. an n-intensive strategy) and the transfer of existing products to new national markets (i.e. an m-intensive strategy) are alternative methods of achieving corporate growth. Pearce (1983) has tested this approach on a sample of the world's largest firms, and has obtained promising results.

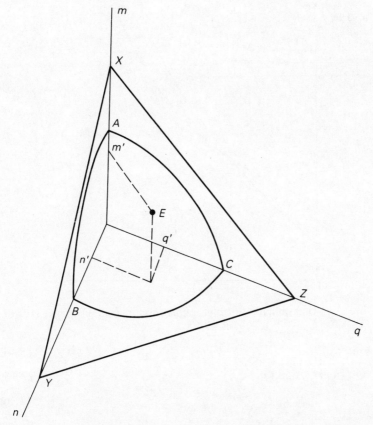

Figure 7.5   Determination of optimal research strategy conditional upon target
rate of overall market growth

The optimizing rate of overall market growth is determined by the
first-order condition with respect to z:

$$A_0(\text{p}^* - \text{c})\, D(\text{p}^*)/(r - z)^2 - \lambda(z,v) = 0 \qquad (7.15)$$

The solution of this equation is illustrated graphically in Figure 7.6.
Note that the marginal valuation of additional market growth, MV,
approaches infinity as market growth, z, approaches the rate of interest,
r, so that for an economically meaningful solution it is necessary that
the marginal cost of market growth, MC, rises from below the marginal
valuation to above before z has reached r. The intersection F determines the equilibrium rate of overall market growth, z^*, and by back-
substitution into (7.14) this gives the optimal research strategy m^*, n^*,
q^*. The full solution is then of the form

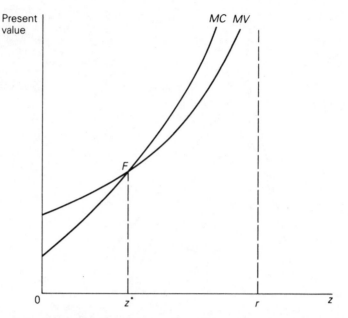

Figure 7.6   Determination of the optimal rate of overall market growth

$$p^* = p^* (c) \tag{7.16a}$$

$$m^* = m^* (A_0,c,v) \tag{7.16b}$$

$$n^* = n^* (A_0,c,v) \tag{7.16c}$$

$$q^* = q^* (A_0,c,v) \tag{7.16d}$$

$$z^* = z^* (A_0,c,v) \tag{7.16e}$$

The model shows, therefore, how the initial size of the world market, A_0, the cost of production and marketing, c, and the research aptitudes of the firm's R&D division, v, simultaneously determine the firm's research strategy and its overall rate of market growth. The research strategy induces a constant proportional rate of growth in the firm's product range, the multinationality of its operations, and its overall product quality, as reflected in its average penetration of the markets which it supplies. Different firms, however, will pursue different strategies which reflect the different aptitudes of their researchers. Some firms will develop highly multinational operations based upon a narrow product range; others will develop a wide product range which is confined mainly to the home market, whilst others still, will concentrate on further deepening their penetration of an existing market niche.

7.7   Conclusions

Judged by criteria of simplicity, elegance and mathematical sophistication, the theory of the MNE does not perform well. But judged by the criterion of relevance, it is highly successful. Indeed, the lack of elegance in the theory is to some extent a reflection of the complexity of the issues with which it deals – and the fact that it does full justice to them. The theory is not devoid of aesthetic appeal, however. At a conceptual level there are certain underlying themes which give an overall coherence to the theory. The subjectivity of knowledge, the universality of transaction costs, the assumptions that purposeful human action encourages the minimization of overall transaction costs, are all very general insights which can be applied to other fields as well. To apply them successfully, however, they need to be combined with specific assumptions about transaction costs, and the appropriate assumptions vary from case to case.

The theory also has a definite logical structure. The direction taken by R&D depends upon the aptitude of the firm's research team, and this determines the strategic issues of organizational form that arise in exploiting the knowledge generated by R&D. For knowledge which is difficult to patent, commercial exploitation requires its deployment to be administered by 'vertical' integration between production and R&D, whilst maximizing monopoly returns calls for horizontal integration amongst producers at different locations. However, the incentive to integrate does not arise solely from proprietary knowledge; it may also be due to more general problems, such as the desire to provide quality assurance through the distribution channel.

This framework generates a range of specific models, rather than just a single one. Each of the models is based upon essentially plausible assumptions. Taken together, moreover, the specific models collectively explain all of the stylized facts that were summarized in the list on pp. 134–5. The relevant explanations are displayed in the list below. Thus – strange as it may seem to many economists – the theory of the MNE is an example of an economic theory which is not merely plausible, but actually 'works'. There still remain gaps in the theory, but by rigorous analysis of special topics these gaps may be filled in due course.

Explanations of the Stylized Facts Presented on Pages 134–5

(1) *Historical pattern of growth.*   MNEs have replaced cartels in the post-war period because (a) greater political stability in Europe

has reduced the expropriation risk of foreign direct investment, (b) improvements in communications and management techniques have facilitated tighter control of international operations, and (c) cartel arrangements are ill-suited to the growing number of progressive industries in which there is a proliferation of new and/or differentiated products. Similar changes explain the switch from sales agencies to wholly owned sales subsidiaries.

(2) *Country of origin and the structure of international production.* US-based MNEs exploit mass-production technologies, harnessed to mass-market sales methods, originally developed in the large multi-ethnic US market, and therefore well adapted to other large markets in developed countries – notably the European Community market. European-based MNEs processed the raw materials obtained from colonies, and integrated backwards to secure further supplies against pre-emption by rivals. In the 1950s and 1960s they learnt mass-production methods from US enterprises, and during the early 1970s developed a temporary technological leadership of their own in a few industries. The Japanese MNEs have taken mass-production methods one stage further than US firms. They have evolved new methods of managing a complex inter-industry division of labour through tight inventory management and quality control. They have split up production processes within an industry so that different stages can be carried out at different locations. Unskilled labour-intensive operations have been concentrated upon low-wage, newly industrializing countries.

(3) *Industry characteristics.* These characteristics reflect the fact that technological progress derives from R&D and that successful product innovation (and differentiation) relies heavily on advertising. Mass-production methods make intensive use of supervisory staff and economize on manual labour. The high set-up costs associated with the dedicated production line generate economies of scale, which are reflected in high industrial concentration. The high fixed costs of R&D, and the prevalence of patents and trade secrets also create barriers to entry. While the market is expanding, rivalry between the firms behind the barrier generates innovation. (If the market is static in future, however, inter-firm collusion may result.)

(4) *Firm characteristics.* Because knowledge has the characteristics of a 'public good', the firm with privileged knowledge tends to become multinational. Thus the multinationality of the firm discriminates, within a progressive industry, between the firms that

have privileged knowledge, and those that do not. The MNEs, therefore, are the firms that highlight the characteristics of a progressive industry. Firms that are skilful in differentiating products to local conditions will tend to concentrate on this to the exclusion of new product development. Conversely, firms that are skilful in product development will tend to hand over their products, through licensing or profit-sharing arrangements, to firms that are good at local adaptation. Thus specialization according to corporate comparative advantage, in the field of R&D, generates an inverse relationship, in a cross-section of firms, between the multinationality of the firm and the range of its products.

(5) *Contractual alternatives to the MNE.*   Licensing is easiest when patent protection is secure, and when the global market is easily segmented. Patent protection is fairly secure for process technologies and the printed word, and segmentation is easy for services since they are difficult to transport. Joint ventures are a useful method of rationalizing production in an oligopoly, or sharing risks under bilateral monopoly, when there are significant economies of scale. Political opposition to foreign control of production – particularly in developing countries – has recently encouraged the exploitation of these alternative contractual arrangements.

(6) *Vertical integration.*   There are economies of scale in smelting aluminium, copper and tin, but the supplies of ores are more concentrated for aluminium and copper than they are for tin. The resolution of bilateral monopoly conflict encourages integration in the first two cases, therefore, but not in the third. Economies of continuous flow, and the hazards of transportation, are more significant in oil than in coal, so that centralized control of the sequential stages is more important. Integration is therefore more common in oil. Bananas pose serious problems of quality control which can be resolved through skilled plantation management and the integration of growing, shipping and ripening. In the case of other agricultural products, the problems are not so acute. Agribusiness operations by vertically integrated MNEs are therefore confined mainly to bananas and tobacco (though a few other instances are known).

Acknowledgements

The author is grateful to Wilson Brown, Roger Clarke, Tony McGuinness and John Dunning for comments on an earlier draft of this chapter.

Further Reading

This chapter has focused on the relationship between the multinational enterprise and the theory of the firm. It has presented in relatively non-technical fashion material which is discussed in a more technical way in Buckley and Casson (1985). Much has also been written on wider issues, such as the role of multinationals in world trade and in the international capital market. For a survey of these wider issues see Dunning (1981) and Caves (1982). The role of foreign investment by multinationals in developing countries has been a subject of considerable controversy, particularly over whether foreign investment promotes growth, or merely distorts the process of development. These issues are reviewed in Lall (1981, 1985) and UNCTC (1983). There has recently been a resurgence of research on the historical aspects of the evolution of the modern multinational; the economic aspects of this subject are covered in Casson (ed.) (1983).

8 Conclusions

ROGER CLARKE and TONY McGUINNESS

8.1 Introduction

This book has examined recent developments in the economics of the firm. Its chapters indicate the diversity of modern literature on the firm and we make no claim to have covered all areas of current analysis.[1] Nevertheless, the topics included cover some of the key areas in which developments have taken place and provide a basis for understanding current thinking in the subject. Such thinking, even in the last 10 or 15 years, has experienced considerable development and hence the need for a book such as this.

In this remaining chapter we draw together some of the ideas of the earlier chapters and offer brief suggestions for further developments. Section 8.2 discusses three underlying themes in recent work: the interest in explaining institutional arrangements found within firms rather than taking the existence of firms for granted; the attempt to analyse problems posed by the failure of markets, due, in particular, to the existence of uncertainty, imperfect information, and small numbers' bargaining; and the attention paid to efficiency as a basis for explaining firm development. These ideas have been important in certainly some of the recent work on the economics of the firm and we provide comments on each in turn.

Section 8.3 then considers areas for further development. This section argues that there is a need to synthesize the rather different theoretical approaches and ideas currently being considered in the literature and suggests that further theoretical and empirical work needs to be done.

Some brief comments on welfare issues are also made. Finally, Section 8.4 offers a brief summary and conclusions.

8.2   Some Recent Themes

It is not necessary to go too far in the past to find the economic analysis of the firm being regarded as little more than an adjunct of the broader theory of markets. Nor is it uncommon, even today, to find the firm analysed primarily as a production function; as an institution that can be represented satisfactorily by a functional relationship between output and input levels. Only a cursory look at more recent work is needed to reveal, however, that, though the above approaches clearly have their uses, a great deal more diversity and depth now exist in the economic analysis of the firm. In the popular jargon, modern analyses have begun to look inside the firm rather than merely regard it as a 'black box' for converting resources into outputs.

This change in perspective, which can be traced back to the work of Coase (1937),[2] provides our first theme of modern analysis. In contrast to the view of a firm as a given institution, setting policy variables (price, output, advertising, etc.) in accordance with profit or non-profit objectives, recent work has taken an increasing interest in why firms exist, and what influences their structure and development. In Coase's conception, firms allocate resources by administrative decision in contrast to the price mechanism in the market, and do so because costs of market operation can, thereby, be avoided. The emphasis, therefore, is on the way in which economic activities can be divided up between firms, and on cost-reducing ways of organizing economic transactions. Within this approach, work has focused increasingly on institutional arrangements found within firms and on comparative analysis of the ways in which they deal with resource allocation problems.

Various examples of these ideas have been considered in this book. Authors such as Williamson (1979) (see also Alchian and Demsetz, 1972; Jensen and Meckling, 1976; and Aoki, 1983) attempt to explain one or more of the variety of contracts, explicit or implicit, that exist within the firm. Similarly, although the spatial allocation of resources and the existence of diversified firms had not gone unnoticed by earlier writers, only recently have serious efforts been made to explain the geographic and product boundaries of the firm. Casson (Chapter 7 of this book), for example, attributes to McManus (1972) the first application to the MNE of Coase's ideas on internalization. Whilst, more recently, considerable attention has been devoted to organizational issues in the context of vertical integration, diversification and multinational operation (see Chapters 5–7 of this book). Clearly considerable work has been done on internalization issues in recent years and further work in this area seems likely in the next few years.

One feature of recent work on the institutional organization of firms has been the recognition that contracts and institutional arrangements are more varied than was suggested by Coase. In contrast to Coase's simple distinction between markets and administrative coordination of resources, it is increasingly recognized that more complex alternatives exist. Contractual arrangements between firms, for example, can involve a variety of short- and long-term contracts, franchising, sale or lease, licensing arrangements and so on. Thus transactions typically do not take place in simple 'spot' markets, and, in the case of some long-term contracts in particular, the distinction between market and administrative relations can be blurred. Similarly, as we have seen, organizational relations within the firm between owners, managers and workers, as well as the general organization of the management function, are also diverse; contrasting again with Coase's simple view of entrepreneurial coordination within the firm. It is some of this diversity and the underlying reasons why it arises which recent analysis has sought to explain.

A second theme which we mention is the emphasis placed on uncertainty, limited information and small numbers' bargaining in the modern analysis of the firm. Whilst interest in the nature and scope of the firm has no doubt been spurred by the growth of large vertically integrated, conglomerate and multinational firms since 1945, developments in economic theory have also been important in shaping recent analysis. Modern economic theory has, in particular, been concerned to examine economic relations at a more micro-orientated level than had previous work, incorporating such problems as uncertainty, limited information, bargaining and strategic behaviour. This emphasis in economic theory in general has been applied recently in the context of the firm to analyse organization and behaviour both between and within firms.

Several examples of this may be briefly noted. First, adopting the viewpoint of Coase, economic transactions will be internalized and subject to administrative authority when costs of using markets are comparatively high. As emphasized by Williamson (see Chapter 3) this is likely to be the case when small numbers' conditions lead to costly bargaining between resource owners, a situation which in turn is closely associated with problems of uncertainty or imperfect information. One instance of this is the opportunistic re-contracting motive for vertical integration discussed by Davies (see Section 5.3.1 of this book). In the absence of vertical integration, bargaining problems are anticipated, in this case because of the difficulties one party has in establishing the truth of representations made by the other. Vertical integration, in contrast, enables the use of authority to resolve any asymmetry of information between the parties. The same principle is at work in the 'innovation' and 'quality assurance' motives for vertical integration discussed by Davies (see Sections 5.3.2 and 5.3.3 respectively), and in Casson's discussion of the relevance of marketing strategy to vertical integration of firms across national boundaries (see Section 7.5). All these instances can be regarded as cases where vertical integration (hence authority) is a relatively efficient way of dealing with information asymmetry, and ensuing problems, between resource owners. The most general treatment of this problem is provided by Williamson (see Section 3.3.1).

The principal–agent literature provides a second example of the preoccupation with uncertainty and imperfect information in the recent analysis of the firm. In this case, limited and asymmetric information between actors within the firm creates problems of monitoring agents' behaviour. As Strong and Waterson point out in Chapter 2, information asymmetries drive a wedge between the interests of principals and agents and lead to problems of agent discretion in how to behave. This in turn raises the question of which kind of institutional arrangements and/or contractual incentives are needed to harness the agent's actions more closely to the principal's interests. The principal–agent literature is concerned, therefore, with the implications of incomplete (non-costless) monitoring of agents' actions in the presence of delegation of authority in typically large administrative units. As noted in Chapter 2, this idea encompasses not only shareholder–manager relations but indeed many other possible relationships within the firm.

Much of the principal–agent literature is concerned with the formal analysis of optimal contracts between principals and agents. Our third example, Williamson's work on hierarchical decomposition (see Chapter 3), provides a somewhat less formal approach. In this case, information problems again arise, most importantly in the bounds on the information-processing capacities of managers. The inability of managers to process and utilize large quantities of information gives rise to the need to divide decision-taking authority within the firm, in particular in the separation of strategic and operational decisions in the M-form firm. In this analysis, therefore, bounded rationality on the part of managers in a complex and uncertain world is seen as an important factor in the administrative organization of the firm.

A basic feature of each of the examples cited above is their emphasis on one (or several) aspects of market or organizational failure. If agents are strictly rational and information and other transaction costs are zero then no, or at least limited, economic analysis of the firm is required. Relaxation of these assumptions gives rise to the existence of firms, and, on the Coasian view, influences both the size and the scope of the firm. The converse also applies, however, namely, that administrative 'failures' will, for various reasons, arise within the organization and, ultimately, *limit* the size and scope of the firm. Much of the recent work on the economic analysis of the firm can be seen as considering one or other of the two sides of this coin.

One final theme can be briefly mentioned; namely, the emphasis which a number of authors place on efficiency arguments in the theory of the firm. These ideas flow naturally from Coase's (1937) work which sees administrative control as a means of economizing on market transaction costs, and they underlie subsequent developments in the work of Williamson (1975) and others. One way of viewing these developments is to see them as redressing the balance with what Williamson calls the 'inhospitality' tradition of the 1950s and 1960s, in which any unusual non-standard commercial arrangement was suspected of creating or enhancing monopoly. This was the aim, for example, of Williamson's (1971) work on the efficiency advantages of vertical integration, which suggested that vertical mergers should not be assumed indiscriminately to be against the public interest. From this point of view, therefore, reducing costs of organizing transactions offers an alternative explanation of vertical (or more general) firm development.

It is important to recognize, however, that efficiency considerations are not the only or indeed necessarily the most important explanations of the nature and scope of firms. Ample evidence of this has been provided in Chapters 5–7 where monopolistic and other motives have been extensively discussed. Clearly efficiency is a factor which may have an important role to play in understanding organizational development, but (as argued further below) economic analysis is some way from knowing how important a factor it is likely to be.

8.3 Future Developments

A number of possible future developments can be mentioned. One obvious point concerns the rather disparate nature of some of the current work in the field. This is most clearly seen in the separate development of the principal–agent literature and the work of Williamson on markets and hierarchies. Whilst this largely reflects historical and/or individual factors, it is clear that both literatures offer important insights into the nature of firms. The former emphasizes the problems of controlling agent behaviour for the organization of firms whilst the latter considers general problems of cost economizing as determinants of organizational form. In the former case, problems of *moral hazard* and *adverse selection* are given emphasis, whilst the latter considers implications of *bounded rationality* and *opportunism* for the organization of the firm.

Clearly these separate approaches overlap and/or are complementary to each other to some extent. They overlap, for example, in that problems of controlling the opportunism of middle managers in complex hierarchies can arise for asymmetric information reasons (see Section 3.3.3). They are complementary in this case in that Williamson's confidence that some kinds of organizational form can overcome such opportunism can be subject to formal principal–agent analysis. More generally, information asymmetries highlighted by the principal–agent approach can provide complementary insights into how firms behave. For example, top managers may seek to reduce employment risk (e.g. by indulging in conglomerate mergers). This then provides an added dimension to the analysis of M-form firms put forward by Williamson. These and other complementarities suggest that it would be desirable to consider these ideas in an integrated way and hopefully future work will move in this direction.

A similar point can be made in relation to analysis of the various types of firm. As we have seen in Chapters 5–7, analyses of vertically integrated, conglomerate and multinational firms rely to some extent on specialized analyses developed within each particular area. Thus, for example, writers on conglomerates have traditionally been influenced by the finance literature and questions of reducing risks, whilst international trade and international finance theory have been important inputs to the analysis of MNEs. These different inputs are, of course, important in understanding the particular nature of different types of firm. At the same time, however, they contribute to a diversity of approach in the analysis of firms which needs to be looked at. If ideas on the nature and scope of firms are to be adequately developed then there is a need to adopt a more common method of approach in these different areas.

It could, of course, be argued that different principles apply in the formation of different types of firm. Thus, for example, transactions involving investment in specific assets may be important factors in the decision to integrate vertically (in a national or international context) but managerial risk-reduction motives (say) are particularly important for conglomerates. Again, transaction-cost considerations may be important in some decisions to diversify production (as, for example, where technical knowhow is involved) but problems need not be associated merely with the specialized nature of the assets involved (see

Chapter 6). Monopoly and strategic behaviour can be important in each of the spheres but different arguments could be involved in each case. Clearly, more attention is needed in comparing the different types of firm in order to determine whether more general principles can be applied incorporating some of the diversity of analysis currently observed.

As noted in the previous section, recent work has increasingly emphasized the importance of uncertainty, small numbers' bargaining, and strategic behaviour to the analysis of the firm. This reflects a move away from a broader frictionless view of economic activity towards a more micro-orientated focus on economic institutions. Specific hypotheses which have been suggested concern the incentives of different economic actors under conditions of uncertainty and asymmetric information; the relevance of specific investments in bargaining and game-theoretic situations; and other features of transactions in market and non-market situations. In each case attention is shifted to rational or strategic actions of individual decision-makers in specific micro-orientated circumstances. These developments are clearly to be welcomed if one is concerned with the nature of contracts and institutions in the market. Important theoretical developments have been made and clearly further theoretical work needs to be done.

There is also a need (and perhaps even more so) for more empirical work on the economics of the firm. Recent work has developed many new ideas, some of which at least are capable of empirical test. Up to the present time, however, empirical work has been limited or, in some cases, non-existent in the field. Data limitations and so on are, of course, a factor here, but also a tendency (on the part of some authors) exists to deal in truisms and otherwise fail to see the importance of developing testable predictions. This, it appears to us, is a weakness in the current literature which is in need of rectification.

Examples of hypotheses needing empirical verification include the idea that M-form firms have superior capital-allocation advantages and hence (presumably) superior rates of return (see Chapter 6); that asset-specificity is an important factor in vertical integration (see Chapter 5); that marketing and research are important factors in multinational and/or conglomerate activity (see Chapters 6 and 7); and that management control leads to more risk-averse decisions (see Chapter 6). Whilst some empirical work has been done on some of these hypotheses, more work is needed both to develop testable hypotheses and to carry out the necessary tests. In the absence of such work an important check on the progress of new ideas is missing, and with it the certainty that secure foundations for the economic analysis of firms have been laid.

Finally, we briefly comment on welfare aspects of the analysis of firms. As noted in Section 8.2, recent emphasis on cost economizing as an explanation of firms has led to a significant shift in ideas on the nature and scope of firms. This shift has led some writers to suggest that firms (and especially large firms) raise no problems from a welfare point of view.

It is important, however, to recognize that large firms can (at least potentially) have undesirable effects. This is, of course, most obviously the case when they possess market power in individual markets. In addition, however, market power effects can arise from multi-market activity; be it through vertical integration, or conglomerate or multinational activity. Diversified firms, for example, can take advantage of predatory pricing or mutual forbearance and such effects lead to important reductions in competition. Again, multinational firms can exert power in avoiding taxes or countering union power in individual countries. Hence it would be wrong to ignore the fact that size can have power as well as (or indeed instead of) efficiency effects.

For this reason it would be unwise to view efficiency-based explanations of the nature of firms as justifying large-firm activity. As in the case of the more clearly positive aspects of recent theory, there is a need to subject supposed normative propositions to further investigation.

8.4 Summary and Conclusions

In this chapter we have briefly considered some of the themes of recent analysis of the firm and offered some brief suggestions for further developments. Underlying themes identified have been an increased concern with firms *as* firms rather than as mere production relationships between inputs and outputs; an emphasis on uncertainty, imperfect information and small numbers' bargaining in the theory of the firm; and an increased emphasis on efficiency as an explanation of organizational form. Each of these themes has been an important feature of some recent work in the field, and comments on each were made in this chapter.

The chapter also briefly discussed what future developments may be needed in the economics of the firm. In this section, we emphasized the need to synthesize the somewhat disparate work which has currently been produced both with regard to general principles and applications. More attention to theoretical and (more especially) empirical testing is also needed. Finally, brief comments were made on welfare aspects of the economics of the firm and it was suggested, again, that more work is required.

Notes

1 For mention of some recent work not considered explicitly in this book see the Further Reading section in Chapter 1.
2 In his more recent paper on 'Industrial organization: a proposal for research', Coase comments that his earlier paper has been 'much cited and little used' (Coase, 1972, p. 63). This comment, whilst applicable in 1972, is clearly less applicable today.

References

Adelman, M. A. (1961) The anti-merger act: 1950–60. *American Economic Review*, Papers and Proceedings, 51, 236–44.

Akerlof, G. (1970) The market for lemons: qualitative uncertainty and the market mechanism. *Quarterly Journal of Economics*, 84, 488–500.

Alchian, A. A. and Demsetz, H. (1972) Production, information costs and economic organization. *American Economic Review*, 62, 777–95.

Amey, L. R. (1964) Diversified manufacturing businesses. *Journal of the Royal Statistical Society*, Series A, 127, 251–90.

Amihud, Y. and Lev, B. (1981) Risk reduction as a managerial motive for conglomerate mergers. *Bell Journal of Economics*, 12, 605–17.

Aoki, M. (1983) Managerialism revisited in the light of bargaining-game theory. *International Journal of Industrial Organisation*, 1, 1–21.

Aoki, M. (1984) *Co-operative Game Theory of the Firm*. Oxford: Oxford University Press.

Arrow, K. J. (1975) Vertical integration and communication. *Bell Journal of Economics*, 6, 173–83.

Arrow, K. J. (1984) The economics of agency. *Technical Report No. 451*, Center for Research on Organizational Efficiency, Stanford University.

Baiman, S. (1982) Agency research in managerial accounting: a survey. *Journal of Accounting Literature*, 1, 154–213.

Baiman, S. and Demski, J. S. (1980) Economically optimal performance evaluation and control systems. *Journal of Accounting Research*, 18 (Supplement), 184–220.

Bain, J. S. (1956) *Barriers to New Competition*. Cambridge, Mass.: Harvard University Press.

Bain, J. S. (1968) *Industrial Organisation* (2nd edn). New York: John Wiley.

Batra, R. N. and Ramachandran,R. (1980) Multinational firms and the theory of international trade and investment. *American Economic Review*, 70, 278–90.

Baumol, W. J. (1959) *Business Behaviour, Value and Growth*. New York: Macmillan.

Baumol, W. J. (1962) On the theory of the expansion of the firm. *American Economic Review*, 52, 1078–87.

Baumol, W. J. (1982) Contestable markets: an uprising in the theory of industry structure. *American Economic Review*, 72, 1–15.

Baumol, W. J., Panzar, J. C. and Willig, R. D. (1982) *Contestable Markets and the Theory of Industrial Structure*. New York: Harcourt Brace Jovanovich.

Ben-Ner, A. (1984) On the stability of the cooperative type of organization. *Journal of Comparative Economics*, 8, 247–60.

Berle, A. A. and Means, G. C. (1932) *The Modern Corporation and Private Property*. New York: Commerce Clearing House.

Blair, R. D. and Lanzillotti, R. F. (1981) *The Conglomerate Corporation: an Antitrust and Law Symposium*. Cambridge, Mass.: Oelgeschlager, Gunn and Hain.

Bork, R. H. (1978) *The Anti-trust Paradox*. New York: Basic Books.

Brown, W. B. (1976) Islands of conscious power: MNCs in the theory of the firm. *MSU Business Topics*, 24, 37–45.

Brown, W. B. (1984) Firm-like behaviour in markets: the administered channel. *International Journal of Industrial Organisation*, 2, 263–76.

Buckley, P. J. (1983) New theories of international business: some unresolved issues. In Casson (1983).

Buckley, P. J. (1985) Testing theories of the multinational enterprise: a review of the evidence. In Buckley and Casson (1985).

Buckley, P. J. and Casson, M. C. (1976) *The Future of the Multinational Enterprise*. London: Macmillan.

Buckley, P. J. and Casson, M. C. (1985) *The Economic Theory of the Multinational Enterprise: Selected Papers*. London: Macmillan.

Buckley, P. J. and Enderwick, P. (1984) *The Industrial Relations Practices of Foreign-owned Firms in British Manufacturing Industry*. London: Macmillan.

Bulow, J. I., Geanakoplos, J. D. and Klemperer, P. D. (1985a) Multimarket oligopoly: strategic substitutes and complements. *Journal of Political Economy*, 93, 488–511.

Bulow, J. I., Geanakoplos, J. D. and Klemperer, P. D. (1985b) Holding idle capacity to deter entry. *Economic Journal*, 95, 178–82.

Buzzell, R. D. (1983) Is vertical integration profitable? *Harvard Business Review*, 61, 92–102.

Cable, J. (1985) Capital market information and industrial performance: the role of West German banks. *Economic Journal*, 95, 118–32.

Carlton, D. W. (1979) Vertical integration in competitive markets under uncertainty. *Journal of Industrial Economics*, 27, 189–209.

Casson, M. C. (1979) *Alternatives to the Multinational Enterprise*. London: Macmillan.

Casson, M. C. (1982a) *The Entrepreneur: An Economic Theory*. Oxford: Martin Robertson.

Casson, M. C. (1982b) Transaction costs and the theory of the multinational enterprise. In A. M. Rugman (ed.) *New Theories of the Multinational Enterprise*. Beckenham, Kent: Croom Helm; reprinted in Buckley and Casson (1985).

Casson, M. C. (ed.) (1983) *The Growth of International Business*. London: Allen and Unwin.

Casson, M. C. (1984a) General theories of the multinational enterprise: a critical examination. *University of Reading Discussion Papers in International Investment and Business Studies*, No. 77.

Casson, M. C. (1984b) The theory of vertical integration: a survey and synthesis. *Journal of Economic Studies*, 11, 3–43.

Casson, M. C. (1985) Multinational monopolies and international cartels. In Buckley and Casson (1985).

Casson, M. C. and associates (1985) *Multinationals and World Trade: Vertical Integration and the Division of Labour in World Industries*. London: Allen and Unwin.

Caves, R. E. (1971) International corporations: the industrial economics of foreign investment. *Economica*, n.s., 38, 1–27.

Caves, R. E. (1980) Corporate strategy and structure. *Journal of Economic Literature*, 18, 64–92.

Caves, R. E. (1982) *Multinational Enterprise and Economic Analysis*. Cambridge: Cambridge University Press.

Chamberlin, E. H. (1966) *The Theory of Monopolistic Competition*, 8th edn. Cambridge, Mass.: Harvard University Press.

Chandler, A. D. Jr (1962) *Strategy and Structure: Chapters in the History of Industrial Enterprise*. Cambridge, Mass.: MIT Press.

Chandler, A. D. Jr (1976) The development of modern management structure in the US and UK. In L. Hannah (ed.) *Management Strategy and Business Development*. London: Macmillan.

Clarke, R. (1985) *Industrial Economics*. Oxford: Basil Blackwell.

Clarke, R. and Davies, S. W. (1983) Aggregate concentration, market concentration and diversification. *Economic Journal*, 93, 182–92.

Clarke, R. and Davies, S. W. (1984) On measuring concentration and diversification. *Economics Letters*. 15, 145–52.

Coase, R. M. (1937) The nature of the firm. *Economica*, n.s., 4, 386–405. Reprinted in G. J. Stigler and K. E. Boulding (1952) *Readings in Price Theory*. Homewood, Ill.: Irwin. (Page references to latter source.)

Coase, R. H. (1972) Industrial organization: a proposal for research. In V. R. Fuchs (ed.) *Policy Issues and Research Opportunities in Industrial Organization*. New York: National Bureau of Economic Research.

Comanor, W. S. (1967) Vertical mergers, market power, and the anti-trust laws. *American Economic Review*, 57, 254–65.

Cournot, A. A. (1960) *Researches into the Mathematical Principles of the Theory of Wealth* (1838), trans. N. T. Bacon. New York: Augustus Kelley.

Cowling, K. (1984) The internationalisation of production and de-industrialisation. University of Warwick, mimeo.

Cowling, K., Stoneman, P., Cubbin, J., Hall, G., Domberger, S. and Dutton, P. (1980) *Mergers and Economic Performance*. Cambridge: Cambridge University Press.

Crew, M. A., Jones-Lee, M. and Rowley, C. K. (1971) X-theory versus management discretion theory. *Southern Economic Journal*, 38, 173–84.

Cubbin, J. and Leech, D. (1983) The effect of shareholding dispersion on the degree of control in British companies: theory and measurement. *Economic Journal*, 93, 351–69.

Cyert, R. M. and March, J. G. (1963) *A Behavioural Theory of the Firm*. Englewood Cliffs, N.J.: Prentice-Hall.

Davies, S. W. (1971) The clay brick industry and the tunnel kiln. *National Institute Economic Review*, 58, 54–71.

Davies, S. W. and Lyons, B. R. (in press) *Surveys in Industrial Economics*. London: Longman.

Dayan, D. (1975) Behaviour of the firm under regulatory constraint: a re-examination. *Industrial Organisation Review*, 3, 61–76.

Diamond, D. W. (1984) Financial intermediation and delegated monitoring. *Review of Economic Studies*, 51, 393–414.

Diamond, D. W. and Verrecchia, R. E. (1982) Optimal managerial contracts and equilibrium security prices. *Journal of Finance*, 37, 275–87.

Dixit, A. K. (1980) The role of investment in entry deterrence. *Economic Journal*, 9, 95–106.

Dixit, A. K. (1982) Recent developments in oligopoly theory. *American Economic Review, Papers and Proceedings*, 72, 12–17.

Dunning, J. H. (1958) *American Investment in British Manufacturing Industry*. London: Allen and Unwin.

Dunning, J. H. (1977) Trade, location of economic activity and the multinational enterprise: a search for an eclectic approach. In B. Ohlin, P. O. Hesselborn and P. M. Wijkman (eds) *The International Allocation of Economic Activity*. London: Macmillan.

Dunning, J. H. (1981) *International Production and the Multinational Enterprise*. London: Allen and Unwin.

Dunning, J. H. (1983) Changes in the structure of international production: the last 100 years. In Casson (ed.) (1983).

Dunning, J. H. (1985a) The eclectic paradigm of international production: an up-date and a reply to its critics. Mimeo.

Dunning, J. H. (1985b) *Japanese Participation in UK Manufacturing Industry*. A Report prepared for the Department of Industry.

Dunning, J. H. and McQueen, M. (1982) The eclectic theory of the multinational enterprise and the international hotel industry. In A. M. Rugman (ed.) *New Theories of the Multinational Enterprise*. Beckenham, Kent: Croom Helm.

Dunning, J. H. and Rugman, A. M. (1985) The influence of Hymer's dissertation on the theory of foreign direct investment. *American Economic Review, Papers and Proceedings*, 75, 228–32.

Easterbrook, E. (1984) Two agency-cost explanations of dividends. *American Economic Review*, 74, 650–9.

Eaton, C. B. and Lipsey, R. G. (1978) Freedom of entry and the existence of pure profit. *Economic Journal*, 88, 455–69.

Edwards, C. D. (1955) Conglomerate bigness as a source of power. In National Bureau of Economic Research, *Business Concentration and Price Policy*. Princeton: Princeton University Press.

Fama, E. F. (1980) Agency problems and the theory of the firm. *Journal of Political Economy*, 88, 288–307.

Fama, E. F. and Jensen, M. C. (1983a) Separation of ownership and control. In Symposium (1983), 301–25.

Fama, E. F. and Jensen, M. C. (1983b) Agency problems and residual claims. In Symposium (1983), 327–49.

Feinberg, R. M. (1981) On the measurement of aggregate concentration. *Journal of Industrial Economics*, 30, 217–22.

Fellner, W. (1949) *Competition Among the Few: Oligopoly and Similar Market Structures*. New York: Alfred A. Knopf.

Firth, M. (1979) The profitability of takeovers and mergers. *Economic Journal*, 89, 316–28.

Firth, M. (1980) Takeovers, shareholder returns, and the theory of the firm. *Quarterly Journal of Economics*, 94, 235–60.

Fitzroy, F. and Mueller, D. C. (1984) Cooperation and conflict in contractual organisations. *Quarterly Review of Economics and Business*, 24, 24–50.

Flaherty, M. T. (1981) Prices versus quantities and vertical financial integration. *Bell Journal of Economics*, 12, 507–25.

Fudenberg, D. and Tirole, J. (1984) The fat-cat effect, the puppy-dog ploy, and the lean and hungry look. *American Economic Review, Papers and Proceedings*, 74, 361–66.

Galai, D. and Masulis, R. (1976) The option pricing model and the risk factor of stock. *Journal of Financial Economics*, 3, 53–81.

Gorecki, P. K. (1975) An inter-industry analysis of diversification in the U.K. manufacturing sector. *Journal of Industrial Economics*, 24, 131–46.

Gort, M. (1962) *Diversification and Integration in American Industry*. Princeton: Princeton University Press.

Goudie, A. W. and Meeks, G. (1982) Diversification by merger. *Economica*, n.s., 49, 447–59.

Grant, R. M. (1977) The determinants of the inter-industry pattern of diversification by U.K. manufacturing enterprises, *Bulletin of Economic Research*, 29, 84–95.

Gravelle, H. and Rees, R. (1981) *Microeconomics*. London: Longman.

Greenhut, M. L. and Ohta, H. (1976) Related market conditions and inter-industrial mergers. *American Economic Review*, 66, 267–77.

Greenhut, M. L. and Ohta, H. (1979) Vertical integration of successive oligopolists. *American Economic Review*, 69, 137–41.

Grossman, S. and Hart, O. (1982) Corporate financial structure and managerial incentives. In J. J. McCall (ed.) *The Economics of Information and Uncertainty*. Chicago: University of Chicago Press.

Hall, R. L. and Hitch, C. J. (1939) Price theory and business behaviour. *Oxford Economic Papers*, 2, 12–45.

Haltiwanger, J. and Waldman, M. (1985) Rational expectations and the limits of rationality: an analysis of heterogeneity. *American Economic Review*, 75, 326–40.

Hart, O. (1983) The market mechanism as an incentive scheme. *Bell Journal of Economics*, 14, 366–82.

Hay, D. A. (1976) Sequential entry and entry-deterring strategies in spatial competition. *Oxford Economic Papers*, 28, 240–57.

Hay, D. A. and Morris, D. J. (1979) *Industrial Economics: Theory and Evidence*. Oxford: Oxford University Press.

Hay, G. A. (1973) An economic analysis of vertical integration. *Industrial Organisation Review*, 1, 188–98.

Hennart, J. F. (1982) *A Theory of Multinational Enterprise*. Ann Arbor: University of Michigan Press.

Holmstrom, B. (1979) Moral hazard and observability. *Bell Journal of Economics*, 10, 74–91.

Horst, T. O. (1971) The theory of the multinational firm: optimal behaviour under different tariff and tax rates. *Journal of Political Economy*, 79, 1059–72.

Horst, T. O. (1974) The theory of the firm. In J. H. Dunning (ed.) *Economic Analysis and the Multinational Enterprise*. London: Allen and Unwin.

Hymer, S. H. (1960) *The International Operations of National Firms: A Study of Direct Foreign Investment*. Ph.D. thesis, Massachusetts Institute of Technology, published by MIT Press, 1976.

Hymer, S. H. (1979) The multinational corporation and the international division of labour. In R. B. Cohen *et al.* (eds) *The Multinational Corporation: A Radical Approach; Papers by Stephen Herbert Hymer*. Cambridge: Cambridge University Press.

Jensen, M. C. (1983) Organization theory and methodology. *Accounting Review*, 58, 319–39.

Jensen, M. C. and Meckling, W. H. (1976) Theory of the firm: managerial behaviour, agency costs and ownership structure. *Journal of Financial Economics*, 3, 305–60.

Jensen, M. C. and Ruback, R. S. (1983) The market for corporate control: the scientific evidence. *Journal of Financial Economics*, 11, 5–50.

Johnson, H. G. (1970). The efficiency and welfare implications of the international corporation. In C. P. Kindleberger (ed.) *The International Corporation*. Cambridge, Mass.: MIT Press.

Kahn, A. E. (1961) The chemical industry. In W. Adams (ed.) *The Structure of American Industry*, 3rd edn. New York: Macmillan.

Kaserman, D. L. (1978) Theories of vertical integration: implications for antitrust policy. *Antitrust Bulletin*, 23, 483–510.

Kindleberger, C. P. (1969) *American Business Abroad*. New Haven: Yale University Press.

Kindleberger, C. P. (1984) Plus ça change – a new look at the literature. In C. P. Kindleberger, *Multinational Excursions*. Cambridge, Mass.: MIT Press.

Knight, K. (1976) Matrix Organisation: a Review. *Journal of Management Studies*, 13, 111–30.

Koutsoyiannis, A. (1979) *Modern Microeconomics*, 2nd edn. London: Macmillan.

Lall, S. (1981) *The Multinational Corporation: Nine Essays*. London: Macmillan.

Lall, S. (1985) *Multinationals, Technology and Exports: Selected Papers*. London: Macmillan.

Lambert, R. A. and Larcker, D. F. (1985) Executive compensation, corporate decision-making and shareholder wealth: a review of the evidence. *Midland Corporate Finance Journal*, 2 (4), 6–22.

Lawriwsky, M. L. (1984) *Corporate Structure and Performance*. Beckenham, Kent: Croom Helm.

Lev, B. (1983) Observations on the merger phenomenon and a review of the evidence. *Midland Corporate Finance Journal*, 1 (4), 6–16.

Levy, D. (1984) Testing Stigler's interpretation of the division of labor is limited by the extent of the market. *Journal of Industrial Economics*, 32, 377–89.

Levy, H. and Sarnat, M. (1970) Diversification, portfolio analysis and the uneasy case for conglomerate mergers. *Journal of Finance*, 25, 795–802.

Lindblom, C. E. (1977) *Politics and Markets*. New York: Basic Books.

Lyons, B. R. (1984) The pattern of international trade in differentiated products: an incentive for the existence of multinational firms. In H. Kierzkowski (ed.) *Monopolistic Competition and International Trade*. Oxford: Oxford University Press.

Machlup, F. and Taber, M. (1960) Bilateral monopoly, successive monopoly and vertical integration. *Economica*, n.s., 27, 101–19.

Magee, S. P. (1977) Information and the multinational corporation: an appropriability theory of direct foreign investment. In J. N. Bhagwati (ed.) *The New International Economic Order*. Cambridge, Mass.: MIT Press.

Malcomson, J. (1984) Efficient labour organisation: incentives, power and the transactions cost approach. In F. H. Stephen (ed.) *Firms, Organisation and Labour: Approaches to the Economics of Work Organisation*. London: Macmillan.

Mallela, P. and Nahata, B. (1980) Theory of vertical control with variable proportions. *Journal of Political Economy*, 88, 1009–25.

Marcus, A. J. (1982) Risk sharing and the theory of the firm. *Bell Journal of Economics*, 13, 369–78.

Marglin, S. (1975) What do bosses do? In A. Gorz (ed.) *The Division of Labour*. Hassocks: Harvester Press.

Marris, R. (1964) *The Economic Theory of Managerial Capitalism*. London: Macmillan.

Marris, R. and Mueller, D. C. (1980) The corporation, competition, and the invisible hand. *Journal of Economic Literature*, 18, 32–63.

Marx, T. G. (1980) Political consequences of conglomerate mergers. *Atlantic Economic Journal*, 8 (1), 62–3.

Masten, S. (1984) The organisation of production: evidence from the aerospace industry. *Journal of Law and Economics*, 27, 403–18.

McManus, J. C. (1972) The theory of the international firm. In G. Paquet (ed.) *The Multinational Firm and the Nation State*. Toronto: Collier Macmillan.

Meeks, G. (1977) *Disappointing Marriage: A Study of the Gains from Merger*. Cambridge: Cambridge University Press.

Miller, R. A. (1969) Market structure and industrial performance: relation of profit rate to concentration, advertising intensity and diversity. *Journal of Industrial Economics*, 17, 104–18.

Monopolies Commission (1969) *Beer*. London: HMSO.

Monopolies and Mergers Commission (1975) *The NFU Development Trust Ltd and FMC Ltd. Report on the Proposed Merger*. London: HMSO.

Monopolies and Mergers Commission (1977) *Pilkington Brothers Ltd and UKO International Ltd. Report on the Proposed Merger*. London: HMSO.

Monopolies and Mergers Commission (1981) *S&W Berisford Ltd and British Sugar Corporation Ltd. Report on the Proposed Merger*. London; HMSO.

Monroe, M. (1981) Conglomerate mergers: financial theory and evidence. In Blair and Lanzillotti (1981), Chapter 7.

Monteverde, K. and Teece, D. J. (1982a) Supplier switching costs and vertical integration in the automobile industry. *Bell Journal of Economics*, 13, 206–13.

Monteverde, K. and Teece, D. J. (1982b) Appropriable rents and quasi-vertical integration. *Journal of Law and Economics*, 25, 321–8.

Mueller, D. C. (1969) A theory of conglomerate mergers. *Quarterly Journal of Economics*, 83, 643–59.

Mueller, D. C. (1972) A life cycle theory of the firm. *Journal of Industrial Economics*, 20, 199–219.

Mueller, D. C. (ed.) (1980) *The Determinants and Effects of Mergers*. Cambridge, Mass.: Delgeschlager, Gunn and Hain.

Mueller, D. C. (1981) The case against conglomerate mergers. In Blair and Lanzillotti (1981), Chapter 5.

Nabseth, L. and Ray, G. F. (1974) *The Diffusion of New Industrial Processes*. Cambridge: Cambridge University Press.

Nicholas, S. J. (1982) British multinational investment before 1939. *Journal of European Economic History*, 11, 605–30.

Nicholas, S. J. (1983) Agency contracts, institutional modes, and the transition to foreign direct investment by British manufacturing multinationals before 1939. *Journal of Economic History*, 43, 675–86.

Palay, T. (1984) Comparative institutional economics: the governance of rail freight contraction. *Journal of Legal Studies*, 13, 265–88.

Panzar, J. and Willig, R. D. (1975) Economies of scale and economies of scope in multioutput production. *Economic Discussion Paper No. 33, Bell Laboratories*.

Panzar, J. and Willig, R. D. (1981) Economies of scope. *American Economic Review, Papers and Proceedings*, 71, 268–72.

Pearce, R. D. (1983) Industrial diversification amongst the world's leading multinational enterprises. In Casson (ed.) (1983).

Porter, M. and Spence, A. M. (1977) Vertical integration and different inputs. *Warwick Economic Research Paper No. 120*.

Prais, S. J. (1976) *The Evolution of Giant Firms in Britain*. Cambridge: Cambridge University Press.

Putterman, L. (1982) Some behavioural perspectives on the dominance of hierarchical over democratic forms of enterprise. *Journal of Economic Behaviour and Organisation*, 3, 139–60.

Putterman, L. (1984) On some recent explanations of why capital hires labour. *Economic Inquiry*, 22, 171–87.

Radner, R. (1968) Competitive equilibrium under uncertainty. *Econometrica*, 36, 31–58.

Radner, R. (1982) The role of private information in markets and other organisations. In W. Hildenbrand (ed.) *Advances in Economic Theory*. Cambridge: Cambridge University Press.

Radner, R. (1986) The internal economy of large firms. *Economic Journal*, 96 (supplement), 1–22.

Raviv, A. (1985) Management compensation and the managerial labour market: an overview. *Journal of Accounting and Economics*, 7, 239–45.

Rhoades, S. A. (1973) The effect of diversification on industry profit performance in 241 manufacturing industries: 1963. *Review of Economics and Statistics*, 55, 146–55.

Rhoades, S. A. (1974) A further evaluation of the effect of diversification on industry profit performance. *Review of Economics and Statistics*, 56, 557–9.

Richardson, G. B. (1972) The organisation of industry. *Economic Journal*, 82, 883–96.

Robertson, D. H. (1923) *The Control of Industry*. London: Nisbet.

Robinson, E. A. G. (1941) *Monopoly*. London: Nisbet.

Robinson, J. (1969) *The Economics of Imperfect Competition*. London: Macmillan.

Ross, S. A. (1973) The economic theory of agency: the principal's problem. *American Economic Review*, 62, 134–9.

Rowthorn, R. (1979) The future of the world economy: introduction. In R. B. Cohen *et al.* (eds) *The Multinational Corporation: A Radical Approach; Papers by Stephen Herbert Hymer*. Cambridge: Cambridge University Press.

Rugman, A. M. (1981) *Inside the Multinationals: The Economics of Internal Markets*. London: Croom Helm.

Salant, S., Switzer, W. and Reynolds, R. (1983) Losses due to merger: the effects of an exogenous change in industry structure on Cournot Nash equilibrium. *Quarterly Journal of Economics*, 98, 185–99.

Salop, S. C. (1979) Strategic entry deterrence. *American Economic Review, Papers and Proceedings*, 69, 335–8.

Salop, J. and Salop, S. (1976) Self-selection and turnover in the labour market. *Quarterly Journal of Economics*, 90, 619–22.

Sawyer, M. C. (1979) *Theories of the Firm*. London: Weidenfeld and Nicolson.

Schelling, T. C. (1960) *The Strategy of Conflict*. Cambridge, Mass.: Harvard University Press.

Scherer, F. M. (1980) *Industrial Market Structure and Economic Performance*, 2nd edn. Chicago: Rand McNally.

Schmalensee, R. (1973) A note on the theory of vertical integration. *Journal of Political Economy*, 81, 442–9.

Schmalensee, R. (1978) Entry deterrence in the ready-to-eat breakfast cereal market. *Bell Journal of Economics*, 9, 305–27.

Schmalensee, R. (1983) Advertising and entry deterrence: an exploratory model. *Journal of Political Economy*, 90, 636–53.

Shavell, S. (1979) Risk sharing and incentives in the principal and agent relationship. *Bell Journal of Economics*, 10, 55–73.

Silver, M. (1984) *Enterprise and the Scope of the Firm*. Oxford: Martin Robertson.

Simon, H. A. (1955) A behavioural model of rational choice. *Quarterly Journal of Economics*, 69, 99–118.

Simon, H. A. (1957) *Models of Man*. London: John Wiley.

Simon, H. A. (1959) Theories of decision-making in economics and behavioural science. *American Economic Review*, 49, 253–83.

Simon, H. A. (1960) The new science of management decision. Reprinted in

D. S. Pugh (ed.) (1984) *Organisation Theory*, 2nd edn. Harmondsworth: Penguin Books.

Simon, H. A. (1978) Rationality as process and as product of thought. *American Economic Review*, 68, 1–16.

Singh, A. (1971) *Takeovers*. Cambridge: Cambridge University Press.

Smirlock, M. and Marshall, W. (1983) Monopoly power and expense preference behaviour: theory and evidence to the contrary. *Bell Journal of Economics*, 14, 166–78.

Spence, A. M. (1974) *Market Signalling; Informational Transfer in Hiring and Related Screening Processes*. Cambridge, Mass.: Harvard University Press.

Spence, A. M. (1977) Entry, capacity, investment and oligopolistic pricing. *Bell Journal of Economics*, 6, 163–72.

Spence, A. M. and Zeckhauser, R. (1971) Insurance, information and individual action. *American Economic Review*, 61, 380–7.

Steer, P. and Cable, J. (1978) Internal organisation and profit: an empirical analysis of large U.K. companies. *Journal of Industrial Economics*, 27, 13–30.

Stigler, G. J. (1951) The division of labour is limited by the extent of the market. *Journal of Political Economy*, 59, 185–93.

Stigler, G. J. and Friedland, C. (1983) The literature of economics: the case of Berle and Means. In Symposium (1983), 237–68.

Stiglitz, J. E. (1974) Incentives and risk sharing in sharecropping. *Review of Economic Studies*, 41, 219–55.

Stiglitz, J. E. (1975) Incentives, risk, and information: notes towards a theory of hierarchy. *Bell Journal of Economics*, 6, 552–79.

Stiglitz, J. E. (1985) Credit markets and the control of capital. *Journal of Money, Credit and Banking*, 17, 133–52.

Stuckey, J. A. (1983) *Vertical Integration and Joint Ventures in the Aluminium Industry*. Cambridge, Mass.: Harvard University Press.

Sullivan, L. A. (1977) *The Law of Antitrust*. St Paul, Minn.: West Publishing.

Sutton, C. J. (1980) *Economics and Corporate Strategy*. Cambridge: Cambridge University Press.

Swedenborg, B. (1979) *Multinational Operations of Swedish Firms*. Stockholm: Almqvist and Wiksell.

Symposium (1983) Corporations and private property. *Journal of Law and Economics*, 26, 235–496.

Teece, D. J. (1980) Economies of scope and the scope of the enterprise. *Journal of Economic Behaviour and Organisation*, 1, 223–47.

Teece, D. J. (1982a) A transaction cost theory of the multinational enterprise. *University of Reading Discussion Papers in International Investment and Business Studies, No. 66*; an abstract appears in Casson (ed.) (1983).

Teece, D. J. (1982b) Towards an economic theory of the multiproduct firm. *Journal of Economic Behaviour and Organisation*, 3, 39–63.

Teece, D. J. (1985) Multinational enterprise, internal governance and industrial organisation. *American Economic Review, Papers and Proceedings*, 75, 233–8.

Tucker, I. B. and Wilder, R. P. (1977) Trends in vertical integration in the U.S. manufacturing sector. *Journal of Industrial Economics*, 26, 81–94.

Tucker, I. B. and Wilder, R. P. (1984) Trends in vertical integration: a reply. *Journal of Industrial Economics*, 32, 391–2.

UNCTC (1983) *Transnational Corporations in World Development: Third Survey*. New York: United Nations Centre on Transnational Corporations.

Utton, M. A. (1979) *Diversification and Competition*. Cambridge: Cambridge University Press.

Vaitsos, C. V. (1974) *Intercountry Income Distribution and Transnational Enterprises*. Oxford: Clarendon Press.

Vernon, J. M. and Graham, D. A. (1971) Profitability of monopolisation by vertical integration. *Journal of Political Economy*, 79, 924–5.

Vickers, J. (1985) Delegation and the theory of the firm. *Economic Journal*, 95 (supplement), 138–47.

Walkling, R. A. and Long, M. S. (1984) Agency theory, managerial welfare and takeover bid resistance. *Rand Journal of Economics*, 15, 54–68.

Warren-Boulton, F. R. (1974) Vertical control with variable proportions. *Journal of Political Economy*, 82, 783–802.

Waterson, M. (1982) Vertical integration, variable proportions, and oligopoly. *Economic Journal*, 92, 129–44.

Waterson, M. (1984) *Economic Theory of the Industry*. Cambridge: Cambridge University Press.

Weiss, A. and Stiglitz, J. E. (1981) Credit rationing in markets with imperfect information. *American Economic Review*, 71, 393–410.

Weiss, L. W. (1983) The extent and effects of aggregate concentration. In Symposium (1983), 429–55.

White, L. J. (1981a) What has been happening to aggregate concentration in the United States? *Journal of Industrial Economics*, 29, 223–30.

White, L. J. (1981b) On measuring aggregate concentration: a reply. *Journal of Industrial Economics*, 30, 223–4.

White, M. (1981) *Payment systems in Britain*. Aldershot: Gower Press.

Wilkins, M. (1970) *The Emergence of Multinational Enterprise: American Business Abroad from the Colonial Era to 1914*. Cambridge, Mass.: Harvard University Press.

Wilkins, M. (1974) *The Maturing of Multinational Enterprise: American Business Abroad from 1914 to 1970*. Cambridge, Mass.: Harvard University Press.

Williamson, J. H. (1966) Profit, growth and sales maximisation. *Economica*, n.s., 33, 1–16.

Williamson, O. E. (1963) Managerial discretion and business behaviour. *American Economic Review*, 53, 1032–57.

Williamson, O. E. (1964) *The Economics of Discretionary Behaviour: Managerial Objectives in a Theory of the Firm*. Englewood Cliffs, N.J.: Prentice-Hall.

Williamson, O. E. (1970) *Corporate Control and Business Behaviour*. New Jersey: Prentice-Hall.

Williamson, O. E. (1971) The vertical integration of production: market failure considerations. *American Economic Review, Papers and Proceedings*, 61, 112–23.

Williamson, O. E. (1975) *Markets and Hierarchies: Analysis and Antitrust Implications*. New York: Free Press.

Williamson, O. E. (1979) Transaction-cost economics: the governance of contractual relations. *Journal of Law and Economics*, 22, 233–61.

Williamson, O. E. (1980) The organization of work: a comparative institutional assessment. *Journal of Economic Behavior and Organization*, 1, 5–38.

Williamson, O. E. (1981) The modern corporation: origins, evolution, attributes. *Journal of Economic Literature*, 19, 1537–68.

Williamson, O. E. (1983) Credible commitments; using hostages to support exchange. *American Economic Review*, 73, 519–40.

Williamson, O. E. (1984) The economics of governance: framework and implications. *Zeitschrift für die gesamte Staatswissenschaft*, 140, 195–223.

Williamson, O. E. and Ouchi, W. G. (1983) The markets and hierarchies programme of research: origins, implications, prospects. In A. Francis, J. Turk and P. Willman (eds) *Power, Efficiency and Institutions: A Critical Appraisal of the 'Markets and Hierarchies' Paradigm*. London: Heinemann.

Willig, R. D. (1979) Multiproduct technology and market structure. *American Economic Review*, 69, 346–51.

Wolf, B. M. (1977) Industrial diversification and internationalisation: some empirical evidence. *Journal of Industrial Economics*, 26, 177–91.

Wonnacott, T. H. and Wonnacott, R. J. (1972) *Introductory Statistics*, 2nd edn. New York: John Wiley.

Yarrow, G. K. (1976) On the predictions of managerial theories of the firm. *Journal of Industrial Economics*, 24, 267–79.

Yarrow, G. K. (1985) Shareholder protection, compulsory acquisition and the efficiency of the takeover process. *Journal of Industrial Economics*, 34, 3–16.

Index